DICTIONARY OF PSYCHOLOGY

Edited by
B.R. BHATIA
M.A. Ph.D.
SUNITA SHARMA
M.A.

ANMOL PUBLICATIONS PVT. LTD.
NEW DELHI - 110 002 (INDIA)

ANMOL PUBLICATIONS PVT. LTD.
Regd. Office: 4360/4, Ansari Road, Daryaganj,
New Delhi-110002 (India)
Tel.: 23278000, 23261597, 23286875, 23255577
Fax: 91-11-23280289
Email: anmolpub@gmail.com
Visit us at: www.anmolpublications.com

Branch Office: No. 1015, Ist Main Road, BSK IIIrd Stage
IIIrd Phase, IIIrd Block, Bangalore-560 085 (India)
Tel.: 080-41723429 • Fax: 080-26723604
Email: anmolpublicationsbangalore@gmail.com

Dictionary of Psychology

First Edition, 1989

Reprint, 1991, 1993, 1995, 1998, 2003, 2006, 2010

PRINTED IN INDIA

Printed at Mehra Offset Press, Delhi.

Preface

This dictionary has been carefully compiled and edited to provide students of Psychology at all levels with a handy and reliable source for the entries taken from experimental psychology, abnormal psychology, perception and personality, learning and memory, cognition, motivation and emotion, developmental psychology, child psychology, animal behaviour and psychology, the brain and nervous system, sensory physiology, applied psychology, social psychology, and general psychology. Some terms are explained quite briefly, others at some length.

Every effort has been carefully made to write the entries in a clear and lucid style to provide both straight forward definitions and invaluable back ground information.

The dictionary will be of immense value to undergraduate and post-graduate students and to those appearing for competitive examinations, research scholars, teachers and authors.

When a dictionary of this kind is being compiled, it becomes essential to draw upon the work of many authorities and seek the advice of colleagues to all of whom the authors are deeply indebted.

Finally, the authors express their sincere thanks to the publishers and printers for printing this book promptly.

The Authors

A

A. Used as a Rorschach symbol for classifying responses wherein the content refers to animals.

Aasmus. Asthma that is due to physiogenic causes.

Abacá. Manita hemp, that is often used for narcotic purposes, though cannabis indica is preferred by addicts.

Abasia. Refers to inability to walk due to impairment in motor coordination.

Abaxial. Means out of the axis line.

Abducent Nerve. Refers to the VIth cranial nerve.

Abdominal Reflex. Contraction of the abdominal muscles when the overlying skin is stroked lightly.

Abclution. Refers to the rejection of acculturation.

Abdominal Reflex. A contraction of muscles in the abdominal wall in response to a sudden stroking of the skin in that region.

Abducens Nucleus. It is a mass of nerve cells in the fourth ventricle which gives rise to the abducent nerve.

Abduct. Means to draw away from the midline.

Abduction. Lateral movement of a limb away from the median plane of the body.

Abductor. Any muscle which, upon contraction, moves a limb away from the body.

Aberrant Behaviour. Behaviour which deviates from the normal.

Aberration. Refers to a departure from normal.

Abience. Avoidance. *Abient behaviour* moves the organism away from a stimulus.

Ability. It refers to the proficiency in carrying out various skills, understandings, or adjustments. Specific abilities may be illustrated by, academic, arithmetical, athletic, mechanical, musical, reading, social, and the like.

Abiotic. Not compatible with life.

Ability Grouping. Refers to the practice of dividing pupils into relatively homogeneous groups on the basis of their scholastic ability.

Ability Test. Refers to a standardized examination for the purpose of measuring either general ability or some specialized ability.

Abiotrophy. Means degeneration of tissues or a general deterioration of body.

Abjection. Depressed feeling-tone due to a loss of the sense of personal worth.

Ablation Experiments. Animal experiments wherein portions of the brain are excised after a habit like maze-learning has been established. The relationships between the amounts of destroyed tissues and their location on the one hand, and retention of the skill, on the other hand are then noted by the observer.

Ablutomania. Means incessant washing of body.

Abnormal. Means deviating from the norm.

Abnormal Psychology. It is the branch of psychology that investigates abnormal behaviour.

Abortive Jump. It is the manner in which rats avoided bumping their noses and falling into the net, by learning to strike the barrier with their paws and to turn their heads aside.

Aboulia (Aboulia). Refers to chronic indecision, with eventual loss of initiative. It is a pathology of conation.

Abreaction. The expression of emotion connected with a repressed mental conflict, now brought into the conscious mind of the patient.

Abrosia. It is a condition of fasting. In some types of hysteria (*anorexia*) and in catatonia, negative impulses may induce refusals to eat.

Abscissa. The X-axis ; In representations of psychological data, the line of the graph that is at right-angles to the ordinate (or perpendicular axis).

Absence. Means a brief lapse of consciousness, as in attack of petit mal epilepsy.

Absent-Mindedness. Not paying attention to those phases of a situation which other persons consider to be of major importance.

Absolute Brilliance Limen. It is the minimum intensity of brilliance needed to elicit a sensation of just noticeable difference from the other parts of the visual field.

Absolute Error. It is equal to the observed value or score plus or minus the true value or score. The absolute error is a positive or negative deviation on either side of the mean.

Absolute Impression. Refers to a judgment of intensity, brightness, weight, etc., when the stimuli are presented without any standard for comperison.

Absolute Luminosity. It is the luminosity expressed in absolute terms.

Absolute Measurement. Any measurement taken without regard to algebraic sign.

Absolute Pitch. Refers to the pitch of a tone as a function of its rate of vibration.

Absolute Scale. A scale provided with an absolute-zero point and having intervals that are equal.

Absolute Sensitivity. The absolute threshold or minimal stimulus magnitude needed to arouse a sensation.

Absolute Value. The mathematical value of a number without any consideration of its algebraic sign.

Absolute Zero. Refers to the point on a psychological scale where the variable being measured ceases to exist.

Absorption. Refers to a state of preoccupation or high degree of attention to one object or activity.

Abstract. Any thing that which has been taken out of the whole or is being considered apart from its constituent elements.

Abstract Ability. Refers to the ability to use abstract ideas in problem solving end in dealing with novel situations.

Abstract Ideas. Refers to mental states or activities which lack images.

Abstract Intelligence. It is the ability to use symbols and concepts while dealing with unfamiliar problems and difficulties. This type of intelligence can be measured by verbal and mathematical symbols and abstract concepts.

Abstract Learning. Learning that does not involve concrete objects.

Abstract Set. Refers to the tendency to perceive things in terms of abstractions.

Absurdity Test. It is a task wherein the testee must point out the incongruity or absurdity in a story or picture.

Abulia, Aboulia. Refers to inability to come to a decision.

Abundancy Motive. It is the tendency to seek satisfactions beyond those involved in fulfilling deficits or eliminating needs.

Acalculia. A type of aphasia wherein the subject cannot carry out simple numerical calculations.

Acarophobia. Means fear of mites or of small objects or animals.

Acanthesthesia. A variety of paresthesia wherein the individual experiences pin pricks.

Acathisia. Means inability to remain in a sitting position, as in certain forms of hysteria.

Acathisia. *Akathisia.*

Acataphasia. Refers to the inability to connect words properly in a sentence.

Acceptance. Refers to a positive or adient attitude or recognition of the individual's worth without implying either approval of his conduct or emotional attachment on the part of the therapist.

Accessory Nerve. The eleventh cranial nerve. This nerve is a helper, or accessory, to the vagus, or tenth nerve, and is distributed with it to the muscles of the pharynx and larynx.

Accessory Parts. Includes all parts of sense organs except the receptor cells themselves. Accessory parts contribute to the more effective functioning of sense organs.

Accident Proneness. Refers to the tendency for certain persons to have a disproportionately large number of the accidents that occur within a given group of employees.

Accidental Error. See discussion under error.

Accommodation. Refers to the adjustment of the eye for vision at various distances.

Accommodation Time. It is the time that lapse between a change in viewing distance and the achievement of accommodation.

Accomplishment Quotient. It is the ratio of actual accomplishment to possibilities for achievement.

Accretionary Growth. Refers to multiplication of tissues without qualitative change in the functions of an organ or an organism.

Acculturation. It is the process of absorbing the folkways and mores of a culture that originally was alien to the immigrant.

Accuracy, Compulsion. Refers to pathological zeal in accurate work, even with minute details and trivia. It is considered to be a maladjustive habit whereby the individual seeks to escape from anxiety conflicts.

Accuracy Test. Any test that emphasizes accuracy of performance independent of the time it takes to complete it.

ACE Test. The American Council on Education test of intelligence, designed primarily for college freshmen.

Acetylcholine (ACH). A complex organic compound liberated at the endings of parasympathetic fibers and at muscle end plates. Acetylcholine is a neurotrasmitter.

Acetylcholinesterose (ACHE). The enzyme that breaks down acetylcholine at the transmitter site, thus stoping its effects.

Ache. Refers to an intense, throbbing pain.

Acheiria. Means lacking hands.

Achievement Age. It is the calendar or chronological age equivalent to a given level of proficiency on an achievement test.

Achievement Motive. Refers to the tendency to strive for success or the attainment of a desired end.

Achilles Tendon Reflex. Refers to contraction of the muscles of the calf when the tendon back of the heel is sharply tapped.

Achloropsia. Means green-blindness, or deuteranopia.

Achondroplasia. Refers to defects in the cartilage at the epiphyses of long bones ; children with this disorder have difficulty in locomotion.

Achromatic Response. It includes several subcategories for responses determined by texture, shading, or any factor not involving color.

Achromatism. Refers to total color blindness because of the congenital absence of cones.

Achromatopsia. Refers to total color-blindness.

Acolasia. Refers to general intemperance, with special reference to sex indulgence. It reveals a character defect rather than a somatic pathology.

Acomon. The incus, or anvil; Refers to one of the three small bones of the middle ear.

Acouasm. Refers to a subjective noise in the ears which may be due to impacted cerumen, charges of air pressure in the middle ear, blocked eustachian tubes, quinine, or inflammation of tympanum or middle ear.

Acoumeter. Apparatus used for determining auditory thresholds.

Acoustic Filter. A device used for screening out certain sound frequencies.

Acoustic Pressure. It is the force per square centimeter exerted upon the eardrum.

Acoustic Spectrum. Refers to the range of sounds audible to the human ear—from 20 to 20,000 Hz in young adults.

Acoustics. It is the science of sound also refers to the properties of a room that influence the distinctness with which sounds can be heard.

Acroanesthesia. Refers to loss of sensitivity in the extremities.

Acrocinesia, Acrocinesis. Excessive motility as observed in patients suffering from manic-depressive psychoses.

Acroparesthesia. Refers to numbness of the extremities.

Act Psychology. Refers to the view that emphasizes activities, rather than contents, of consciousness.

Acting-Out. Means gratifying a repressed desire by social behaviour that brings unhappiness and suffering (Freud).

Actual Neuroses. Refers to disturbances caused by toxemia due to such impairments of sex function as masturbation, coitus interruptus, and abstinence (Freud).

Acupuncture. Refers to a techique that is used for producing regional anesthesia. Anesthesia is produced by inserting a long thin needle at the critical point and either twirling it or passing a mild electric current through it.

Acute Brain Disorder. Refers to any disability due to a reversible (hence, temporary) impairment of brain tissue.

Acquiescent Response Set. The tendency to agree with an item on an attitude scale or questionnaire irrespective of its content.

Acquisition. Refers to a new response added to the organism's repertory of responses through learning.

Action Current. Refers to the change in electrical potential in nerves and muscles that is correlated with activity.

Action Potential. It is the change in electrical potential associated with the activity of nerves and muscles.

Action Research. Refers to a research whose ends are practical as opposed to theoretical.

Action System. Refers to the complex of nerves, muscles, and glands which participate in a response.

Activation. Means arousal or preparation for action. For example, the reticular formation alerts or activates the cerebral cortex.

Activation-Deactivation Adjective Checklist. A personality inventory designed to assess the testee's customary level of activation.

Activation Pattern. On the electroencephalogram refers to a fast, irregular wave pattern accompanying arousal.

Active Avoidance. Refers to a learning situation wherein the subject must perform a specific act so as to avoid punishment.

Active Introversion. Refers to a voluntary, deliberate withdrawal from reality.

Active Therapy. Refers to an analysis wherein the therapist assumes a more directive or active role than is customary, for the purpose of breaking down resistance.

Activity Drive. Refers to the hypothetical drive to account for an animal activity even though all physiological drives are satiated.

Activity Quotient. It is a proposed index of emotionality using the ratio of activity words to qualifiers in a sample of the individual's speech or writing.

Activity Sempling. The determination of what an individual does during a specified period of time.

Activity System. Refers to a group of closely interrelated behaviors which serve the same general function. For example, crawling, running, walking, and happing.

Actone. 1. (*Murray*) an action pattern considered from the point of view of the action itself and without regard to its effects.

Act Psychology. Refers to the viewpoint that the subject matter of psychology should be acts, as opposed to contents. If, for example, we see a color, the act of seeing is a process that leads to a content of what is seen. This arose in opposition to structuralism, which held that the subject matter of psychology was conscious contents to be studied by means of the method of introspection.

Act Regression. The reappearance of a previously extinguished conditioned response when a barrier is interposed to a conditioned response related to the extinguished response.

Actual Neurosis. Refers to a neurosis resulting from an organic difficulty.

Acuity. Refers to sharpness of perception.

Acuity Grating. Refers to a printed square of closely spaced, alternating black and white lines used to determine the minimum separability of objects necessary for their perception as two.

Acute Preparation. An animal that must be destroyed for humane reasons at the termination of an experiment involving radical surgical procedures.

Adaptation. Refers to structural or functional change that enhances the organism's survival value.

Adaptation Level. It is a subjective point of equality at which stimuli are indifferent or neutral.

Adaptive Act. It is the basic unit of behaviour involving a motivating stimulus and a sensory situation leading the animal to make responses which reinforce behaviour leading to a goal, thereby satisfying the motivating condition.

Adaptive Behaviour. Refers to the behavior that helps the individual interact more effectively with his environment.

Adaptometer. A device used for measuring changes in sensory adaptation.

Addiction. It is the state of being physically dependent upon a drug. In general, addiction means increased tolerance to a drug, physical and psychological dependence, and withdrawal symptoms when administration of the drug is stopped.

Additive Scale. A scale whose units can be summated since they are equal at all points along the scale. A yardstick is an additive scale.

Adductor. Refers to a muscle which, upon contraction, moves a limb towards the medial plane of the body.

Adenine. One of four nucleotide bases that make up both *deoxyribonucleic acid* and *ribonucleic acid.*

Adenohypophysis. The anterior pituitary gland.

Adequate Stimulus. Refers to a stimulus that excites a receptor.

Adience. Refers to behavior that moves the organism toward the the source of stimulation.

Adipsia. It is a pathological condition that is characterized by failure to drink when body water level is low.

Adjuvant Therapy. Supplementary or corollary techniques used in therapy.

Ad Hoc. Refers to a hypothesis or hypothetical explanation developed to explain a particular set of data that does not fit into an existing theoretical framework.

Adipocytes. Means *fat cells.* It has been found that obese people have more and larger adipocytes than those of normal weight.

Ad Lib. Refer to ad lib body weight, that is the weight approached by a fully nature organism given unlimited access to a balanced diet, *i e.*, one on ad lib feeding.

Adolescence. It is the period of development marked at the beginning by the onset of puberty and at the end by the attainment of physiological or psychological maturity.

Adrenal Cortex. The outer portion of the adrenal glands.

Adrenal Gland. A gland located adjacent to and covering the upper part of the surface of the kidney.

Adrenaline. It is, a hormone secreted by the adrenal medulla.

Adrenergic. Means having an adrenaline-like action or characterizing the action of autonemic fibers of the sympathetic nervous system which secrete sympathin, an andrenalinelike product.

Adrenocorticotrophic Hormone (**ACTH**). A hormone secreted by the anterior pituitary that functions in the growth and development of the adrenal cortex. It also plays a critical role in the continued functioning of the adrenal cortices by stimulating the production of glucocorticoids and has been implicated in subpressing the production of testosterone.

Adult Intelligence. The measured intellectual level at which the curve of mental growth has ceased to rise. It is estimated at between 16 and 19 by most authorities, but some would advance the point to the early twenties.

Adventitious Deafness. Deafness caused by injury.

Aerial Perspective. Refers to the loss of distinctness and fading-out of colors with increased distance.

Aero. Combining form meaning *air* or *gas*.

Aerobic. Pertaining to or characteristic of organisms (or tissues) that need or are not destroyed by free oxygen.

Aerobic Exercise. Any exercise designed to increase oxygen uptake in the body.

Aesthetics. It is the branch of psychology dealing with the experimental study of beauty.

Affect ; Affection. It is a broad class of mental processes, including feeling, emotion, moods, and treatment. Historically.

Affective Attack. Refers to a violent, highly emotional attack on one animal by another.

Affective Congruency. Refers to the consistency between an individual's feelings about a segment of his self concept and related behavior and the feelings of others toward these same components.

Affective Experience. Refers to an emotional experience.

Affective Logic. It is made up of sequences of judgments or reasoning that superficially resemble logical chains of reasoning but upon closer examination are found to be linked by emotional factors.

Affective Psychosis. Psychotic reaction especially characterized by severe emotional disturbances, like those occurring in manic-depressive reaction.

Affective Ratio. (*Rorschach*). It is the ratio of the total number of responses to the colored cards to the total responses to the un-colored cards.

Affective Syndrome, Organic. Refers to persons displaying serious disturbances of mood that are traceable to some particular organic factor, generally a toxic reaction to a drug or a metabolic disturbance.

Affective Tone. It is the feeling tone associated with any experience.

Afferent. Refers to the conduction of nerve impulses from the periphery to or toward the central nervous system.

Afferent Code. Refers to the pattern of neural input to the brain corresponding to the pattern of environmental stimulation.

Afferent Stimulus Interaction. (*Hull*) the postulate that all afferent impulses interact in such a way as to modify one another.

Affiliation (*Murray*). Refers to the need for friendly association with others ; formation of friendships ; joining of groups.

Affordance. Refers to the "invitational" quality of a percept or an event. In a sense, affordance refers to the intrinsic properties of items and events.

Affricate. Refers to a speech sound that in simplest terms, is made up of a *stop* and a *fricative*.

Aftereffect. It is the continuation of a sensory experience after cessation of a stimulating condition.

Afterimage. It is the continuation of a sensory experience after removal of the stimulus. In visual experience, after images may be positive or negative. If positive, they are of approximately the same hue and brightness as the original stimulus. If negative, they are less saturated, duller, and approximately the complementary colour of the original stimulus.

Attersensation. It is the continuation ot a sensory experience after cessation of the stimulus.

Agamogenesis. Asexual reproduction or Parthenogenesis.

Age, Carpal. Bone development as determined by the degree of ossification of the carpal (wrist) bones.

Age Equivalent. Refers to the level of development of any trait expressed in age unit.

Age-equivalent Scale. A test whereon the scores are expressed in age units.

Age-grade Scaling. The standardizing of educational materials by determining the norms for a population of children who are at the appropriate grade level for their age.

Agenesis. Lack of reproductive capacity or Complete or partial failure of an organ or organ part to develop properly.

Age Norm. The average score on a standardized test observed in a large, representative sample of children at a particular age.

Agent. Refers to anything that produces an effect. The "thing" may be a chemical substance, a force, a person, a group of persons, etc.

Age, Physiological. Refers to a person's age in terms of level of physiological development. Rough estimates are based on such factors as hormonal levels, glandular secretions, musculature, neural development, etc.

Agerasia. Refers to vigorous, healthy appearance in a person of advanced years.

Age Regression. In hypnosis the subject's reliving through fantasy events based on early memories.

Age Score. Refers to score on any standardized test expressed in terms of the age at which the average child achieves that score.

Age Test. Refers to a score on a test that has been standardized for various ages.

Ageusia Means. Partial or complete loss of the sense of taste.

Agglutination. In physiology a term used in a variety of contexts wherein substances (microorganisms, tissues, blood corpuscles. etc.,) become clumped by mutual adhesion.

Aggregation Theory. A theory of intelligence according to which abilities are a function of dispersed localized areas in the cerebral cortex.

Aggression, Weaning. It is a mild form of aggressive response by parents directed against their offspring who are showing resistance to being weaned.

Agitated Depression. Refers to a pathological condition characteristic of certain psychotics wherein there is restlessness, apprehension, delusions of self-depreciation, feelings of worthlessness, and despair.

Agitated Melancholia. Refers to a psychotic state of profound depression accompanied by anxiety. Typically occurs in later life.

Agitation. Restlessness.

Agitophasia. Refers to extremely rapid speech with slurring and omission of words.

Agnosia. Refers to partial or total inability to attach meaning to sensory impressions. Agnosia may take place in any sensory modality and is generally the result of brain injury.

Agnosia, Auditory Means. Inability to recognize of interpret the meanings of spoken words.

Agnosia, Tactile Means. Inability to recognize or interpret objects by touch.

Agnosia, Visual Means. Inability to recognize or interpret objects in the visual field.

Agoraphobia. Refers to morbid fear of open places.

A-ha Experience. Refers to the feeling that accompanies the moment of insight, that instant when the various disparate aspects of a problem-solving situation suddenly fit together to yield the solution.

Aim-Inhibited. A term that characterizes an action or a relationship wherein there is no conscious recognition of the underlying motive or drive.

Akinesia. Refers to partial or complete loss of motor control.

Alallia. Refers to loss of ability to speak.

Alarm Reaction. It is the first stage of the general adaptation syndrome which characterized by an emergency reaction involving the mobilization of energy through adrenal and sympathetic activity.

Albedo. The reflectance of any surface ; particularly, the percentage of light that is reflected by a surface measured against the total light falling on that surface.

Albinism. A category of pigment disorders characterized by a less than normal production of melanin in the skin.

Alcohol Hallucinosis. Refers to a syndrome of vivid auditory hallucinations following the sudden cessation of alcohol intake after an extended history of alcohol abuse.

Alcoholic. A person who suffers from alcoholism (*q.v.*).

Alcoholic Jealousy. Refers to an irrational, paranoid-like jealousy often observed in cases of chronic alcohol abuse.

Alcohol Withdrawal. Refers to an organic mental disorder that is characterized by coarse trem or of the hands, eyelids and tongue, nausea, weakness, sweating, depressed, mood anxiety and irritability.

Aldosterone. The most active of the mineralocorticoids produced by the adrenal cortices, aldosterone is important in the regulation of the metabolism of sodium, potassium and choline.

Alexia. Means without words. A languagerelated disability characterized by the partial or complete loss of the ability to identify the printed word. The disorder is often quite specific in that alexics do not have impairment of vision and can identify spoken words normally. Sometimes called *word blindness* and *visual aphsia.*

Alexithymia. It is a disruption in both affective and cognitive processes. It is not treated as a "true" psychiatric syndrome. Typically the alexithymic person has relatively undifferentiated emotions and thinking tends to dwell excessively on the mundane.

Algedonic. Pertaining to the pleasantness-unpleasantness dimension of feeling or emotion.

Algesimeter. It is a device for measuring sensitivity to pain. A variety of such devices exists. In all cases, the basic data are the subjects' reports of subjective experience.

Algethesia. Means the subjective experiencing of pain.

Algethesis. The sense of pain.

Algia. Combining form meaning pain. Generally used as a suffix.

Alg(o). Combining form meaning *pain.*

Algolagnia. Means painlust. Hence, the arousal of sexual feelings through pain.

Algophobia. An extreme fear of or aversion to pain.

Algorithm. Refers to a method or procedure for solving a particular problem that is guaranteed to lead, eventually, to the solution.

Alienist. Refers to a physician, usually a psychiatrist, who is a qualified specialist in mental disorders.

Alimentary canal (or tract). The system of organs made up of a tubular passage from mouth to anus that serves digestive functions. It includes the mouth, pharynx, esophagus, stomach, small and large intestines, and the rectum.

Allele. One of a pair of genes located at corresponding positions on a pair of chromosomes. Each pair of alleles controls or influences a specific trait, like eye color. One allele is generally dominant and the other recessive.

Allelótropia. Refers to the apparent shifting in lateral position of an element in the visual field when a similar element is presented to a disparate position in the other eye.

Allergy. It is a condition of heightened sensitivity to foreign substances that would be harmless to most people but, in the susceptible individual, causes reactions ranging from mild irritation to shock and, in rare cases, death.

Allocentric. Means outside the self.

Allochiria, Allocheiria. Refers to a condition wherein touch is referred to a corresponding point on the opposite side of the body being stimulated.

Alloeroticism. Refers to the focusing of sexuality toward others.

Allomorph. One of two or more linguistic forms that have the same meaning but differ in their form.

Allophone. Refers to one of two or more elementary sounds in a particular language that differ in acoustic or articulatory properties but without conveying any difference in meaning.

Alloplasty. It is a process of adaptation whereby modifications in the outside world are made. Alloplastic changes are changes in the external environment.

Allopsychic. Descriptive of psychic processes wherein the primary reference point is in the external world.

All-or-none Law. It is the principle according to which individual neurons and muscle fibers fact with maximum strength or not at all.

Allotropic. Refers to persons who are not self-centered, who are concerned with the well-being of others.

Alpha, Beta, Gamma Hypotheses. These are three hypotheses that state the relationship of frequency of repetition to rate of learning. Alpha : frequency promotes learning ; Beta :

frequency has no influence; Gamma : frequency hinders learning.

Alphabet Content. It is a scoring code used when letters of the alphabet are given in response to the inkblots.

Alpha Block. Refers to the inhibition of the resting alpha wave of 8-10 Hz by asynchronous and rapid beta waves when a novel stimulus is presented.

Alpha Blocking. A change in the alpha rhythm of an EEG because of any shift away from normal, waking, relaxation. Alpha rhythms may be "blocked" by the person orienting toward a stimulus such as a sound or light, by a state of apprehension or anxiety, or by a mental activity such as performing multiplication covertly.

Alpha Examination. Refers to a group verbal test made up of eight subtests; the Army Alpha Test was administered extensively to military personnel during World War I.

Alpha Male. Refers to the male at the top of a *dominance hierarchy* of a troop.

Alpha Motor Neuron. Refers to one of the large motor neurons that controls the voluntary or skeletal muscles.

Alpha Response. It is a rapid, low-amplitude response that is assumed to be an unconditioned response that develops as a result of sensitization during training.

Alpha Rhythm. The alpha rhythm has a normal frequency of 8-12 cycles per second and an amplitude of 5-15 microvolts. It is affected by age, drugs, mental activity, sleep, and sensory stimuli.

Altercasting. Means influencing the role of another by choosing a specific role oneself, thereby reducing alternative behavior for the other.

Alter Ego. Refers to a very intimate friend so close as to be "another self".

Alternate Form. It is a scale of items quite similar to another scale such that the two are considered as different versions of the same test.

Alternate-response Test. Refers to any test that presents two responses for each question, the subject is required to choose the correct alternative.

Alternating Personality. Refers to a dual personality, one component of which tends to alternate in its appearances with the other component.

Alternating Perspective. Refers to the shift in *perspective* that takes place when one fixates on a particular stimulus for a period of time.

Alternating Vision. Refers to the use of first one and then the other eye in seeing. For most purposes one of the eyes is dominant over the other, whose sensory information is suppressed.

Altitude. It is a proposed dimension of intelligence measured by the level of difficulty of problems solved by the subject on a power test.

Altitude Test. Refers to a test designed to measure the maximum difficulty level the individual can achieve.

Altruism. It is the disposition to act in behalf of others for unselfish reasons.

Alveolar. Refers to a speech sound produced by placing the tip or blade of the tongue against the alveolar ridge.

Alzheimer's Disease. It is a progressive form of presenile dementia that is superficially similar to senility except that it strikes relatively early in life. The first sign is impaired memory, generally followed by disturbed speech and thought and ultimately complete helplessness.

Amacrine Cells. Cells present in the retina which link the bipolar and the second-order neurons.

Amathophobia. Refers to the fear of dust.

Amaurotic (Familial) Idiocy. Refers to a group of related, genetically transmitted diseases which are marked by retardation and vision deficits and produced by faulty metabolism.

Amaxophobia. Refers to fear of being in a vehicle.

Amazon. Refers to a myth of a race of, female Greek warriors, a tall, muscular woman. Such women are falsely considered as lesbians , there is no relationship between a woman's physical stature and her sexual preferences.

Ambi. Prefix meaning *both*, with the connotation of equality of the two things under consideration ; *e.g., ambidextrous.*

Ambidextral. Refers to the use of both sides of the body, specially the hands.

Ambiequal. Refers to one who is well balanced in extratensive and introtensive tendencies ; neither egocentric nor excessively dependent upon others.

Ambiguity Tolerance. It is the ability to withstand conflicting or complex situations without undue psychological distress.

Ambiguous. Means to have two possible meanings or interpretations, as in *ambiguous figures*.

Amblyaphia. Refers to a diminished sense of touch.

Amblygeustia. Refers to a dulled or deficient sense of taste.

Amblyscope. It is an instrument used for determining the fusion point of separately presented visual stimuli.

Ambrosiac. Refers to musk like odour.

Ambulatory Psychotherapy. Refers to outpatient treatment of persons suffering from psychological disorders.

Ameliorate. Means to improve. Used specially with respect to improvement in diseases, dysfunctions or other conditions.

Amenorrhea. Refers to absence of menstrual period.

Ament. Refers to one who has amentia, or mental deficiency.

Amentia. Refers to any serious mental deficiency.

Ames Room. It is a specially constructed room designed by the artist/psychologist Adelbert Ames. It provides a striking demonstration of the cues for depth perception. The room is of distorted construction, three of the walls are actually trapezoidal and the ceiling slants markedly. However, due to the use of the cues of shading, size constancy and interposition, the room appears normal to an outside observer. Looking into the room produces many illusions, objects and persons appear distorted particularly in their apparent size, round objects seem to roll uphill, etc.

Ametropia. Refers to any refractive deficit in the eye, *e.g., hyperopia, myopia, astigmatism*.

Amimia. Refers to loss of ability to communicate by means of gestures.

Amine. Refers to a large group of organic compounds. The ones of primary interest in psychology are the *biogenic amines*.

Amnesia. Refers to any partial or complete loss of memory. Amnesic syndrome which is "physiological" is caused by some form of damage to brain tissue or "psychological" which is caused by any of a variety of factors including alterations in the memorial code or neurotic reactions.

Amok. An acute, murderous frenzy. It is often regarded a *culture-specific syndrome* specially to certain Malaysian groups.

Amuck. From the Malay *amoq* or *amok*, a state of uncontrolled, homicidal frenzy.

Amygdalotomy. A form of psychosurgery where in amygdaloid fibers are severed. It has been used in cases of extreme uncontrollable violence, *psychosurgery* for discussion of this and other procedures.

Amytal ; Sodium Amytal. It is the proprietary name for one of the barbiturates used extensively as a sedative and hypnotic. It is also called "truth serum," because under its influence inhibitions may be lowered with the result that the individual will discuss his problems more freely. Contrary to popular opinion, criminals do not confess against their will when given hypnotic drugs.

Anabolic. Means, promoting a buildup or restoration of a structure or body. Anabolic agents like testosterone or similar steroids stimulate anabolism.

Anabolism. Refers to conservation phase of bodily metabolism where in tissues are restored and built up, in contrast to catabolism or the expenditure and breaking down of tissue.

Anaclisis. Refers to emotional dependence on others, generally used in reference to infantile dependency.

Anacusia. Means total deafness.

Anaglyph. Refers to a picture printed in two complementary colors slightly offset from each other so that when viewed through lenses of corresponding colors (one color to each eye) the effect is one of stereoscopic depth. This process is that used in the production of 3-D movies.

Anaglyptoscope. It is a device which shifts the angle of lighting on a test object, resulting in a reversal of areas of shadow and light. It is used to demonstrate the role of shadows in the perception of depth.

Anal. Pertaining to the anus or exterior opening of the large intestine.

Analgesta. It is the absence of pain sensation.

Anal Expulsive (Stage). Some psychoanalytic theorists hypothesize two distinct aspects to the *anal stage*, one characterized by anal expulsiveness, where in pleasure is derived from the passing of feces, and the other characterized by anal retentiveness, wherein pleasure is associated with the withholding of feces.

Anal Impotence. Refers to the inability to pass feces in the presence of other persons.

Anal Intercourse. Refers to sexual intercourse with the penis inserted in the anus. The term is used for hetero- and homosexual relations.

Anality. That part of libidinous energy associated with the anal region.

Analog. A thing or event is said to be an analog of another if there is a coherent correspondence between their parts, function, roles, etc.

Analogical Reasoning. Reasoning by which decisions about objects, events or concepts depend upon perceived similarities in the relationships between pairs.

Analogies Test. A test wherein a relationship between two terms is given and the person is asked to complete an analogous relationship.

Analogy. It is the a functional correspondence in organs that are anatomically different or found in different species.

Anal Sadism. It is a form of sadism originating in an individual's resentment due to punishment he received during toilet training.

Anal Sadistic. Refers to any sadistic pleasure hypothesized to originate in the *anal stage*. Such behavior derives from harsh punishment during toilet training.

Anal-Sadistic Stages. Refers to an infantile period of development characterized by anal eroticism and sadistic impuluses directed toward the parent.

Analysand. Refers to the individual being psychoanalyzed.

Analytical Scale. It is a test that is used for diagnostic purposes.

Analyzer. Refers to a receptor and its central neuronal connections.

Anancasm. Refers to repetitious, stereotyped behavior that if not carried out results in anxiety.

Anandria. Refers to absence of normal male characteristics.

Anaphia. Refers to loss of or diminution in the sense of touch.

Anaphrodisia. Refers to the condition of diminished or absent desire for sex.

Anaphylaxis, Psychological. Refers to psychological hypersensitivity resulting from a previous traumatic experience so that later presentation of the original circumstances causes deep psychological distress.

Androgen. Refers to the male sex hormone that is responsible for the structural and functional changes associated with "maleness" at maturity.

Androgenization. It is the process of becoming a male. It refers to the complex processes in the developing embryo initiated by exposure to androgens and resulting in the development of male sex organs.

Androgyneity. In anthropology refers to the concept that the individual has bipolar potentiality in sex until he is turned into a definite sex by tribal ritual.

Androgynous. Refers to a characteristic of a male who shows structures characteristic of the female.

Andromania. Refers to excessive sexual desire in a female.

Anergasia. Refers to a loss of function.

Anergia. Refers to a loss of energy.

Anesthesia; Anaesthesia. Refers to a complete or partial loss of sensitivity to external and/or internal stimuli due to drugs, lesions, or functional causes.

Anger. A state of an acute emotional reaction elicited by any of a number of stimulating situations, including threat, overt aggression, restraint, verbal attack, disappointment, or frustration. It is characterized by strong responses in the autonomic nervous system, specially by emergency reactions of the sympathetic division and by implicit or overt attack responses that may be either somatic or verbal.

Angina. Refers to a feeling of suffocation, of being choked. It is a disease of the pharynx characterized by attacks of choking.

Angiotensin. It is a protein produced in the blood that helps to regulate blood pressure and water balance.

Animal. Refers to a member of one of the two divisions of living organisms distinguished from plants (the second of the two) primarily by lack of photosynthesizing ability. In psychology, references to animals typically mean organisms lower than man.

Animal Content. It is a scoring category for animal references.

Animal Magnetism. Refers to hypnotism in which the hypnotic state was induced by the flow of magnetism from the operator to the subject.

Animal Psychology. It is a branch of psychology that deals with the systematic study of animal behaviour, particularly from a comparative point of view.

Animatism. Refers to the belief that a kind of impersonal supernatural force exists in all things, animate or inanimate.

Animosity. Refers to intense and enduring hostility with the implication that the feelings are open and active.

Anisocoria. Refers to a condition wherein the diameters of the pupils are of unequal size.

Anisocoria. Refers to inequality in the size of the pupils.

Anisometropia. Refers to unequal refractive power in the two eyes.

Ankle Clonus. It is the process of repetitive contraction-relaxation of the ankle muscles and is a common symptom of neurological diseases of the central nervous system.

Anniversary Reaction. Refers to a strong emotional reaction to an earlier event occurring at the same time of the year as the original event.

Annoyer. Refers to any stimulus possessing noxious or unpleassant properties.

Annulment. Refers to the process through which painful, anxiety-provoking ideas and images are neutralized or "annulled."

Annulus. Refers to a ring-shaped structure.

Anodyne. An analgesic, or agent to reduce pain.

Anoesia. Means lacking the ability to comprehend or understand ; idiocy.

Anorchism. Refers to congenital lack of one or both testes.

Anorectic. Means lacking in appetite.

Anorexia. Refers to pathological loss of appetite. It is a common symptom in mental disorders.

Anorexia, Sexual. Refers to a lack of appetite for sex, a loss of sexual desire.

Anorgasmia. It is a condition that is characterized by a total inability to achieve orgasm.

Anosmia. Refers to any deficiency in the sense of smell.

Anoxia. Refers to a marked deficiency in the supply of oxygen to the body tissues.

Antecedent. Refers to something which precedes a phenomenon in a mander that "invites" the inference of causality.

Anterior Horns. Refers to the ventral portion of the gray matter in the spinal cord. These are the site of origin on the large motor neurons controlling muscular movement.

Anterior Nucleus. Refers to a thalamic nucleus which receives input from the mamillary bodies and projects to the limbic cortex.

Anterograde. Means extending forward in space or progressing forward in time.

Anthropology. It is the study of mankind. It includes archeology, linguistics, psychology, sociology and smatterings of biology, anatomy, genetics and comparative literature.

Anthropopathy. Refers to attributing human feelings or emotions to gods or animals.

Antianxiety Drugs. Refers to several classes of drugs that function primarily to reduce anxiety.

Acticipation Method. It is a technique used in verbal learning where the subject is prompted upon hesitation and corrected upon making an error.

Anticipatory Error. Refers to a premature response in serial learning.

Antidiuretic Hormone. It is a hormone secreted by the posterior lobe of the pituitary gland that regulates water balance in the body.

Antidiuretic Hormone (ADH). It is a hormone released by the posterior pituitary which increases the capacity of the kidney tubules to reabsorb water, thus reducing urinary output.

Antihistamine. Refers to any substance or agent that inhibits or blocks the effect of *histamine.* They are useful in controlling rashes and allergic reactions due to release of histamine and are helpful to sufferers of hayfever. They are also used as mild sedatives as they tend to produce drowsiness in most (but not all) persons.

Anti-Intraception. Refers to a tendency to be opposed to that which is subjective, imaginative, humanistic. It is considered as a characteristic of the *authoritarian personality.*

Antimania Drugs. Drugs which are used for the treatment of *hypomania* and *manicdepressive psychosis,* The drug of choice here is one of the lithium compounds. These drugs also help in preventing the depressive aspect of manic-depression.

Antimetropia. Refers to condition wherein the two eyes have differences in refractive power, *e.g.*, one eye is myopic and the other hyperopic.

Antonym Test. It is a verbal test where the subject is given a word and must supply its antonym as quickly as possible.

Anvil. It is one of the small bones in the middle ear.

Anxiety Neurosis. A neurosis wherein the most prominent symptom is anxiety that cannot be identified with any particular cause and that in many cases is pervasive and affects major areas of the individual's life.

Apanthropy. It is an aversion to society or human companionship.

Apareunia. Refers to inability to have sexual intercourse. The term is used for problems such as vaginal obstructions.

Aperture Color. Color as seen in holes in neutral screens. Aperture colors are classified as film colors.

Aphemia. Refers to inability to speak.

Aphephobia. It is the fear of being touched by another person.

Aphonia. Means loss of speech due to laryngeal defects or emotional disorders.

Aphrasia. Refers to the functional inability or refusal to utter correct words or phrases even though separate words may be spoken.

Aphoresis. Refers to lack of energy, weakness, poor endurance.

Aphrodisiac. Refers to anything that excites sexual desire.

Apnea. Refers to transitory cessation in breathing.

Apomorphine. It is a drug which mimics the action of dopamine (*q.v.*) at the synapse. It may be used to induce vomiting.

Apostilb. It is equal to one tenth of a millilambert.

Appeal. It is an attempt to arouse emotion or motivation by verbal or pictorial communication.

Applied Psychology. Refers to all those subdisciplines within psychology that seek : (*a*) to apply principles, discoveries and theories of psychology in practical ways in related areas like education, industry, marketing, opinion polling, sport, etc. ; and/or (*b*) to discover basic principles which can be so applied.

Apport. Refers to the hypothesized moving of an object to a particular place by paranormal means.

Apprehension. It is the act of seizing or of grasping. Apprehension is generally considered as a rather primitive, immediate act and distinguished from *comprehension*, that involves more in the way of reflection and interpretation.

Apprehensiveness. Refers to a relatively mild sense of anxiety about upcoming events, an uneasiness about future happenings.

Apraxia, Akinetic. It is a form of apraxia characterized by an inability to carry out spontaneous movements.

Approach-approach Conflict. It is a situation wherein the individual is drawn toward equally attractive but incompatible goals. For example, a college senior might receive equally attractive offers from two professional courses to which he has applied.

Approach-avoidance Conflict. It is a situation wherein there are both attracting and repelling aspects to the same goal. For example, a woman wishes to marry but fears sexual relations.

Aqueous Numor. It is the fluid that fills the anterior chamber of the eye.

Aquaphobia. Refers to tear of water in bathing or swimming.

Arachnoid Layer. It is the delicate membrane intermediate between the pia mater and dura mater in the brain and spinal cord.

Arbitrary Response. It is a response that ignores the character of the inkblot whereon it is based.

Arborization. Interlacing, branching. Used of nerve processes that display tree-like conformations.

Area Sampling. Refers to the use of all respondents in a given geographical area. For example, all respondents in a square mile in a given city.

Argot. Means slang. A specialized slang that reflects the common and unique experiences of a particular group. Originally, argot was reserved for the language of criminal groups, now it is more widely used.

Armed Forces Qualification Test. A preliminary screening test consisting of several subtests designed to provide scores of performance on verbal, arithmetic, spatial and mechanical skills as well as a single general score.

Army Alpha (and Beta) Tests. Two general tests of intelligence used in screening recruits for the U.S. Army in World War I. The Beta was a *performance test* designed for illiterates and recent emigres to America whose English was poor ; the Alpha was a standard examination that drew heavily on verbal skills.

Arrest. Means, a stoppage, a cessation of the function, motion, development etc,, of a process.

Arrhythmia. Refers to lack of or disruption in normal rhythm; irregularity.

Arthur Performance Scale. A *performance test* of intelligence based on non-verbal materials. Used with deaf children but has wider applicability.

Artificial Intelligence. The solution by computers or information processing systems of tasks that normally need human intelligence.

Artificialism. Refers to child's tendency to explain natural phenomena in terms of intentions. For example, when asked why the clouds move, the child answers, "The clouds move because they want to."

A-scale. A questionnaire designed to measure intolerance for ambiguity.

Ascendance. Refers to tendency to assume a leadership role in social interactions and groups.

Asceticism. It is a way of living based upon voluntary abstention from sensual, physical pleasures and emphasizing simplicity and self-discipline

Asexual. Means reproduction that does not involving the union of sex cells from two different individuals.

Asitia. Refers to revulsion at the sight or thought of food.

Asocial. Means lacking in social customs or social sense.

Aspartic Acid. An amino acid suspected of being a neurotransmitter.

Assay. Means to examine by test or trial. Hence, the analysis of any complex subject (*e.g.*, a chemical substance, a drug) to determine its components.

A-S Scale. It is an opinion scale for measuring anti-Semitism.

Assets-liabilities Technique. A therapeutic procedure wherein the client compiles two lists of his or her behavioral and personality characteristics, one containing traits regarded as being of value (assets) and the other listing traits seen as personal liabilities. The technique is generally used in behavior therapy for specifying the goals for the client.

Assignment Therapy. Refers to the utilization of small work or play groups for the purpose of psycho-therapy.

Association Neuron. Refers to one of the neurons in the central nervous system which connect sensory and motor neurons or, connect any two centers in the brain

Association-Reaction Time. It is the elapsed time between a stimulus word and the response in a word association test.

Association Test. It is a psychometric or experimental procedure that is designed to assess the subject's reactions to stimuli of various sorts. In *free association* tests, the subject is allowed to respond with word that comes into his mind. In *controlled association* tests he must respond according to a predetermined category, such as synonyms, antonyms, etc.

Associative Thinking. Refers to the thinking that depends on past associations. A train of thought where one idea leads to another illustrates this form of thinking.

Assumption. It is a premise or supposition that something is true for the purpose of theoretical development. The term includes *hypothesis*, a principle to be tested experimentally, and *postulate*, a principle assumed to be true for the purpose of developing a theory.

Asthenic Body Type or Physique. Refers to the long, slender body. A physique Kretschmer believed to be associated with the schizoid personality.

Astigmatism. Refers to the failure of the light entering the eye to come to a focal point due to irregularities in the curvature of the refracting mechanism mostly the cornea.

Astraphobia Refers to abnormal fear of thunderstorms.

Asylum. Refers to any institution for persons unable to care for themselves.

Asymbolia. Refers to a form of language disorder characterized by the inability to use and understand symbols.

Asymptote. It is theoretical limit that a curve approaches but never reaches.

Asynergia. Refers to inability to carry out complex motor activities involving coordination between different muscle groups.

Atropine. It is a drug which acts to block the action of acetylcholine at certain synaptic sites. Once widely used in eye examinations to relax the iris and in research on thirst to block salivation.

Atrophy. It is the wasting away of tissue caused by disease, old age or injury.

Attend. Means to pay attention to a stimulus.

Attention Reflex. Refers to a change in pupillary diameter upon a sudden fixation of attention.

Attitude Type. Refers to classifications of people according to their reactive dispositions.

A-Type Personality. Refers to a personality pattern characterized by competitiveness, aggressiveness, high achievement, impatience, and restlessness.

Atypical. Means differing markedly in some characteristic.

Aubert-Fleishel Paradox. Movement perceived as slower when a moving target is fixated than when the background is fixated.

Audiometer. It is an instrument used for determining auditory acuity.

Audiometry. It is the science of testing hearing.

Auditory Never or Acoustic Never. Refers to the portion of the eighth cranial never that mediates auditory sensation.

Auditory Space. It is the sense of the physical space surrounding one as perceived through sound.

Autistic Child. Refers to an extremely withdrawn child. They appear to be lost in a world of inner fantasy.

Autoeroticism ; Autoerotism. Refers to sexual behavior utilizing one's own body, as in masturbation.

Autohypnosis. Refers hypnosis that is self-induced.

Automatism. Refers to any act performed automatically, that is, without conscious thought or reflection.

Automatization. It is the process of development of a skill to degree wherein acts become so routine as to need little or no conscoùs effort.

Automatograph. It is a device used for measuring and recording involuntary movements.

Autoplasty. It is the process by which one's internal psychic system is developed.

Autopsychic. Descriptive of psychic processes where the primary reference point is in the individual.

Autopsychosis. Refers to a psychotic condition wherein the primary symptoms are displayed as disordered ideas concerning the self.

Autosome. It is a chromosome other than a sex chromosome.

Auxiliary Solution. It is defense mechanism or partial solution to a conflict, like compartmentalization ; externalization ; and intellectualization.

Aversive Therapy. It is a technique that reduces the frequency of maladaptive behavior by associating it with real or imagined aversive stimuli during a conditioning procedure.

Aversive Behavior. Refers to the study of behavior under conditions of noxious stimulation. It includes the three major phenomena of *escape learning, avoidance learning* and the effects of *punishment.*

Aversive Control. Refers to characterize any situation where behavior has been brought under control by unpleasant or painful consequences, *e.g., escape learning.*

Avoidance Learning. Refers to any learning situation where the correct response allows the organism to escape punishment.

Avoidance Response or Reaction. Refers to ambient behavior wherein the individual moves away from a stimulus.

Axial. Pertaining to an axis, situated in or along an axis.

Axiom. Any proposition whose truth is considered self-evident. In logical-theory construction the axioms form the fundamental, primitive elements upon which the whole theory rests.

Axoospermia. Means absence sperm from the semen.

Axotomy. Means severing of an axon.

Azygous. Means not paired, single.

B

B. Rorschach's symbol for resposes determined by perception of human beings in motion in the Inkblot Test.

Babble. Infant vocalizations which are presumably produced without any meaning intended. As babbling gradually starts to include sounds typical of the speech environment and to be used for communication, various qualifiers have been used, *e g., directed babbling, controlled babbling,* etc.

Babble Stage. Period of simple vocalizations which the normal infant uses in play at about two months of age.

Babinski Reflex. Extension of the toes when a blunt object is drawn across, the sole of the foot. In the infant, it is a normal reflex ; in the adult, it indicates a lesion of the pyramidal tract of the cord.

Babyhood. The stage of life which precedes walking. The upper limits are variously set at one year, fourteen months, and eighteen months.

Baby Talk. A basically silly term having two opposing denotations : 1. The speech *of* very young children. 2. The speech of adults and other children *to* very young children.

Bacillophobia. Morbid fear of infection by microbes.

Background. It is the portions of a picture depicted as being in the rear or at some distance from the figure.

1. A person's collective experiences in life as pertains to some task or job. 2. The total environmental setting preceding an event. 3. The background represents the objects and surfaces in the rear of a visual stimulus, the largely undifferentiated portion which contains no figure (as opposed to the foreground). 4. More generally, any secondary sensory stimulus, as in "background music."

Backward. This term is used to characterize one with mild retardation, *e.g.*, a backward child.

Backward Association. Refers to the connection that exists between a given item in a series and a preceding item.

Backward Child. Euphemism for a child of subnormal intelligence. Backwardness, however, may be caused by adventitious factors, such as timidity, malnutrition, illnesses, uncorrected sensory defects, cultural impoverishment of the environment, and the like.

Backward Conditioning. The establishment of conditioned reflex when the adequate stimulus precedes the conditioned stimulus in the training sequence.

Bad. A term which is used frequently in clinical psychoanalysis to qualify the unpleasant, feared or malevolent aspects of a psychodynamically important object. Hence, the *bad* mother is the image of the punishing, love-withholding, persecuting mother.

Bad Trip. The term used for a frightening and occasionally terrifying drug experience.

Bait Shyness. A particular instance of *toxicosis*.

Balance. Refers to any state in which all opposing forces are equalized is said to be "in balance."

Balanced Scale. Refers to any scale (or test or questionnaire) in which items with any potential source of bias get balanced.

Balance Theory. Refers to a general theory of attitudes and attitude change which is due originally to F. Heider. Its main assumption has been that a person will seek to resolve or relate attitudes that are "out of balance" with each other.

Ballism. Refers to a motor disorder (*i.e.*, a *dyskinesia*) which is characterized by violent failing movements. It has been due usually to damage to one of the subthalmic nuclei associated with the *basal ganglia*. When only one side of the body gets affected it is termed as *hemiballism.*

Ballistic. The term characteristic of the motion of projectiles. The eye movements known as *saccades* are generally referred to as ballistic movements as the eye seems to "throw itself" to its next fixation point. Such movements can be seen in normal reading of printed materials.

Ballistic Movements. Sweeping motions of the entire arm. In studies of efficiency in industry, output can sometimes be increased when workers are trained to use ballistic movements rather than jerky motions.

Ballistophobia. Refers to the fear of missiles or thrown objects.

Balsamic. Refers to a class of pine-like odors.

Band Score. Generally a sense of the error variance in a test score is provided by reporting not a raw score but a band score. Thus a person who scored, say, 43% on a particular test would be reported as falling within the band 40%-46%, revealing that a 3% error is not unusual. Band scoring was developed to disallow overinterpretation of scores known to be inexact and variable.

Bandwagon Technique. The term used for a propaganda device in which it is claimed that a majority of people hold a position or belief so as to persuade others to adopt that position or belief.

Bandwidth. Refers to the frequency range of a group of sound stimuli.

Baragnosis. The term used for the inability to provide accurate estimates of the weights of lifted objects. Generally a result of lesions of the parietal lobe.

Barany Chair. Apparatus for rotating a person in a test of vestibular sensitivity.

Barany Test (or **Method**). This involves bodily rotations of a subject in a special chair (the standard method is one full rotation every two seconds for 20 seconds) so that each of the semicircular canals gets ended up in a plane at right angles to the direction of rotation. Such rotation produces a characteristic pattern in *nystagmus*, which could be studied to determine whether the vestibular apparatus is functioning properly.

Barbiturate. Any one of a class of drugs like phenobarbital or seconal, that act as central nervous depressants, inducing drowsiness and muscular relaxation.

Barbiturate Abuse. Generally, chronic, pathological use of barbiturates experiences disturbed and impaired social/occupational functioning as a result.

Barbiturate Amnestic Disorder. An amnestic disorder which follows long-term abuse of barbiturates. Unlike alcohol amnestic disorder. full recovery, may occur once the abuse has ceased.

Barbiturates. The term used for a very large group of drugs classified as *hypnosedatives*. Of the over 2,500 barbiturates which have been synthesized, roughly 15 have been currently used, in a variety of conditions, including (most commonly) as an aid for sleeping, as an anesthetic and in the symptomatic treatment of epilepsy.

Barbiturate Withdrawal. A syndrome which has been classified as an organic mental disorder. It appears following cessation of intake of barbiturates after a history of prolonged and heavy use. The symptoms include nausea, weakness, tachycardia, sweating, anxiety and confusion.

Barbiturate Withdrawal Delirium. *Delirium* that takes place within a week after cessation of or dramatic reduction in heavy use of a barbiturate or similarly acting drug.

Bar Diagram or Chart. A method used representing scores or magnitudes by means of narrow rectangles of uniform width but different lengths. If the bars are made contiguous, the vertical lines are generally omitted and the diagram is called a *histogram*.

Baresthesis ; Baraesthesia. Refers to the sense of pressure.

Bargaining. As a social psychological term it includes those processes which are used by two or more persons or groups in their attempts to settle the give-and-take involved in a transaction between them.

Bar(o). Combining form which means *weight, pressure.*

Barognosis. The term used for the ability to estimate reliably the weight of lifted objects. Distinguish from *baragnosis.*

Baroreceptor. Specialized receptors which respond to changes in barometric pressure. Found primarily in the blood vessels and the heart.

Barotaxis. An automatic orienting response to a pressure stimulus as displayed, for example, by fish species which swim with (or against) water currents.

Barotropism ; Barotaxis. An orienting response where in the organism heads into the current, such as may take place in fishes that inhabit currents of water.

Barrier. Refers to any impediment or block preventing an organism from reaching a goal.

Barrier. Refers to any real or imagined impediment to movement toward a goal. These may be physical, social, or the result of the individual's physical or mental limitations.

Barron Movement Threshold Inkblot Test. A projective test wherein the person is shown a graduated series of inkblots that are progressively likely to produce the perception of human movement.

Baryecoia. Refers to partial deafness or hardness of hearing.

Baryglossia. Means thick tongue, therefore slow, thick speech.

Barylalia. It is indistinct "thick" speech or poor articulation.

Baryphonia. Refers to difficulty in producing articulate speech.

Basal Age. On tests standardized in mental age units the age level at which all items are passed.

Basal Ganglia. They consist of a number of masses of gray matter in the subcortex of the cerebral hemispheres that are important in motor coordination.

Basal Metabolism Rate (BMR). It is the minimum energy in calories output required for minimum bodily functioning.

Base Line. Refers to the abscissa or horizontal axis.

Base Rate. It is the normal frequency of occurrence of any response, statistic or other measure per unit of time. For example, in assessing a new reading curriculum one would compare the new reading scores against the base rate prior to its introduction.

Basi-, Baso-. Prefixes denoting *base* or *walking*.

Basic. Pertaining to a base.

Basic Anxiety. Refers to the child's feeling of being alone and helpless in a potentially hostile world.

Basic Conflict. Refers to fundamental conflicts which emerge when *neurotic needs* are discoordinate.

Basic Needs. Refers to the primary human needs including those that are physiologically based, like food, water, avoidance of pain, etc. and those which are psychologically based, like security, affection, self-esteem, etc. These needs are also called *deficiency needs*, on the assumption that if the object of need is missing the person will seek to make up for the deficiency.

Basic Personality. Refers to the constellation of personality traits common to individuals in a given culture that results from common childhood experience and training.

Basic Skills. Refers those skills to which are considered fundamental for further education and essential for learning other subjects.

Basilar Artery. It is the artery at the base of the brain that connects the blood supply of the vertebral artery and the carotid artery.

Basilar Membrane. The membrane in the cochlea whereon the organ of Corti rests. The hair cells of the organ of Corti change mechanical energy (movements of the basilar membrane) into nervous impulses that are then transmitted to the auditory centers in the temporal lobes.

Basiphobia. Refers to fear of walking or, in extreme cases. of standing erect.

Basket Cell. It is a type of interneuron found in the cerebellum.

Bathophobia. Means, a fear of depth. Also used for a fear of looking down from a high place.

Bathy. Means *deep.*

Bathyesthesia. Refers to deep sensitivity. Used for sensitivity in body parts under the skin, in muscles, internal organs, etc.

Battered Child. Refers to a child who has been repeatedly subjected to severe physical beatings and abuses by parents or guardians.

Battle Fatigue. Refers to *shell shock* or *combat fatigue.*

Bayes' Theorem. It gives a relation between the various conditional probabilities of different events that gives the probability if a particular event (A) is a result of one (X) of a number of mutually independent events (B, C, D, ... , Z) that might have produced A.

Bayley Scales of Infant Development. One of the most commonly used *developmental scales* for assessing the status of infants from 2 months to 2½ years of age. It consists of a *mental* scale, that samples perception, memory, learning, simple problem solving and the like ; a *motor* scale, that measures sitting, standing, walking, stair climbing and manipulatory skills ; and an *infant behavior record* that rates personality development, social behavior, attention span, persistence and goal directedness.

Beat. It is the periodic fluctuation in sound intensity produced when two tones of slightly different frequencies are sounded together.

Beat Tone. It is a rough tone intermediate in pitch between two tones, differing slightly in pitch, and are sounded simultaneously.

Before-After Design. An experimental condition wherein both the experimental and control groups are given a pretest and an aftertest.

Behavioral. Term refers to distinguish sciences whose aims and methods are objective as opposed to subjective or mentalistic.

Behavioral-directive Therapy. Refers to any of a number of behavior therapies all of which share the assumption that neurotic or maladaptive behaviors can be objectively treated independently of the rest of the client's personality.

Behavioral Dynamics. Refers to the pattern of motives that underlies behavior.

Behavioral Genetics. It is a branch of psychology that deals with the investigation of genetic or hereditary influences on behavior.

Behavioral Homology. The generalization that behavioral patterns form a continuity from species to species.

Behavioral Oscillation. Refers to momentary fluctuations in *reaction potential.* Behavioral oscillation is considered to be normally distributed.

Behavioral Pattern. Refers to any complex, act made up of recognizably individual components which are organized into a whole.

Behavioral Rehearsal. Refers to the utilization of role playing by therapist and patient with the goal of helping the patient overcome deficits in interpersonal behavior.

Behavioral Science. Refers to any science that deals with the study of the behavior of organisms including psychology, sociology, social anthropology, ethology, and others.

Behavioral Sink. Refer to the disorganized and aberrant environment that is an outcome of severe overcrowding.

Behavior Determinant. Refers to any variable that is a essential antecedent condition for behavior to occur.

Behavior Disorder. Refers to any aberrant or maladaptive pattern of behavior which is sufficiently severe to warrant the attention of counselors or therapists.

Behavior Episode. Refers to a sequence of actions that have some reasonably well-defined beginning and ending.

Behaviorist. Any person who espouses the theoretical and methodological positions of *behaviorism*.

Behavior Modification. Refers to the process of changing (modifying) a person's behavior.

Behavior Object. Anything toward which reactions tend to be standardized, like a toothbrush, a chair, or a shoe.

Behavior Problem. Refers to a person, generally a child or adolescent, whose behavior is persistently antisocial.

Behavior Rating. Refers to the report of the presence of a specific behavior or class of behavior.

Behavior Sampling. It is a record of what an individual does during a specific period. The period chosen is to be representative of the totality of the behavior under reference.

Behavior Setting. It is the general, ecological mileu within which behavior takes place.

Behavior Therapy. A type of psychotherapy which seeks to change abnormal or maladaptive behavior patterns by using extinction and inhibitory processes and/or positive and negative reinforcers in classical and operant conditioning situations.

Belief Dilemma. Refers to an attitude or opinion whose positive and negative components are in a state of imbalance.

Bell Adjustment Inventory. It is a personality questionnaire which yields scores on home, health, social, and emotional adjustments. Grades 9-16 and adult.

Belle Indifference, La. French for *sublime indifference.* Refers to various psychiatric conditions wherein the patient appears blithely and inappropriately unconcerned about his or her disabilities.

Bell-Magendie Law. It states, that the ventral roots of the spinal nerves are motor in function and the dorsal roots are sensory.

Bell-Shaped Curve. Refers to the normal-distribution curve.

Bem Sex Role Inventory. A scale used for measuring the extent to which an individual displays traits or behavioral characteristics traditionally associated with the masculine and/or feminine poles of sex-role identification.

Beneceptor. Refers to a receptor, or sense organ, whose stimuli are in some way beneficial to the organism.

Benign. Pertaining to the milder forms of mental disorders.

Bennett Differential Aptitude Test. These are the tests of numerical, verbal, mechanical, and abstract reasoning ; spatial relations ; clerical speed and accuracy ; language usage. Grades 8-12.

Benzedrine. It is a synthetic compound that is used as a central nervous stimulant.

Berdache. Refers to an American Indian who dresses and assumes the occupation of a woman.

Bestiality. Means sexual intercourse with animals.

Beta Endorphin. It is the most potent of the known *endorphins.*

Beta Response. It is a response that occurs shortly after presentation of the conditioned stimulus but anticipatory to the unconditioned stimulus in classical eye lid conditioning.

Beta Rhythm ; Beta Waves. These are brain waves of 13-25 Hz observed on the electroencephalograph, that are faster than the alpha waves and are of lesser amplitude.

Beta Test. It is a group performance test for illiterates and was used during the First World War.

Beat Weight. In multiple correlation, the weights are the multipliers of predictors that will produce the highest correlation.

Betz Cell. Refers to the large pyramid-shaped cells of layer V of the motor cortex.

Bezold-Brucke Phenomenon. It is a shift in hues containing red and green toward the yellow and blue side of the spectrum on increasing the intensity of illumination.

Bibliophobia. Refers to an irrational fear of books. Also used for a pathological hatred of books.

Bifactor Method. A method in *factor analysis* that extracts a principal factor first and then extracts other factors.

Bilateral. Pertaining to two sides.

Bilingual. Refers to one who is able to speak two languages with approximately equal fluency.

Bimodal. It is the characteristic of any frequency distribution that has two points or scores which share the property of having the greatest number of cases, that is, a distribution with two *modes.*

Bimodel Distribution. Refers to a distribution having two peaks or maxima.

Binaural. Pertaining to the two ears acting together, as in ordinary hearing.

Binaural Beat. It is a periodic fluctuation in sound intensity produced when two tones of slightly different frequencies are led into the two cars separately.

Binaural Fusion. Refers to the combined effect of stimuli simultaneously presented to the two ears.

Binet Test or Scale. The individual verbal scale designed to assess the relative intellectual ability of French school children.

Binocular. Refers to the simultaneous functioning of both eyes.

Binocular Accommodation. Refers to the simultaneous accommodation of the two eyes.

Binocular Color Mixture. It is the simultaneous. presentation of two different colors to the two eyes by means of a stereoscope.

Binocular Cue. Refers to a visual cue for depth perception that needs both eyes, *e.g.*, *retinal disparity.*

Binocular Disparity. Refers to the slight difference between the two retinal images when viewing a solid object.

Binocular Fusion. Means the blending of two images that fall on the separate retinas into a unitary experience.

Binocular Parallax. It is the disparity in the two retinal images due to the separation of the eyes.

Binocular Perception. It is perception with the two eyes interacting in a way so as to achieve fusion of the two visual fields.

Binocular (or Retinal) Rivalry. A perceptual phenomenon which takes place when the proximal stimuli to the two retinae cannot be resolved into a single percept.

Binocular Vision. Means seeing with both eyes focused on the same object.

Bio. Refers to *life* or indicates a *relationship* to *life* or the *living.*

Bioacoustics. A hybrid field of study including zoology, biology, physics and psychology and investigates the acoustic communication systems of nonhuman species.

Biocybernetics. A relatively new area of research that deals with the relationships between consciousness and biological functioning.

Bioelectrical Potential. It is the electrical potential shown by living tissues, like neurons, the brain, and the heart.

Bioenergetics. Refers to the study of energy transfer between living systems.

Bioethics. A field of study dealing with issues of ethics and values in relation to medicine and related sciences like biology, physioloay, psychology, etc.

Biofeedback. It is the control of internal processes, like heart rate, brain waves, or the galvanic skin response, through conditioning.

Biomedical Therapy (or Treatment). Refers to any form of psychotherapy based on biological techniques. *e g.*, drug, therapies, electroconvulsive shock therapy, and psychosurgery.

Biometry. It is the process of utilization of statistical techniques for the study of living organisms.

Bionics. Refers to the study of living systems with emphasis on the construction of artificial systems that will simulate their functions and characteristics.

Bionegativity. A personality constellation wherein a part is not harmoniously related to the whole, thereby impairing the functioning of the organism.

Biopsychic. Concerning to psychological phenomena as they are related to the life of the individual.

Biorhythms. It covers all forms of periodicity of biological systems.

Biosocial. Concerning the interrelationships between biological and social phenomena.

Biosphere. It is the portion of the earth which supports life. The biosphere in organismic theory includeds the whole person, encompassing the biological, psychological and sociological aspects.

Biostatistics. Means *Vital statistics.* Or the use of statistical procedures and techniques in the study of living organisms.

Biotype. Refers to a group of organisms which share a common complex of hereditary factors.

Biotransformation. Refers to any alteration in a substance within the body.

Bipolar. Anything having branches arising from both ends of a cell body, as bipolar neurons.

Bipolar Cell (or Neuron). Refers to neuron with two extensions or processes (axon and dendrite) running in opposite directions from the cell body.

Bipolar Disorder. It is an *affective disorder* wherein both manic and depressive episodes occur, *i.e.*, both poles on an affect dimension are manifested.

Birth. It is the act or process of being born.

Birth Control. Refers to any procedure or practice that is used to control the number of conceptions and births.

Birth Cry. It is retlex vocalization associated with the initiation of respiration immediately after birth.

Birth Defect. Refers to any congenital abnormality.

Birth Injury. Refers to an injury to the infant that occurs during birth.

Birthmark. Refers to any congenital disfiguration.

Birth Order. The relative age of children in a given family.

Birth, Preterm. Refers to any birth before the completion of the full, normal gestation period, *i.e.*, prior to the 37th week.

Birth Rate. It is the number of live births per 1,000 people in the total population.

Birth Symbolism. It is a symbolic representation in a neurotic symptom or other form of behaviour, that stands for the separation of the newborn child from the mother.

Birth Trauma. Refers to the anxiety experienced by the infant upon being flooded with stimuli at birth.

Biserial Correlation. It is a relationship wherein one variable is divided into two classes and the other into many classes.

Bisexual. Refers to an individual whose sexual preferences include members of his or her own sex as well as members of the opposite sex.

Bisexual Libido. Refers to fixation of the libido on both masculine and feminine objects.

Bit. A contraction of the words "binary digit." A bit is a "piece" of information. In simplest terms it is the amount of information necessary to reduce the alternatives in a choice situation by one half.

Bite. Refers to a sudden reduction in response rate followed by a compensatory increase will, when presented in a graph of cumulative responses, make it look like a "bite,' has been taken out of the otherwise smooth curve.

Bite Bar. Refers to rigid plate that a subject can bite down on firmly so that the head is held steady. Bite bars are generally used in visual research so that the subject dces not move his or her head about needlessly and the experimenter has control over where in the visual field a stimulus is presented.

Bitter. One of the four primary tastes.

Black. An achromatic color having minimum brilliance. It constitutes the extreme lower limit of the gray series.

Black Box. Refer to models that seek to explain the behaviour of organisms by drawing analogies between the organism and a piece of apparatus capable of receiving stimulation (input) and of making responses (output).

Black English. Refers to the dialect of American English spoken by many Americans of African descent.

Blackout. Refers to temporary loss of consciousness. Or the amnesia experienced by some serious alcoholics where they have no memory for a period of time.

Blacky Test. A psychoanalytical test for children based on a set of cartoons depicting a family of dogs in a variety of situations. The child is asked to tell a story about each picture.

Blind Alley. Refers to passage or arm of a maze that is a dead end.

Blend. Means a fusion of sensory experiences, such as the taste blend experienced in lemonade.

Blind Analysis. Refers to any analysis that is carried out without knowledge about conditions or information that might lead to biases in interpretation. For example, in a "blind" clinical diagnosis the psychologist or psychiatrist would proceed without knowing the results of any other diagnosis that may have been made.

Blindness. Refer to complete lack of vision. Strictly speaking, there is a continuum of loss of vision and the point at which a person is considered blind is usually a legel problem. The standard generally adopted is of visual acuity of less than 20/200 after correction or the visual field restricted to 20° of arc or less.

Blending. Refers to the synthesis of phonetic elements.

Block. Refers to any obstruction or barrier that prevents a process from taking place.

Block-design Test. Refers to a test that makes use of colored blocks wherein the testee is required to match designs.

Block Sampling. The phenomenon of grouping of respondents or elements to be sampled into categories representative of the population and selecting from each category a certain number of cases for the final sample.

Blood-brain Barrier. A selectively permeable "barrier" between the circulating blood and the brain that functions by preventing some substances from reaching the brain. It is considered to consist partly of cells making up the walls of the capillaries in the brain mainly of the astrocytes that surround the capillaries.

Blood Levels. Refers to the concentration of a substance in the blood.

Blood Pressure. It is the force exerted by the blood against the arteries. Systolic pressure is the maximum phase, which results from the surge of blood from the left ventricle ; the diastolic phase is the minimal or resting phase. The two are often reported in the form of a ratio. For example, 120/80 means a systolic pressure of 120 and a diastolic of 80.

Blue. One of the four primary colours. The normal eye experiences it when stimulated by a light of approximately 470-75 nm.

Body. Refers to the central portion of an organism bearing the appendages and head.

Body Build. Refers to the individual's structure from the point of view of the proportions of trunk and limb length to girth.

Body Concept or Body Image. Refers to the individual's idea of how his body appears to others.

Body Language. Refers to the complex system by which information about feelings and emotions is communicated through non-verbal channels involving gestures, body position, facial expressions and other *paralinguistic* devices.

Body Size. Refers to the standard score for height times transverse chest measurement.

Bogardus Social Distance Scale. A scale to measure the social distance that people desire to maintain between themselves and members of other races or ethnic groups.

Bogen Cage. An intelligence test in which the tastee is required to move a ball toward the exit by the shortest route using a stick inserted between slates of the apparatus.

Bond. Refers to a connection or like between things.

Bonding. Refers to the strong attachment of the mother to infant and infant to mother that develops shortly after birth.

Bone Conduction. Refers to the conduction or transmission of vibrations through the bones of the skull.

Boomerang Effect. Refers to shift in an attitude away from the position advocated by others.

Boolean Algebra. This is basically a system of symbol manipulation that uses algebraic procedures but independently of specific mathematical interpretation.

Bootstrap. Refers to operations by which one uses existing knowledge or information to develop more powerful routines. The term is used metaphorically in cognitive psychology and artificial intelligence to characterize theoretical procedures wherein the system (organic or mechanical) "builds" useful structures for more powerful procedures than were originally programmed (genetically or artificially) into it.

Borderline. Refers to any class of phenomena lying between two categories.

Borderline Intelligence. It is used to specify the level of intellectual capacity that would differentiate those who were capable of functioning normally and independently in the world from those who would need some form of institutional assistance.

Boundary (*Lewin*). Refers to any limitation or hindrance to moving from region to region within the life space.

Bound Energy. Refers to energy that is available to the ego process for dealing with reality.

Bovarism. Means failure to differentiate between davdreams and reality.

Brachycephalic. Means broad-skulled ; having a short front-to-back ratio.

Bradyarthria. Refers to abnormally slow and hesitating speech.

Bradyesthesia. Refers to any reduced perceptual functioning.

Bradykinesia. Refers to slowness of motor movements.

Bradylalia. Refers to slowness of speech.

Braidism. Synonym for hypnotism.

Braille (or Braille). A touch-based writing and reading system wherein patterns of raised dots are used to represent letters and numerals.

Brain. Refers to that part of the central nervous system that is encased within the skull.

Brain Center. Refers to any one of a number of areas in the brain wherein there are complex interconnections between afferent and efferent fibers. It is used to refer to explicit and identifiable structures like the hypothalamus and also to refer to hypothetical groups of neurons assumed to control a particular function, like the speech center.

Brain Death. Refers to the circumstances wherein standard electroencephalographic (EEG) data indicate that key components of the brain are no longer functioning.

Brain Lesion. Refers to any damage to brain tissue produced by injury, disease, surgery, etc.

Brain Potential. It is the electrical potential of the brain.

Brain Stem. It is the portion of the brain that remains after the cerebrum and cerebellum are removed.

Brainstorm. Refers to a sudden insightful idea, generally accompanied by a compelling emotional reaction.

Brainstorming. Refers to a group problem-solving technique wherein everyone sits around and lets fly with ideas and possible solutions to the problem at hand.

Brainwashing. The process of conversion of an individual from an established orientation to another.

Brain Waves. Refers to the rhythemic, spontaneous electrical discharges of the living brain.

Brawner Decision. A legal decision about the use of an *insanity defense* in the U.S.A. It states, "a person is not responsible for criminal conduct if at the time of such conduct as a result of mental disease or defect he lacks substantial capacity either to appreciate the wrongfulness of his conduct or to conform his conduct to the requirements of law."

Breakthrough. In psychotherapeutic work refers to a progressive quantum step in the client's attitudes, reactions, behaviors, feeling of self, etc.

Breast. In classical psychoanalytic writings, the term refers to both the anatomical part and to a symbolic representation of it in the mind.

B Reaction Test. Refers to a test wherein the subject is required to discriminate or choose between two stimuli.

Bregma. Refers to the juncture in the skull where the sagittal and coronal sutures meet.

Brief Psychotherapy. Refers to any psychotherapy which is specifically designed to be relatively short in duration.

Brief Reactive Psychosis. Refers to an acute psychotic disorder with the defining feature that the duration is of no more than two weeks.

Brightness. It is the intensity of visual experience and is primarily dependent upon the amplitude of the light wave.

Brightness Adaptatian. Refers to a decrease in the brilliance of stimuli because of increasing the general of incident illumination.

Brightness Constancy. Refers to the tendency for a visual stimulus to be perceived as having the same brightness under widely divergent conditions of illumination despite the fact that the different conditions deliver different amounts of physical energy to the eye.

Brightness Contrast. Refers to the intensification of the apparent brightness of a stimulus object as because of either simultaneous or prior stimulation.

Brightness Threshold. It is the minimal intensity of visual stimulation required for any specified wavelength that is recognized as brighter than the surrounding unstimulated field.

Bril. It is a unit of the perceived brightness of a light.

Brilliance. Refers to the dimension of a color that enables the subject to locate it on the black-white-gray series.

Briquet's Syndrome. Refers to a behavior disorder characterized by vague feelings of unease and poorly articulated, indefinite complaints.

Brodmann's Areas. Refers to regions of the cerebral cortex to which Karl Brodmann, a German anatomist, assigned a system of numbers.

Broken Home. Refers to a home wherein one parent is absent because of death, divorce desertion, etc.

Brontophobia. It is pathological fear of thunder.

Brown-Peterson Paradigm. Refers to a design used for measuring short-term retention wherein a distraction stimulus is used to prevent rehearsal.

Brusixm. It is the tendency to grind the teeth during sleep.

Brute Force. A problem-solving technique in which all possible alternatives are attempted or all possible paths to a solution are followed.

B-Type. It is a personality pattern that is associated with low aggressiveness, competitiveness, and achievement motivation. B-type persons are considered to be less prone to coronary attacks than A-types.

Buccal. Concerning the mouth or cheek.

Buffer. It is a storage structure or process that provides for holding information for brief periods, as in short-term memory.

Bug. Refers to problem in a process, an error in a program.

Bugger. Slang for anal intercourse.

Bulb. It is the medulla oblongata.

Bulia. Combining form meaning *will.*

Bulimia. Refers to a pathologically excessive appetite.

Bunsen-Roscoe Law. The principle according to which the visual threshold is a function of the duration of the stimulus multiplied by its intensity.

Burnt. An odor quality that is typified by the smell of burnt wood.

Burst. Refers to any sudden increase in responsiveness.

Butaperazine. One of the *phenothiazine derivatives* used in the treatment of schizophrenia.

Butyrophenones. A group of *major tranquilizers* classified as *antipsychotic drugs.* The most commonly used is *haloperidol.*

Buzz Word. Refers to any word or term that is instantly responded to with a predictable, emotional reaction.

Bystander Effect. It has been found that people are less likely to help in an emergency when they are with others than when alone.

C

C. Refers to a Constant.

Cable Properties. Properties which characterize the ability of axons to conduct impulses passively in a decremental fashion. cachexia ; cachexis. It is a condition of extreme malnutrition.

Cachexia. Means, bad condition, due to ill health, malnutrition, physical wasting away.

Cachinnation. Refers to inappropriate, hysterical laughter.

Cac(O-). Combining form meaning *bad diseased, degenerate.*

Cacoethes. Refers to a bad habit or propensity.

Cacogeusia. Pathological condition wherein ordinarily palatable foods produces a disgusting, putrid taste.

Cacosmia. Refers to an abnormal condition wherein pleasant or neutral smelles are experienced as foul and disgusting.

Caffeinism. Refers to caffeine intoxication. Its symptoms are nervousness, anxiety, insomnia. In sensitive persons as little as 250 mg (roughly 2—3 cups of coffee or 3—5 cups of tea) can produce these effects.

CAL. Computer-assisted learning.

Calcarine Cortex. Refers to the cerebral cortex that surround the calcrine fissure in the occipital lobe. It contains the primary visual area.

Calcarine Fissure. Refers to an invagination on the medial surface of the occipital lobe that separates the cuneus from the lingual gyrus.

Caloric Nystagmus. Refers to nystagmus induced by irrigation of the ears with warm or cold water.

Calyx. An eggcup-shaped dendritic process wherein another cell is embedded.

Camera. Refers to a chamber, room, cavity, box, etc. Used in anatomy for internal chambers and in experimental research for specially constructed chambers.

Campimeter. Refers to the chart used in mapping the visual field.

Canal. It is a narrow channel or tube ; *e.g., groove, duct, foramen, tract*, etc.

Canalization. Means the narrowing or restricting of alternative ways of behavior so as to select one in preference to others.

Cancellation Test. It is a speed test wherein the subject is asked to cancel out a certain symbol whenever it appears scattered at random among a pattern of similar symbols.

Candela. The primary standard unit for measurement of the luminous intensity of light. It is the amount of light radiating from a bar of pure platinum held at the solidification temperature (2,042°K) through a 1.5 mm aperture.

Cannabis Sativa. Indian hemp. The female plant is the source of marijuana and hashish.

Canon. Refers to any working principle or formula and is generally reserved for important, fundamental principles that are likely to lead to meaningful truths.

Canonical. Characterizing or relating to elements or events that are ordered or structured according to some principle or model.

Cannula. Refers to a small tube inserted into the body for the extraction or introduction of substances.

Capacity. In computer sciences and cognitive science refers to the amount of information which a given system can handle ; *e.g., channel capacity, storage capacity.*

Capgras Syndrome. Refers to the delusion that "doubles" have replaced persons whom one knows.

Capillary. Means *hairlike.* The capillary system connects the arterial and venous systems.

Carbon Dioxide Therapy. It requires the inhalation of a mixture of 30 per cent CO_2 and 70 per cent O_2 to the point of unconsciousness several times weekly.

Carboxyl Group. A functional group made up of two oxygen atoms and one hydrogen atom bound to a carbon atom (COOH).

Cardiac. Pertaining to the heart.

Cardinal Point. Refers to that point in a quantitative series of sensations at which the differential threshold begins to increase in accordance with Weber's law—that is, in proportion to the magnitude of the stimulus rather than in an absolute manner.

Cardinal Trait. It is a pervasive and outstanding characteristic which influences nearly all of an individual's behavior.

Cardio. Prefix meaning pertaining to heart.

Cardiogram. A graph of the electrical activity of the heart muscle.

Cardiograph. It is an instrument used for recording the rate and amplitude of the heartbeat.

Cardiophobia. Refers to irrational fear of heart problems.

Cardiovascular. Pertaining to the heart and blood vessels.

Caretaker. Refers to anyone who is intimately involved in the raising of a child.

Carnal. Pertaining to the flesh. Occasionally used as a euphemism for *sexual.*

Carpal. Pertaining to the wrist.

Carpal Age. Refers to the degree of bony development as judged by ossification of the carpal, or wrist, bones.

Carphenazine. A *phenothiazine derivative* that is used to treat schizophrenia.

Case Study (or History). Refers to the detailed account of a single individual. This is used in psychotherapy, where as complete a compilation as possible is made on a single person. In clinical psychology and psychiatry, disciplines which were originally nonexperimental in their approach, case studies often became the basis for generalized theoretical principles.

Caseworker. Refers to any health-related professional (or para professional) who handles individual case over an extended period of time.

Caste. It is a group separated socially from others by social, racial, or religious barriers.

Castration. Refers to the surgical removal of the testes or ovaries.

Castration Complex. (*Psychoan.*) in the male refers to the infantile fear of losing the genital organs. In the female, the fantasy that the girl once possessed the penis but lost it by castration.

Cata. It is a prefix which indicates *from*, *against*, and on occasions *in accordance with* or *repeating*.

Catabolism. It is the processes that is involved in tearing down tissues and expending energy, with the resulting accumulation of waste products.

Catalexia. Refers to a reading disorder wherein words are reread.

Cataplexy. Refers to immobility caused by extreme fear or shock.

Categorical. Absolute, independent of other things.

Cathexis ; Cathection. Refers to the investment of the libido on an object, on another person, or on the self.

Catotrophobia. Refers to fear of mirrors.

Cauded. Toward the tail.

Caudal. Pertaining to the tail.

Ceiling. Refers to the maximum score that is attainable in any test.

Ceiling Effect. Refers to the maximum score on a test or a limit on the performance on some task.

Cell Body. It is the integral "life support" component of a neuron. It contains the nucleus and other supporting structures.

Cellular. Pertaining to, or composed of cells.

Cenesthesia. Refers to the normal collective sense of being alive, of being aware.

Cen (o). Combining form meaning *common frequent.*

Cenogamy. A form of marriage where two or more men and two or more women unite into a single marital tie.

Censorship. It is the process responsible for selecting, accepting, or rejecting from consciousness ideas, memories, and impulses arising from the unconscious. It is a joint function of the ego and superego.

Cent. A unit of pitch equal to 1/1,200th of an octave.

Center. The mid-point of a body, organ or other structure.

Centi. Prefix denoting one-hundredth (1/100th).

Central Refers to something in the middle, or in the main portion of a body or a structure.

Centralism. Refers to the view that behavior could only be understood and explained through appeals to brain processes and brain function.

Central Process. Refers to process that occurs in the central nervous system.

Central Tendency. Refers to tendency for judgments, ratings, or estimates to gravitate toward the center of a scale.

Cephalic. Pertaining to the head.

Cephalad. Toward the head.

Cephalocaudal. Any thing pertaining to the dimension of the body between the head and tail.

Cerebellar Cortex. Refers to the gray, outer covering of the cerebellum.

Cerebral Hemispheres. Refers to the two symmetrical hemispherical halves of the *cerebrum*.

Cerebration. Refers to a physiological activity in the cerebrum.

Cerebrum. It is the largest and most important division of the brain. It consist of two hemispheres, each containing a number of cortical (surface) and subcortical centers that mediate sensory, motor, and complex ideational activities.

Certifiable. A term which indicates that the individual is in need of treatment for a mental disorder.

Cervix. Refers to the neck of any organ or body part, particularly of the womb.

Cerveau Isole. Refers to an experimental animal whose brain has been transected at the upper level of the midbrain between the inferior and superior colliculi.

C Factor. The factor of cleverness, quickness in thinking, reveald in some factor analyses of intelligence tests.

C Group. Refers to the control group in an experiment or study.

Chancroid. It is a veneral disease that is characterized by the eruption of a sensitive, inflamed ulcer in the genital area. Treatment is usually with antibiotics.

Character. Refers to a consistent and enduring property or quality by means of which a person, object, or event can be identified.

Character Analysis. Psychoanalysis oriented toward dealing with the client's character defeness.

Character Neurosis. Refers to a long-standing neurosis or disorder originating in childhood.

Charpentier's Law. According to it the product of the area of the image and the light intensity is a constant for threshold stimuli in the fovea.

Chemoreceytor. Refers to those sense organs which are responsive to chemical action.

Cherophobia. Refers to the fear of fun or gaiety.

Child. Refers to one who has not reached maturity.

Children's Apperception Test (CAT). A type of *Thematic Apperception Test* (TAT) designed for use with children.

Chir (o). Combining form meaning *hand.*

Chlorolabe. It is a green-sensitive pigment found in the cones of the retina.

Choc. Refers to an uncoordinated response elicited by a sudden stimulus for which the organism is not prepared.

Choleric. Means irritable, touchy, easily angered.

Chorea. Refers to any neurological disorder that is marked by muscular twitching and jerky, involuntary movements, *e.g.*, Huntington's chorea, Sydenham's chorea.

Choreiform. Pertaining to movements like those observed in chorea.

Chromatic Color. A color possessing the attributes of hue and saturation.

Chromatics. It is the science of color.

Chronaxie. A value used to express the sensitivity of a nerve to stimulation. It is measured by first determining the threshold of the nerve, the amount of direct current that when applied indefinitely would just excite it. This value is then doubled and the amount of time this current must be applied before the nerve responds is the chronaxie.

Chronoscope. Refers to a clocklike instrument used for measuring short durations of time.

Chronobiology. Refers to the study of biological rhythms, biological clocks, circadian rhythms, etc.

Chronograph. Refers to a device that records and presents graphic records of time intervals.

Cilia. Means Eyelashes. or Hairlike processes projecting from the surface of various cells (*e.g.*, in the bronchi), sing., *cilium.*

Cingulotomy. A form of psychosurgery wherein fibers in the cingulate cortex are severed. It is used in severe cases of manic-depression or severe anxiety.

Circadian. Pertaining to rhythmic biological cycles occurring at approximately 24-hour intervals.

Clairaudience. Refers to the hypothesized extrasensory perception of a distant sound.

Clan. Refers to a social group having common descent.

Clang Association. Refers to an association in a verbal task wherein two words or other stimulus items become linked due to acoustic similarity.

Classification. The process of categorizing things or events into mutually exclusive classes.

Class Limits. Refers to the upper and lower bounds of a class interval.

Clerical Test. Refers to a vocational test of the abilities needed in clerical work.

Clinic. Refers to a place organized for the diagnosis and treatment of physical and mental disorders.

Psychological clinics are similar in organization and function to medical clinics.

Clinical Psychology. It is the branch of psychology that deals with the application of clinical methods to persons suffering from behavior disorders.

Clinical Type. Refers to any individual case wherein the symptoms and behaviours conform to one of the many identifiable syndromes of clinical psychology and psychiatry.

Clonus. Refers to rapid, rhythmic contraction and relaxation of muscles.

Clone. Refers to a cutting taken for the purpose of propagation.

Cluttering. Refers to rapid, often incoherent speech characterized by eliding words and syllables.

Coacting Group. Refers to a group working side by side on a common project but without communication or interaction between the members.

Coccyx. Refers to the small bone at the base of the spine in man and tailless apes. It is formed from four fused rudimentary vertebrae.

Coenesthesia : Coenaesthesia ; Coenesthesis. The mass of undifferentiated sensations from within the body that forms the basis for bodily feelings.

Codeine. An opium alkaloid obtained from morphine. It is an analgesic and has sedative properties and is commonly used in low does as an analgesic and a cough suppressant.

Cognitive Need. Refers to a motive or desire to observe and know the environment.

Cognitive Science. Refers to a cluster of disciplines that studies the human mind. It includes cognitive psychology, epistemology, linguistics, computer sciences, artificial intelligence, mathematics and neuropsychology.

Cohort. Refers to an ancient Roman military unit consisting of from 300 to 600 soldiers. In demography, a number of persons all possessing a common characteristic ; for example, a group of children born in the same year. In ethology, a number of organisms of a given species that function together as a group.

Coition ; Coitus. Refers to sexual intercourses ; the union of the male and female genitals with orgasm. Coition is the process in general whereas coitus is a specific act of intercourse.

"Coke." Street slang for cocaine.

Cold. Refers to the sensation normally aroused by a stimulus whose temperature is below skin temperature.

Coldness. Refers to frigidity, or the inability to enjoy sexual feeling.

Collective Consciousness. Refers to the group or crowd mind.

Color. Refers to the subjective sensation associated with light. Color experience depends on three components of the physical energy : *wavelength, purity* and *intensity.* Wavelength corresponds to the psychological attribute of *hue* purity to *saturation* and intensity to *brightness.*

Colorimeter. It is an instrument used for measuring colors.

Color Mixer. It is an electric apparatus which rotates interleaved colored discs rapidly so as to achieve fusion of the colors.

Color Naming. It is a scoring category for naming the colored cards with appropriate color names as a form of response.

Color Primary. Refers to one of those colors which, when mixed in proper proportions, yield all other colors including white ; within this definition, red, green, and blue are the primaries.

Color Shock. Refers to scoring category for an emotional response to a colored card.

Color Temperature. It is the temperature of a black body at which it yields a color matching that of a given sample of radiant energy. The temperature is measured on the Kelvin or absolute scale.

Color Value. The dimension of brightness.

Coma. It is an abnormal state of deep stupor with total absence of consciousness, loss of all voluntary behavior and most reflexes.

Comatose. In a coma or a coma-like state.

Communication. Means the transmission of energy changes from one place to another, as in nervous transmission.

Comparison Stimulus. Refers to a stimulus, or part of a series of stimuli, that is compared with or judged against a standard stimulus.

Compartmentalization. Refers to the isolation of one's thoughts, feelings and beliefs from each other.

Compatible. Means capable of harmonious coexistence.

Compensation Idea. Means the substitution in fantasy or in dreaming of a superior image for an inferior one.

Compensatory Movement (or reflex). Refers to any movement that functions to restore normal body position or equilibrium.

Competent. In forensic psychiatry refers to a person who has been judged mentally capable to stand trial.

Complement. Refers to that which completes something.

Completion Test. A type of test designed in such a way that the subject must supply the answer by filling in blank spaces.

Compliant Character. Refers to a person who displays neurotic self-effacement, deference and inappropriate yielding. Horney considered such people as displaying a *neurotic compliance.*

Complication. Refers to a combination of sensations derived from different receptors, like the sight and smell of a rose.

Complication Experiment. Refers to experimental procedure the data from which gave rise to Titchener's *law of prior entry.*

Composite. Refers to unitary experience or whole made up of elements belonging to several other experiences.

Compound. A mixture or blend of elements or independent parts.

Compound Eye. A type of eye found extensively in insects, it is made up of a number of rudimentary optical systems which focus images at slightly different points in order to form a mosaic instead of a single image.

Compound Reaction. Forms of the reaction-time experiment wherein the subject either must recognize the stimulus before reacting or must discriminate between two or more stimuli.

Compound Tone. Refers to a tone composed of two or more simple or partial tones.

Compulsive. Characterizing a *compulsion.*

Computational Metaphor. Refers to the use of computers as models of human functioning and to the extended notion that human cognition is a computational process.

Conation. Refers to that aspect of the mental processes that have to do with volition, striving willing.

Concaveation. Means placing nonpregnant animals with young. Maternal behavior may be induced in female animals by this procedure.

Concept Acquisition. Refers to the process by which one learns ("acquires") a concept not known before.

Concept Discovery. Refers to the process by which one discovers which of several previously learned concepts is the proper one for a given situation.

Concordance. Refers to the appearance of the same trait in both members of a pair of twins.

Concrete Image. Refers to a memory image which is recalled in terms of the sensory qualities of an object, like the feel of a hammer or the odor of a skunk.

Concrete Intelligence. Refers to the ability to deal effectively with practical or concrete situations and relationships.

Conduction. The transmission of a neural impulse from one location to another.

Conduction Aphasia. Refers to a speech disorder involving the inability to repeat words as a result of damage to the conduction pathways between Wernicke's area and Broca's area.

Conduction Unit. It is a system of neural connections or bonds that function in a certain adaptive act.

Cones. Refers to the photoreceptors in the retina which mediate color vision. They are most densely packed in the fovea and thin out toward the periphery.

Confabulation. Making up details or filling in gaps in memory.

Confidence Limits. Refers to the limits outside of which an event is not expected to table place by chance with more than some specified probability.

Conformity. Refers to tendency to allow one's behavior to be governed by prevailing attitudes and opinions.

Confound. Means to fail to separate two variables so that their effects cannot be independently ascertained.

Congenital. Refers to those that are present at birth.

Congenital Deafness. Deafness already present at birth due to the defects in the development of the middle or inner ear.

Congruence. Refers to the conscious integration of an experience to become a part of the self.

Conjugate Movement. Coordinated movement, as of the two eyes.

Conjunctiva. Refers to the mucous covering of the eyeball and inner eyelid.

Connate. Appearing at or shortly after birth.

Connection. Refers to any linking between two phenomena, whether physical or mental.

Connector (Nouron). Refers to neuron that lies between and connects two other neurons or a receptor and an effector.

Conscience. Refers to the individual's system of moral values : the sense of right and wrong in conduct formerly believed by the theologians to be an innate character but now generally held by psychologists to be learned.

Conscious Experience. It is that awareness of a mental process of perception, emotion, motivation, etc.

Conscious Need. Refers to a need of which the individual is aware.

Conscious State. Refers to the totality of menntal processes at any given time.

Consequent. Refers to an event or phenomenon which occurred following some other event such that it "invites" the inference that it was caused by that event.

Conservatism. Refers to the point of view that defends the status quo, and maintains that the *conservative* position is to be defended.

Constancy. It is the tendency for perceived objects to give rise to the same perceptual experiences even though there may be wide defferences in the conditions of observation.

Constant. Refers to something that does not vary or is not permitted to vary.

Constellation. Refers to any reasonably well-organized matrix of associations, ideas, images, effects, etc.

Constriction. Refers to diminished or narrowed spontaneity.

Consultant. Refers to an expert brought into provide advice and counsel.

Contact. Refers to any face-to-face interaction between two or more people.

Contact Comfort. Refers to the satisfying feeling that comes from making contact with soft, comfortable objects.

Contagion. Refers to the spread of behavior patterns through a social group as a consequence of suggestion.

Content Word. Any word that has semantic content or meaning.

Context. Refers to conditions that surround a mental process and thus influence its meaning or significance.

Contiguity. Refers to the proximity of two objects or events in space or time.

Continence. Means self-restraint with respect to : (1) retention of urine, feces and other bodily discharges ; (2) sexual impulses.

Contingency Table. Refers to a table showing the frequencies of occurrence of categories of events in vertical and horizontal rows.

Continuant. In phonetics, a distinctive feature for distinguishing the sounds of a language.

Continuity Theory of Learning. The postulate that in discrimination learning there is an increment of learning for every rewarded or reinforced response to the stimulus.

Continuous Scale. A scale wherein the increments of gain are on a continuum.

Continuous Variable. Refers to a variable whose course of change shows no jumps, gaps, or breaks.

Continuum. Refers to a variable, graph, or curve having no discrete gaps between points.

Contour. Refers to the boundary of a perceptual figure.

Contralateral. Pertaining to the opposite side of a body.

Contrasuggestibility. Refers to the tendency to act in a way opposite to that which has been suggested.

Contradictory. Refers to either of two propositions such that if one is true the other necessarily is false and vice versa.

Contrary. Refers to either of two propositions such that if one is true then the other cannot also be true although both of them may be false.

Contrast. A marked awareness of the differences between two stimulus conditions resulting from bringing them together.

Contrectation. Means to touch with the hands.

Control. Means, the exercise of the scientific method by which the various treatments in an experiment are regulated such that the causal factors may be unambiguously identified.

Control Series. Refers to a series or measurements or experiments designed to test the validity of a previous experiment or set of observations.

Converse. Refers to a proposition derived by conversion (reversing the terms) of another proposition.

Conversion. Refers to a rapid, sometime dramatic, change in religious beliefs.

Convolution. A fold of the cerebral cortex.

Convulsant. Refers to an agent which produces a convulsion.

Coolidge Effect. It is the phenomenon by which the males of many species will show high continuous sexual performance for extended periods of time with successive introductions of new, receptive females.

Coordination. Means smooth, harmonious functioning of bodily parts, particularly muscles.

Coping Behaviour. Refers to the characteristic way in which the individual deals with his social and physical environment, specially as he mobilizes his resources to handle stress.

Coping Strategies. Refers to conscious, rational ways for dealing with the anxieties of life.

Copro. Combining form meaning *feces, filth, excrement,* etc.

Coprophagy. Refers to the ingestion of excrement or filth

Copulation. Means sexual intercourse.

Copulin. Refers to a vaginal pheromone isolated in rhesus monkeys that stimulates the male to copulate. The level of secretion is highest at the time of ovulation, thereby maximizing impregnation.

Corium. Refers to the outer portion of the derma, or layer, that lies under the epidermis.

Cornea. It is the transparent outer layer of the eye that covers the iris and the pupil. It is completely free of blood vessels and functions as a refractor of light.

Corollary. Refers to a proposition that follows naturally from something else.

Coronal. Pertaining to a plane of the head passing through the two ears.

Corporal. Pertaining to the body.

Corpuscle. Refers to a free-floating cell in the blood or a small, specialized organ in the skin like a touch corpuscle.

Correction. Refers to the manipulation of data in such a way as to minimize errors of observation and chance.

Correlate. Refers to any of two variables or factors which are systematically related to each other ; that is, they "co-relate".

Correlation Ratio. It is a measure of the extent to which a given regression line departs from linearity.

Correlation Table. It is a statistical technique used for showing the relationship between two variables to be correlated.

Correlation, Tetrachoric (r_t). Refers to correlation which is based on two variables each of which is expressed as a dichotomy (two-valued).

Corresponding Points. Refers to retinal points in the two eyes which give rise to a single visual impression when stimulated simultaneously.

Cortex. Refers to the outer layer of tissue of any organ and specifically to the *cerebral cortex.*

Cortical. Pertaining to the cerebral cortex.

Corticalization. Refers to the gradual subsuming of control of behavioral and psychological processes by the cerebral cortex. It can be seen as an evolutionary process.

Cortical Deafness. Refers to deafness due to injury to the areas for hearing in the cerebral cortex.

Cortin. It is a complex secretion of the adrenal cortex and contains several hormones. *Cortin* is important in the control of salt intake and in the regulation of the gonads.

Cortisone. It is a hormone produced by the adrenal cortex.

Co-twin Control. An experimental procedure by which hereditary factors can be controlled.

Counseling. Refers to a wide variety of procedures for helping individuals achieve adjustment, like giving of advice, therapeutic discussions, the administration and interpretation of tests, and vocational assistance.

Counterego. Refers to the unconscious part of the self which acts antagonistically toward the ego or self.

Counterinvestment. Means attaching an opposite feeling to a repressed idea or impulse. For example, showing hatred for a person whom one unconsicously loves.

Couvade. It refers to the custom among nonliterate peoples of the father taking to bed at the birth of a child as if he were suffering the pains of childbirth.

Covert. Refers to processes that cannot be directly observed like imagery, thought, etc.

Cranial. Pertaining to the *cranium*.

Cranial Index. The cephalic index as taken on a bare skull.

Craniometry. It is the measurement of the skull.

Crawling. Refers to infantile locomotion in a prone position by means of the arms pulling the body forward as the legs or knees push.

C Reaction. Refers to the response of an embryo to stimulation by bending the body into a C shape.

Creative Imagination. Refers to the pattern of ideas that accompany the solution of a problem.

Credulity. Refers to a disposition to believe too readily or on too little evidence.

Creole. In studies of language, refers to a *pidgin* which has become the dominant verbal communication system for a people and has acquired its own native speakers.

Criminal Psychology. It is a branch of psychology that deals with the study of criminal behavior.

Crisis. Refers to a turning point marked by sharp improvement or sharp deterioration.

Criterion. Refers to an independent, outside measure against which a test can be validated or a standard of judgment or belief.

Critical. Pertaining to an important or crucial judgment or evaluation, or a decisive point or the point of transition in a phenomenon or event.

Crossed Reflex. Refers to a reflex on the contralateral (opposite) side of the body from that stimulated.

Cross Education. A type of transfer wherein practice given to one side of the body is carried over to the other side.

Crossing Over. In genetics refers to the mutual exchange of genes between two chromosomes. The exchange takes place between corresponding genes on homologous chromosomes during meiosis.

Cross-validation. It is a technique used for determining the validity of a procedure by testing it for a second time on another sample after its validity has been demonstrated on an initial sample.

Crowd. Refers to a large but temporary gathering of persons having a common interest or focus.

Crowding. Refers to the sensation of stress and unpleasant feelings that are associated with settings involving a high density of people.

CRT. *Cathode ray tube* ; the output "screen" of an oscilloscope.

Crucial Experiment. Refers to a test or experiment which is critical for the acceptance of rejection of a hypothesis or theory.

Crude. In statistics : refers to characterizing data not yet analyzed or transformed.

Crutch. Refers to any supportive device.

Crystallized Intelligence. Refers to intellectual ability as dependent on cultural factors and learning as these interact with fluid intelligence.

Cyptorchidism. A condition wherein one (unilateral) or both (bilateral) testide(s) are undescended.

Cue. Refers to a learned signal for guiding or controlling behaviour or a stimulus used by the organism in making a discrimination.

Cult. Refers to a body of beliefs, rites, and customs associated with an object or person.

Cultural. Pertaining to cultural.

Cultural Items. Refers to test items which are heavily loaded with information which can be acquired only in a specific culture or subculture and are thus unfair to anyone not belonging to that culture.

Cultural Lag. Refers to the carryover of customs, attitudes and cultural products after these become dated or obsolete relative to the standards set by another culture or subculture.

Culture. It is the sum total of the customers, arts, science, and religious and political behaviour taken as an integrated whole that distinguishes one society from another.

Culture Complex. Refers to an organized set of social attitudes and behavior patterns which form an integrated whole ; for example, all activities associated with the hunting, preparation, and eating of meat.

Culture Contact. Refers to any form of interaction between persons of two distinct cultures which results in mutual modification of the cultures through reciprocal assimilation of traits.

Culturgen. Refers to the basic individual unite which make up culture.

Cumulative Record. Refers to a continuous record to which data are added in summative form.

Cumulative Scale. It is an attitude scale wherein the items have been arranged in such a way that a response to any given item may be taken as indicative of agreement with all items of lower rank.

Cuneate Nucleus (or Cuneus). Refers to grouping of neurons located in the lower medulla which relays neural impulses from the upper trunk and arms to the somatic sensory areas of the brain.

Cunnus. Refers to the external genitals in the female.

Cupula. Refers to a gelatinous body in the ampulla of the *semicircular canals* wherein the hair cells of the *crista* are embedded.

Curare. Refers to d-Tubocurarine. It is a chemical substance found in certain South American plants which causes paralysis in striated muscles. It acts by blocking cholinergic transmission at the myoneural junction by competing with acetylcholine at the receptor sites. Its major medical use is to induce muscle flaccidity for surgery, but it has also served psychology in a number of experiments that showed that a paralyzed animal can still learn a stimulus-response connection even through the overt response itself cannot be made during the actual training trials.

Cure. Refers to any procedure or treatment that restores health.

Curiosity. Refers to the tendency to explore, to investigate, to seek knowledge. Curiosity is considered by some psychologists as one of the primary drives, along with sex, hunger, thirst, etc.

Custodial Care. Refers to the minimal institutional care of mental patients without any therapy.

Custodial Case. Refers to an individual who needs institutional care due to mental illness or criminality.

Custom. Refers to a mode of relatively permanent behavior characteristic of a society.

Cutaneous. Pertaining to the skin or sense organs in the skin.

Cutting Score. Refers to a critical score which serves as a dividing point in a distribution of scores.

Cyan. Bluish-green color.

Cybernetics. A discipline primarily concerned with control mechanisms and their associated communications systems, particularly those that involve feedback of information to the mechanism about its activities.

Cyberphobia. Refers to fear of computers, a relatively recently acknowledged affliction.

Cycle. Refers to a recurrent series of events, or a complete vibration in sound or light waves.

Cyclic Disorder. Refers to a mental disorder, like manic-depressive psychosis, which tends to recur periodically.

Cycloid. Characterizing a personality pattern which shows relatively marked alternations of depression and excitement.

Cyclothymia. It is a tendency toward alternating periods of elation and depression which is serious cases, is manifested as manic-depressive psychology.

Cyesis. Means Pregnancy.

Cynophobia. Refers to irrational fear of dogs.

Cypridophobia. Refers to fear of sexual activity or fear of venereal disease.

Cytoarchitectonics (or Cytoarchitecture). Refers to the study of the architecture of the cells within the cerebral cortex.

Cytoarchitecture. Refers to the organization and patterning of cells within the cerbral cortex.

Cytogenetics. It is a branch of the study of heredity specializing in the structure and function of chromosomes and genes.

Cytology. It is the branch of biology that deads with the study of cells.

Cytogenic Syndrome. Refers to a condition marked by a variety of physical and behavioral symptoms due to some abnormality in the size, number, or shape of the chromosomes.

Cytoplasm. It is the protoplasmic substance of cells exclusive of the material in the nucleus.

Cytosine. It is one of the four nucleotide bases that make up ***deoxyribonucleic acid*** and ***ribonucleic acid.***

D

D. In Hull's theory, it stands for *drive*. In statistics it represents, a difference score.

Dactology. It is the art of communication by making use of signs made with the fingers.

Dactyl. Derived from the Greek for *finger* and, by extension, *toe*.

Daltonism. Refers to red-green colorblindness.

Damping. Refers to diminution in the amplitude of a wave.

Dance Therapy. It is based on the use of the physical and esthetic aspects of dance as a therapeutic medium.

Dancing Mania. Refers to an epidemic of obsessive dancing that has appeared from time to time in Europe.

Dark. Refers to a state of color of low illumination or brilliance.

Dark Light. Not light at all. It refer to the fact that the receptors in the eye have a level of spontaneous activity that, under the proper conditions, can be phenomenologically real and detected as a sense of "light".

Daseinanalyse. Refers to *existential analysis* or *existential psychology*.

Data. Refers to a collection of facts or numerical values.

Datum. It is the singular of *data* ; a fact or value.

Day Blindness. Refers to an abnormality of the eye in which the individual sees better in dim light.

Daydream. Refers to mental meandering, fantasies while one is awake. Interestingly, a good deal of research suggests that daydreaming is associated with mental health and stability.

Daymare. Refers to an acute anxiety attack.

Day Residue. Refers to the fragments of recent experiences during waking hours that emerge as dream images.

Deaf-mute. Refers to a person who can neither hear nor speak.

Deafness. Refers to the partial or complete inability to hear.

Deafness, Nerve. Refers to deafness caused by any neurological impairment of the auditory receptors in the cochlea or the auditory nerve.

Death. Refers to the point when an organism ceases to be alive.

Death Instinct. Refers to the instinct for destruction and death, and when fused with pleasure, inward and outward directed drives for pain.

Death Feigning. Refers to a response to threatening situations which a number of species have developed. The organism goes into a state of *tonic immobility* and seems to be dead.

Death Wish. Refers to an underlying element of the death instinct. It typically stands for a hypothesized motivational syndrome which is arguably responsible for individuals who consistently put themselves into situations which are life-threatening.

Debility. Refers to weakness in function, loss of ability. Generally of organic and motor functions, sometimes of cognitive.

Debriefing. It is the process of telling the subject in an experiment what it was about and, when necessary, revealing any deception or withholding of information that may have been a necessary element in the study.

Debug. Means to detect, identify and correct an error in a program, a research project, a logical argument, a complex piece of equipment, etc.

Decerebration. Refers to the removal of the cerebrum.

Decibel. It is a unit of measurement of the perceived differences in sound. The decibel is a $10 \times \log_{10}$ of the ratio between thresh hold intensity of 1000 Hz 2nd a comparison sound. A bel is ten times the threshold intensity. A whisper is about 10 decibels, conversation about 60, and thunder about 120.

Decile. Refers to any one of 9 points which devides a distribution of ranked scores into equal intervals. Each interval, thus, contains 1/10th of the scores.

Deciduous Teeth. Refers to the first, or baby teeth, that give way to the permanent teeth.

Declarative. It is a *speech act* wherein one tells someone something, *i.e*,, one makes a *declaration*.

Decoding. It is the process by means of which a receiver translates signals into messages.

Decompensation. Refers to a progressive loss of normal functioning in favor of psychotic behaviour, or disorganization of the personality under stress.

Decorticate. Refers to the state of being without a cortex. Certain classes of behavior requiring little or no functioning of the "higher mental processes" are sometimes referred to as decorticate activities. Sometimes the term is used of species of animals that never evolved a neocortex ; *e.g.*, avians.

Decorticate Conditioning. Refers to a conditioned response that has been established in the absence of the cerebral cortex.

Decrement. Refers to any decrease in anything. The term is used of behavioral performances, of knowledge, of memory, etc.

Decryption. Within cryptography, it is the act or process of converting a coded message back into normal form ; *decoding.*

Deduction. Refers to an inference made from formal premises or propositions, or the formulation of a hypothesis or set of hypotheses.

Deep Means below the surface, as in anatomical descriptions of underlying organs and tissues. In acoustics, pertaining to low-pitched tones. In vision, pertaining to richly saturated colors. In psychoanalysis, characteristic of material which the client brings to the analysis which derives from early life experiences or from experiences which have been repressed.

Deep Sensitivity (or Sensibility). Refers to sense of pressure, the receptors for which are in deep subcutaneous layers of the skin or in muscles.

Deep Structure. In psycholinguistics refers to the idea underlying a sentence.

Defect. Refers to flaw, an imperfection or a failure to function owing to such flaws.

Defective. Means lacking in some manner or having less than normal intellectual ability.

Defendence. Means to defend oneself from criticism, to justify verbally one's actions.

Defense. Refers to behavior that protects the ego against guilt, anxiety, and shame.

Defense Mechanism. Refers to any behavior pattern which protects the psyche from anxiety, shame, or guilt. Some common defense mechanisms are : repression ; regression ; projection ; identification ; fantasy ; compensation ; sublimation ; reaction-formation ; aggression.

Defence Reflex. A reflexive response, like as the sudden withdrawal of a limb to a painful stimulus.

Defensiveness. Refers to the personality characteristic of being overly sensitive to criticism.

Deference. Refers to the need to admire and follow a leades, or to serve a superior happily.

Deficiency. Means a lack of something, a condition wherein some important element is missing.

Definition. A boundary between two classes or phenomena. For example, a figure may be said to have good definition if it stands out clearly from the background because of having a well-defined border.

Definitional Validity. It is the assumed validity of a test whose items are taken as the definition of the variable to be measured.

Deflection. A defense mechanism which functions by diverting attention or awareness away from the object that arouses anxiety.

Defusion. Refers to a separation of the life and death instincts mostly fused in the unconscious.

Degenerate. Refers to one who deviates markedly from normal standards of acceptable conduct. Refers to individuals who have committed sexual offenses and in such cases implies a constitutional deficiency.

Dehoaxing. Means revealing any deceptions practiced on a subject during an experiment.

Deiter' Cells. These are elongated supporting cells present in the outer portion of the organ of Corti in the cochlea.

Delayed Reaction. Refers to a response in a reaction-time experiment which does not occur immediately.

Delayed Reward. Refers to the presentation of the reward following an interval of time after the subject has made his response.

Delinquent. Refers to someone who commits a crime or who violates a legal code.

Delinquency. It is a relatively minor offense against the legal code, by a minor.

Delirium. Refers to disoriented condition having clouded consciousness, generally accompained by hallucinations, illusions, misinterpretations of events and a mostly confused quality with reduced capacily to sustain attention to things in the environment.

Delphi Methods. It is a procedure used for predicting future events based on the pooling of judgements made by a number of experts.

Delta (△). A notation (the symbol △) used to refer to an increment in some variable or factor.

Delta Rhythm. An electroencephalographic wave of 1-3 Hz of high voltage (150 microvolts) that is characteristic of deep sleep.

Delusion. A false belief which cannot be modified by reasoning or a demonstration of the facts. Delusion should be distinguished from *illusion*, that is a distorted perception, and from *hallucination*, that is a false perception.

Delusion or Reference. A false belief that the behavior of others has malign significance for the self

Demand Character. Refers to the need-arousing attributes of objects. A shiny red apple "demands" to be eaten ; a striking painting "demands" to be looked at.

Dementia. Refers to a deterioration of intellectual, judgmental, and emotional processes that are characteristic of certain forms of senility and psychoses.

Dementia, Alcoholic. Refers to dementia observed in the last stages of severe, chronic alcoholism.

Democratic Atmosphere. Refers to the general socio-political climate established when a group is led by a person having democratic values, where free exchange of ideas and open discussion of issues are encouraged.

Demography. It is the study of population variables including geographic distribution, vital statistics, physical situations, and the like.

Demonology. It is a legitimate area of study of folklore and cultural myths concerned with demons and spirits.

Demonomania. Refers to the delusion on the part of an individual that he is under the influence of a demon or evil spirit.

Dendrite. It is the receiving end of a neuron. It is the first part of the neuron to receive impulses conveyed toward the cell body from other neurons or receptors.

Denervation. Refers to the removal of the nerve supply to an organ or part of the body.

Denial. A defense mechanism which simply disavows or denies thoughts, feelings, wishes or needs which cause anxiety.

Denotation. Refers to the object or objective events designated by a word.

Density. It is the attribute of solidity or compactness that according to some psychologists, tones possess.

Dental. Refers to a speech sound that is produced by placing the tongue against the teeth.

Dental Age. It is a measure of the child's dental development comparing the number of permanent teeth that have erupted to the average number for the child's age.

Deoxyribonucleic Acid (DNA). A large complex molecule consisting of four nucleotide bases (*adenine, guanine, cytosine* and *thymine*) and a "backbone" of a sugar molecule (specifically, 2-*deoxy-D-ribose*). The nucleotide basis are arranged in pairs down the center of the double-helix-shaped molecule and it is the specific arrangement that carries the genetic code determining the functioning of every cell. The code is based on sequences of 3 nucleotide bases each specifying one of 20 amino acids. Since there are 64 possible arrangements there is considerable flexibility in the arrangement and more than enough to code any given protein's sequence of amino acids. Each of the chromosomes in the nuclei of all cells is made up of DNA ; it is, therefore, the chemical basis for all heredity and the carrier of all genetic information.

Dependence. It is a relationship of causality between two phenomena, in such a way that a change in one is accompanied by a change in the other.

Dependence, Psychological. Refers to drug dependence produced by alterations in physiological states due to repeated administrations of the drug. Sever physiological dysfunctions emerge if the drug is suddenly discontinued or if an antagonist is administered. The opiates and the barbiturates both produce such dependence after prolonged use.

Dependence, Psychological. Refers to drug dependedce characterized by a pervasive drive to obtain and take the substance. It is used for dependences on drugs whose action does *not* produce fundamental biochemical changes like that continued doses of the drug are required for normal functioning. Drugs like marijuana are cited as likely to produce psychological dependence with habitual use.

Dependency. Refers to a condition wherein one individual must rely upon another, or upon society, for his maintenance.

Dependent. That which is influenced by another or is contingent upon the appearance of another event.

Depression. Refers to, a state of despondency characterized by feelings of inadequacy, lowered activity, and pessimism about the future or in pathological cases, an extreme state of unresponsiveness to stimuli, along with self-depreciation, delusions of inadaquacy, and hopelessness.

Depressor Nerve. It is a branch of the vagus (Xth cranial) nerve that functions to lower blood pressure.

Deprivation. Refers to the loss or removal of something desired or loved.

Deprogramming. It is a procedure used for reversing the effects of extreme indoctrination characteristic of brainwashing in cults. The victim is encouraged to think critically, flexibly, and independently after removal from the cult.

Depth. Refers to the perceived dimension of distance away from the observer.

Depth Analysis. Psychoanalysis is often called depth analysis as the assumption is that the analysis is probing deeply below the well-defended conscious level of mind to the underlying dynamic factors which presumably motivate the person.

Depth Interview. Refers to an interview which attempts to get at underlying or dynamic factors which motivate the individual and are responsible for observed behavior patterns.

Depth Perception. It is, the perception of depth, viewing the world in three dimensions. It refer to the distance of objects from the viewer and also refer to the three-dimensionality of objects themselves.

Depth Psychology. Refers to any psychological system which assumes that explanations of behavior are to be found at the level of the unconscious.

Deranged. Means disturbed or disoriented. Used with regard to cognitive, intellectual abilities.

Dereistic. Characterizing thinking that is autistic or governed by personal factors.

Derivation. Refers to that which is the result of a formal set of inferences, the outcome of a deductive process.

Derived. Meads developed out of, transformed from, acquired from, adapted from, etc.

Derived Emotion. Refers to an emotional reaction associated with the outcome of any intense motive or instinct, like joy or despair.

Derived Need. It is a need developed from or learned by close association with a primary need.

Derived Property. In psychology refers to the postulate that parts derive their characteristics from the whole.

Derived Scale. Refer to any scale which is a result of a transformation from another scale.

Derived Score. Refers to any score which is a result of a transformation from another score, *e.g.*, the *z-score*.

Derma ; **Dermis**. It is the skin under the epidermis.

Dermal. Cutaneous.

Dermal Sense ; **Dermal Sensitivity**. Refers to the sensations associated with receptors in the skin.

Dermatitis. Refers to any inflamation of the skin. Several types are known and generally associated with specific causes, but according to many authorities psychosomatic factors lead to a predisposition and exacerbation of many forms.

Dermatographia. Skin writing ; the appearance of raised welts on the skin upon being lightly stroked. It is believed to be because of hyperirritability of the dermal capilaries.

Dermatome. It is a section of the skin innervated by a particular spinal nerve root.

Dermographia. An incorrect, but sometimes used, spelling for dermatographia.

Descriptive Psychiatry. Refers to any system of psychiatric diagnosis that is used on the relatively straightforward descriptions of overt, observable symptions.

Desensitization. Means lessened reactivity, or a decreased emotional sensitivity with respcct to a personal defect or social problem after counseling.

Desexualization. Refers to to any procedure which results in the "removal" of sexual significance from something.

Design. Refers to a plan involving forethought, or a graphic or schematic representation.

Desire. Refers to a conscious longing or want, or a conscious wish to be rid of an unpleasant or aversive stimulus or situation.

Destination. It is the place where messages arrive.

Detached Affect. Kefers to affect that has been removed ("detached") from the painful, anxiety-producing idea or thought with which it was originally associated.

Deterioration. Refers to a progressive impairment or loss of function. The deteriorative psychoses are those in which the predominant system pattern is one of loss of judgment, emotional and intellectual deterioration, and progressive loss of memory.

Deterioration Index. It is a way of estimating the degree of deterioration of mental functioning. The index is based on the observation that certain abilities that the test measures decline with age.

Determinant. Refers to a cause or antecedent condion, or a factor that is decisive or final in a cause-and-effect relation.

Determiner. Refers to a cause, an antecedent condition that results in some particular outcome.

Determinism. Refers to the doctrine that for every effect there is a cause. According to determinism, given a complete knowledge of the individual's past and of present environmental conditions, his behavior could be predicted precisely.

Detour Behavior. Refers to any form of indirect action which leads to a goal.

Detour Problem. Refers to an experimental setting which requires subjects initially to move away from a goal so as to obtain it eventually. The problem was first introduced by the Gestalt psychologists under the German term *Umweg Problem.*

Detoxification. It is the process of treatment making use of rest, fluids and changes in diet to restore proper physiological functioning following disruption by overuse of drugs.

Detraction. Refers to the lessening of attention without loss of the local point of what one attending to.

Detumescence. Refers to subsidence of swelling.

Deuteranomaly. It is a visual condition wherein there is a slight diminution in sensitivity to green wavelengths. A deuteranomalope will need more green light to achieve color matching than one with normal vision.

Deuteranopia. It is a form or red-greed blindness wherein weakness for green is the predominant symptom. Shades of gray are seen in place of red and green, but the relative brightness value of the spectral colors remains unchanged.

Development. Refers to the progressive and continuous change in the organism from birth to death.

Developmental. Pertaing to *development*, in any of its senses.

Developmental Age. It is a measure of development stated in age units, or a combined index of all developmental estimates or scores.

Developmental Level. Refers to a division of the span of life according to arbitarily fixed chronological ranges. The period of infancy lasts from birth to approximately one year ; childhood from 1 to 12 years ; adolescence from 12 to 21 years ; maturity from 21 to 65 years ; and old age from 65 years to death.

Developmental Norm. It is a norm that is based on the representative performance to be expected of children at a given age or developmental level.

Developmental Psychology. It is a branch of psychology which studies the processes of pre- and post-natal growth and the maturation of behavior. It is interested in the various stages of development, the principles or laws of maturation, and the effects of early experience and later practice on development.

Developmental Quotient. It is equal to the developmental age, or any measure of development divided by the chronological age.

Developmental Scale. It is an inventory of behavior for the purpose of assessing the level of development reached by a child.

Developmental Sequence. It is the order of appearance of maturational patterns characteristic of the species.

Developmental Stage. Refers to any period of development during which certain characteristic behaviors appear.

Developmental Tasks. Refers to skills, levels of achievement, and social adjustment considered important at certain ages for the successful adjustment of the individual.

Developmental Unit. Refers to an interval in a scale of measurement that is equal or approximately equal at different ages.

Developmental Zero. It is the hypothetical point where development starts ; the point of fertilization of the ovum.

Deviance. Refers to any pattern of behavior which is markedly different from the accepted standards within a society.

Deviate. Refers to one who differs markedly from normal, or whose standards of conduct and attitudes are sharply in conflict with accepted standard, a sexual pervert.

Deviation IQ. Refers to a standard score on an intelligence test like the Stanford-Binet. The interpretation of the deviation IQ is similar to that of the conventional IQ.

Deviation Score. A value giving the degree to which any single score deviates from the mean of all the scores in a sample. Generally denoted as x or d.

Device. Any instrument, piece of apparatus or cognitive procedure used for some specific purpose

Devolution. Means reversal or undoing of evolution.

Dexter. Means *right* or *favourable.*

Dexterity Test. Refers to a test which requires both speed and accuracy in manual operations. Such tests utilize peg boards and simple assembling operations.

Dextrad. Toward the right side of the body.

Dextral. Meaning to the right side of the body.

Dextrality. Means preference in handedness for the right hand or the right side of the body.

Diachisis. Refers to a temporary increase in the threshold for excitability in a nerve center.

Dialectic (al) Psychology. It argues that conflict and change are the basic principles of life. Dialectics had its origins in Heraclitus and was further developed in philosophical and political forms by Hegel and Marx respectively. On this position, man transforms his environment by action which, in turn, changes him.

Dialysis. It is the process of purifying a liquid by passing it through a membrane.

Diazepam. A *minor tranquilizer* used in the treatment of anxiety.

Dich (o). Means *in two parts.*

Dichotic. Pertaining to differential stimulation of the two ears.

Dichotomy. It is a division in two classes according to some predetermined criterion.

Dichromacy. Refers to any of several kinds of color-vision deficiencies. Two forms of dichromacy involve weakness in the perception of reds and greens two others involve blues and yellows synonyms for dichromacy are *dichromatism, dichromatopsia, dichromopsia, dichromia* and *dichromasy.*

Dichromat. Refers to an individual having any of the various forms of *dichromacy.*

Diet. Means *way of living.* Thus Food substances and liquids normally consumed in day-to-day living.

Differential. Pertaining to factors or features that make one thing different from another.

Differential Aptitude Tests (DAT). A multi-aptitude battery made up of 8 separately administered tests designed to measure skills relevant to educational and vocational performance.

Differential Conditioning. Refers to the establishment of a conditioned response to one of two or more stimuli by selectively reinforcing the desired conditioning stimulus and not reinforcing the rest.

Differential Diagnosis. It is the process of distinguishing between two similar diseases or abnormalities by discovering a critical symptom that is present in one but not in the other.

Differential Extinction. Refers to selective extinction of responding by withholding reinforcement for that response while continuing to reinforce other responses.

Differential Growth. Refers to growth or development of an organ at a rate different from that of other organs in the same organism.

Differential Inhibition. Describes the gradual elimination of responding to stimuli that are similar to, but, discriminably different from, the original, conditioned stimulus.

Differential Psychology. Refers to study of psychology which focuses on individual differences in behaviour.

Differential Reinforcement. Refers to the application of reinforcement to one of two alternative responses. For example, if an animal is responding to both a tone of 260 Hz and one of 290 Hz, rewarding only the 260 Hz tone would be differential reinforcement leading to a discriminated response.

Differential Response. Refers to any response that is elicited by a particular stimulus among many possible different stimuli.

Differential Scoring. Refers to the scoring of a test battery in several ways so as to obtain measures of several different variables.

Differential Threshold. Refers to the minimally effective stimulus difference which is reported correctly as a difference 75 per cent of the time.

Differentiation. Refers to a biological process whereby a group of initially similar cells generates a number of different kinds of cells or a mathematical process of carrying out a differential or in sociology, refers to the process by which groups, roles, statuses, etc. develop within a society. In psychology proper there are two distinct uses. In conditioning studies, whenever an organism must learn to make two or more different responses to two or more similar stimuli.

Differentiation of Life Space. Refers to the organization of the life space into different regions, like the past, the present, and the future, and on the levels of reality and unreality.

Difficulty Scale. Refers to a test whose items are arranged and graded in the order of difficulty.

Difficulty Value. It is a measure of the discriminating power of a test item in terms of the percentage of individuals who passed the item.

Diffraction. It is the process cf bending of light or sound waves around the edges of some object in the path of the wave.

Diffraction Grating. Refers to a polished surface ruled by fine lines that is used for producing a spectrum.

Diffuse. Means lacking in specificity or coordination like the diffuse responses in infants which show a lack of goal direction and coordination.

Diffusion. It is the spread of cultural traits from one group to another or the spread of a stimulus through cutaneous tissues or the scattering of light in the eye because of spherical aberration.

Digital. Pertaining to the numbers in any given numbering system; *e.g.*, 0—9 in the decimal system, 1—2 in the binary, etc. or The fingers and toes.

Digit-span Test. Refers to a test of immediate recall wherein the subject repeats a random series of digits following a single presentation.

Digraph. Refers to any 2 letters in a word which are pronounced as a single phonetic unit; *e.g.*, the *ch's* in *church.*

Diglottic. Refers to the simultaneous stimulation of two areas of the tongue with the same substance.

Dilantin. It is an anticonvulsant drug that is used in the treatment of epilepsy.

Dilation. Means expansion, enlargement.

Dildo (e). Means artificial penis.

Dilemma. Refers to a situation wherein one is faced with two or more mutually exclusive or mutually incompatible alternatives from which to choose when none can be taken as truly satisfactory.

Dimension. Refers to three characteristics of physical space: height. width and depth. Now a days one speaks of color as having three dimensions (brightness, hue, saturation) or of a pure tone as having three (amplitude, frequency, phase).

Dimming. Refers to the enhancement of an afterimage by reducing the intensity of the area wherein the image is projected.

Dimorphism. Means having two forms of manifestations. Refers to species of which there are two distinguishable forms, as in juvenile and adult or male and female.

DIN Color System. Refers to color-classification system used widely in Europe. It is based on the three primary dimensions of hue, brightness and saturation.

Dionysian. Pertaining to the emotional.

Diopter. It is a unit for measuring the power of a lens for bringing parallel rays of light to a focus.

Diotic. Stimulation of the 2 ears with the same stimulus.

Diphenylbutyl Piperidines. Refers to group of *major tranquilizers* classified as *antipsychotic drugs* and used primarily in the treatment of schizophrenia.

Diphthong. Refers to speech sound produced by gliding from one vowel to another.

Diplacusis. Refers to an auditory disorder wherein a tone is heard as two tones differing slightly in pitch in the two ears.

Diplegia. Refers to paralysis on both sides of the body.

Diploid. Characterizing the two sets of chromosomes present in all cells except the gametes.

Direct Association. Refers to memory bonds between items without intermediary connections. For example, the linkage between $2 \times 2 = 4$ is direct.

Directions Test. Refers to a series of ordered tasks given to examinees as items on an intelligence test assuming that the ability to carry out verbal instructions is one indication of intelligence.

Direct Reflex. Refers to any reflex where the receptor and effector involved are homolateral, or on the same side of the body.

Dirhinia. Means of both nostrils.

Dis. A prefix meaning ***apart, away from, lack of, separation from, reversal.***

Disability. Refers to a severe, handicapping, loss, or impariment of a bodily organ, with corresponding functional loss.

Disabled. Refers to one suffering from a ***disability.***

Disambiguation. Refers to the act of determining the contextually appropriate meaning(s) of an ambiguous word, phrase, sentence, or other situation.

Discharge. Means the firing of a stimulated neuron or the release of pent-up tensions or the flowing away of a bodily secretion or the secretion itself.

Discipline. Refers to a branch of knowledge or control of subordinates.

Discontinuous. Means lacking continuity ; characterized by gaps or breaks or pertaining to measures that do not form a continuum of infinitely small steps but represent instead whole numbers.

Discord. Refers to a combination of musical tones that sounds harsh or inharmonious.

Discordance. Refers to failure of a trait to appear in both members of a twin pair.

Discourse. Refers to most speech-act longer than a sentence.

Discrete. Means separate, distinct, individually identifiable, discontinuous.

Discrete Measure. Refers to a measure taken from separate or discontinuous values.

Discriminanda. Refers to those properties or characteristics of stimuli that made them discriminable.

Discriminating Range. Refers to the spread of scores at which a test separates or measures subjects on the dimension measured.

Discrimination. Refers to the process of distinguishing between two objects or the process of distinguishing differences between stimuli.

Discussion Leader. In small groups, refers to one whose function is to promote discussion.

Disease. Refers to an abnormal condition within the body, involving a serious impairment of function.

Disfiuency. Refers to any nonfluent speech, *e.g.*, stuttering.

Disgust. Refers to the emotional feeling accompanying attitudes for repulsion, rejection, and withdrawal.

Disinhibition. Means the temporary removal of inhibition by introducing an outside or irrelevant stimulus or a loss of self-control upon overindulgence in alcohol or while under the influence of drugs.

Disjunctive Concept. Refers to concept that can be defined by the presence of any one of 2 or more aspects.

Disorder. Refers to a disease or lack of organization or meaningful relations among phenomena.

Disorganized. Refers to that which has lost or had disrupted its previous structure and functioning.

Disorganized Behavior. Refers to extreme emotional conditions where the individual's behavior lacks harmony and may show unintelligible relationships with environmental conditions, like those occurring in hysterical laughter induced by a tragic loss or disaster.

Disorientation. Refers to inability to orient oneself with regard to spatial, temporal and contextual aspects to the environment.

Disparation. Refers to the doubling of images nearer or farther than the point of fixation.

Dispersion. Refers to the scatter of a group of scores plotted in a frequency distribution or on a scatter diagram.

Dispersion Circle. Refers to the circle of light seen when looking at a single point source.

Displaced Vision. Refers to the research on perceptual experiences produced by various modifications of the visual field brought about by wearing special lenses that alter incoming light.

Displacement. Refers to the distortion of an eidetic image wherein there is inversion and reversal of the image or the transference of an affect or emotional attachment from its proper object to a substitute.

Disposition. Refers to the organized totality of the individual's psychophysical tendencies to react in a particular way.

Dissimilation. It is an antonym of *assimilation.*

Dissonance. Refers to the harsh, unpleasant effect produced by two notes sounded simultaneously which do not blend or fuse.

Distal. Means distant, away.

Distal Effects. Refers to responses which alter the environment in some manner.

Distance. It is the distance between a source of stimulation and the organism or on graphic rating scales, the linear distance between two data points.

Distance Receptor. Refers to any receptor or receptor system which responds to stimuli arising some distance from the body.

Distance Vision. Refers to the visual discrimination of objects more than twenty feet distant from the observer.

Distorted Room. It is a room constructed in a way such that the subject perceives it as rectilinear when, in reality it is not.

Distortion. Refers to any twisting or contorting that changes the shape of something so that it no longer lurely represents the object. In psychoanalysis as a defense mechanism which functions to alter or "disguise" dream content that would be unacceptable in nondistorted form.

Distractibility. Refers to tendency to be drawn away from that to which one is attending.

Distributed Practice. Refers to the spacing of periods of practice over a period of time rather than massing the practice in one long learning session.

Distribution. It is a table or graph of the frequency of scores plotted against their appropriate numerical values.

Distribution, Probability. It is similar to frequency distribution except that instead of pairing each class or category with the frequency with which it occurred it is paired with its probability of occurrence.

Distribution, Sampling. Refers to any distribution which results from taking samples of specified size from a population.

Disulfram. It is a drug that is used for treatment of alcoholism. It causes acetaldehyde, a breakdown product of alcohol, to accumulate in the blood resulting in a variety of most unpleasant experiences including dizziness, nausea, vomiting, sweating and a throbbing headache. Its success rate in treating alcoholism is not high and one likely reason for the failure is that the alcohol is not the unusual or novel stimulus that the conditioned aversion response needs for effective learning.

Disuse, Law of. Refers to the assumption that responses or associations which are not practiced will weaken and disappear.

Disutility. It is the opposite of *utility*, but with a wrinkle.

Diuresis. Refers to secretion and passage of large volume of urine.

Diuretic. Refers to a substance that causes increased secretion and passage of urine.

Diurnal. Means occurring during daylight hours.

Divagation. Refers to a tendency to disgress and ramble while speaking confused thought.

Divergence. Refers to the property of moving away from a central point or of lying in different directions.

Divination. Fore telling the future by magical or supernatural means.

Dizygotic Twins. Refers to fraternal twins, or twins arising from two separate eggs.

Dizziness. Refers to the sensation of falling or whirling generally accompanied by nausea.

DNA. *Deoxyribonucleic acid.*

Docile. One that is easily trainable, teachable. Tractable, manageable.

Doctrine. Refers to a teaching ; a set of beliefs, generally without adequate supporting evidence but with the implication that given further research adequate supportive evidence will be forthcoming.

Dogmatic. That which is stated on authority as a matter of faith.

Dogmatism Scale. It is a questionnaire designed to measure rigidity and inflexibility in thinking.

Dolichocephalic. Anything having a longs narrow head.

Dolor. Pain ; may be physical, or psychic.

Dolorology. It is the study of the causes and treatment of pain.

Dominance. Refers to the trait of desiring to be on top.

Dominance Need. Refers to the need to control others or to lead or dictate to others.

Dominant. Means displaying the characteristic of *dominance.*

Dominant Wavelength. Refers to the spectral wavelength which when mixed with white, will match a sample hue.

Dominator. Refers to a retinal ganglion cell which responds over the entire visible spectrum. Such cells do so in a nonuniform fashion and display peak sensitivity a particular wavelength.

Donders' Law. Refers to a principle of visual fixation which states that regardless of how an ocular position is reached, every position of the line of fixation corresponds to a definite, invariable angle of torsion of the eyes.

Dopamine. Refers to one of the catecholomines important in neural transmission. Also used in the treatment of depression and in Parkinson's disease.

Doppler Effect. It is the shit in hue or pitch when a source of light or sound is moving rapidly in reference to an observer.

Dorsad. Means toward the back.

Dorsal. Pertaining to the back.

Door-in-the-Face Technique. It is device used for obtaining compliance wherein the individual initially requests something very large, so large that it will surely be denied and than de-escalates to a more modest request.

Dopaminergic. Pertaining to pathways, fibers or neurons wherein dopamine is a neurotransmitter.

"Dope." Street slang for drugs.

Dorsoventral. Refers to the axis extending from the back to the ventral side of the body.

Dosage. It is the amount of a medicine or other preparation prescribed to be given.

Dotting Test. It is a paper-and-pencil test of mechanical ability wherein the subject is asked either to make as many dots as possible (tapping test), or to put dots in small circles as quickly as possible (aiming test).

Double Bind. Refers to the situation faced by a person who is receiving contradictory messages from another, powerful person.

Doubtful Judgment. In psychophysical experiments refers to a judgment of difference between stimuli of which the subject is uncertain.

"Downers." Street slang for any drug that has relaxing, anti-anxiety effects.

Dowsing. Means locating underground sources of water or minerals by prospecting with a divining rod of forked twig held by the two branches in the two hands. When the rod or twig dips toward the earth, the dowser takes this as a sign of success. Psychologists generally account for the phenomenon as unconscious muscle movements.

DQ. *Developmental quotient.*

Dramatization. Refers to the transformation of repressed wishes or impulses into symbolic forms, as in dreams.

Dream. Refers to a more or less coherent train of imagery and ideas coming during sleep, or in drugged or hypnotic conditions.

Dream Analysis. Refers in psychoanalysis to the contents of dreams that are analyzed for underlying of disguised motivations, symbolic meanings or evidence of symbolic representations.

Dream Content. Refers to the images and ideas expressed in the dream.

Dream Determinant. Refers to any factor in the environment which plays a part in the causation of a particular dream and lends it is particular flavor.

Dream Ego. Refers to a separate component of the ego which was considered to be responsible for dreaming.

Dream Interpretation. It is the process of deciphering the meaning of a dream. The procedure used by psychoanalysts is to have the patient free-associate around the dream content until its wish-fulfilment nature has become apparent.

Dream-series Method. It is technique used for studying dreams.

Dream Symbolism. Refers to the disguised expressions in dreams in which one thing is a "stand-in" or a symbol for something.

Dream Wish. Refers to the symbolic representation of a repressed or unconscious wish in a dream.

Drill. Refers to practice by systematic repetition to the point of mastery.

Drive. It is an aroused, goal-directed tendency of an organism that is based on a change in organic processes.

Drive Arousal. Refers to the activation of a drive by an internal or external condition, or, by a combination of both.

Drive Displacement. Refers to the arousal of behavior appropriate to one drive upon the frustration of another.

Drive Specificity. Refers to the assumed relationship between drive stimuli and the responses which satisfy the drive.

Drive State. It is the hypothetical intraorganic state which gives rise to drive behavior. Such states are considered to reach a certain critical level before initiating goal-seeking behavior.

Drive Stimuli. Refers to the afferent nervous impulses which are considered to arise in organs in a drive state.

Dromomania. Refers to an abnormal impulse to travel.

Drug Abuse. Refers to improper use of drugs.

Drug Addiction. Refers to the habitual use of drugs, with psychological and physiological dependence.

Drug Effect. Refers to any change in behavior or in a psychological state which is systematically related to drug dosage.

Drug Holiday. Refers to a period of time during which a drug is discontinued.

Drug Interaction. Refers to the effects of two (or more) drugs taken together, when their combined effects are different from what would be produced by only one of them taken alone. For example alcohol and a sedative where the interaction produces central nervous depression far greater than either drug alone would yield.

DSM (I, II, III). Refers to *Diagnostic and Statistical Manual.* Having been revised twice in recent years the three versions are denoted as I, II and III.

D-Tubocurarine . It is a drug whose active ingredient is *curare.*

Dual-Code Hypothesis. Refers to the belief that human memory is made up of two coding systems one based on a visual-imagery process and one on a verbal-coding process.

Dualism. Refers to any of a number of philosophical positions that admit of two separate states of nature or two sets of fundamental principles in the universe.

Dull Normal. It is a category for persons having IQ's between 70 and 90.

Dumb. Means mute, unable to speak.

Dumbness. Refers to an inability or unwillingness to speak.

Dummy. Synonym of *placebo.*

Duplicity Theory. The theory—now considered as established fact—that there are separate visual receptors for brightness vision (rods) and for color vision (cones).

Dural Sinus. It is the space between layers of the dura mater, or hard outer covering of the brain, that carries blood from the cerebral veins into the neck.

Dura Mater. It is the tough, outermost membrane covering the brain and spinal cord. Below it lie the arachnoid layer and the pia mater.

Durance. It is an interval of time during which a life activity takes place.

Duration. It is the time of occurrence of an event.

Dvorine Test. It is a test used for defective color vision it is similar to the Ishihara test.

Dyad ; Diad. Refers to a social group made up of two persons or a chord composed of two tones.

Dynaception. Refers to the self-perception of one's own need state.

Dynamic Equilibrium. It is the state equilibrium in which, although shifting and changing the overall pattern of forces or energy is in a stable, organized configuration.

Dynamic Psychology. Refers to any number of theoretical. systems.

Dynamic System. A term applicable to any system in which the several elements are all interwoven or interrelated so that changes in one sector of the system have systematic effects on the rest of the system.

Dynamics. In field theory refers to the forces which act upon a psychological field.

Dynamic Subsidiation. Refers to a sequence of subgoals leading to a final goal.

Dynamic Trait. It is a trait which has motivating characteristics or is manifested in goal-directed behavior.

Dynamism. Refers to a mechanism of adjustment. Whose primary function is to fulfill drives and motives and to protect oneself from stress and discomfort.

Dynamogenesis ; Dynamogen. Refers to the initiation of motor responses due to sensory stimulation or the correlation of effector responses with receptor activities.

Dynamograph. Refers to a recording dynamometer.

Dynamometer. It is an instrument used for measuring strength of muscular response, usually hand-grip.

Dyne. A unit of force defined as the force needed to accelerate 1 gram of matter through 1 centimeter per second.

Dys. A prefix meaning ***faulty, ill, bad, difficult***, etc.

Dysacousia. Refers to a psychological condition in which ordinary noise causes discomfort.

Dysarthia. Refers to speech impairment due to brain lesions.

Dysbasia. Refers to a difficulty in walking ; a form of *ataxia*.

Dyschiria. Refers to inability to tell which side of one's body has been touched.

Dyschromatopsia. Refers to any deficiency in color vision.

Dyschronism. Refers to disturbed time sense, specially one caused by flight across 5 to 10 time zones, which maximally disrupts biological rhythms.

Dyseneia. Refers to defective articulation of words, due to deafness.

Dysesthesia. Refers to a diminished sensitivity to pain.

Dysfunction. Refers to any disruption in normal functioning.

Dysgenic. Pertaining to influences detrimental to heredity or biologically deficient.

Dysgeusia. Refers to a disruption of the sense of taste.

Dysgnosia. Refers to any impairment of intellectual functioning.

Dysgraphia. Refers to inability to write, due to cerebral lesions.

Dyshomophilla. A psychosexual disorder wherein the sufferer is severely distressed and rendered highly anxious by his or her sexually arousing fantasies about homosexuality.

Dyskinesia. Refers to defects in voluntary movement.

Dyslalia. Refers to defective speech without demonstrable brain damage.

Dyslexia. Refers to inability to read ; impairment of the reading function.

Dyslogia. Refers to a deficiency in the ability to express ideas verbally.

Dysmnesia. Means impaired memory.

Dyspareunia. Refers to painful sexual intercourse. Considered as a functional disorder not associated with any physical or matomical dysfunction.

Dysphagia. Refers to any abnormal eating pattern.

Dysphasia, Aphasia. Refers to impairment or inability in any of the language functions.

Dysphoria. Refers to depression accompanied by anxiety.

Dysphrenia. Refers to any mental disorder.

Dysphrasia. Refers to impairment in writing or skeaking due to mental disorders.

Dysplasia. Abnormal growth because of an abnormal physique.

Dysstasia. Refers to difficulty in standing upright.

Dysthymia. Means despondency, depression.

Dystonia. Refers to a lack of muscular tonus.

Dystrophy. Refers to faulty nutrition leading to wasting and muscular weakness.

Dysuria. Refers to painful or difficult urination.

DZ. *Dizygotic.*

DZA (or DZa). Abbreviation for a set of dizygotic twins raised apart from each other.

E

E. A Multifunctional abbreviation used for 1. Experimenter. 2. Experimental group. 3. Energy. 4. Error are : $_sE_R$= excitatory potential ; $_sE_R$=reaction potential (from generalization) ; $_sE_R$=effective reaction potential.

Eccentric Projection. Refers to the experiencing of a locus of stimulation as "out there" in the world rather than at the receptors stimulated.

ECG. *Electrocardiogram.*

Echo. Combining form meaning ***repetitive.***

Echoic. It is the auditory analog of *iconic*.

Echoic Behavior. Refers to imitations of verbalizations of others.

Echolalia. Means the compulsive and apparently senseless repetition of a word or phrase just spoken by another person.

Echolocation. Refers to the location of objects in space using the echoes of self-produced sounds.

Echopathy. Refers to any pathological mimicking of the speech, gestures, actions or mannerisms of others.

Ecmnesia. Refers to loss of memory for recent materials while retaining memory for more remote events.

Ecological. Pertaining to ***ecology.***

Ecological Niche. Refers to position or function of an organism in a particular environment.

Ecological Optics. The notion of ***ecological validity*** applied to the study of visual perception.

Ecological Psychology. Refers to the approach to psychology that elaborates on J.J. Gibson's theory of *direct perception*.

Economic. It is thoughly equivalent to or pertaining to energy. Hence, the so-called *economic concepts* are those pertaining to the origin, distribution, transfer and use of psychic energy or libido.

Ecosphere. Refers to those portions of the natural environment which are habitable by life forms.

Ecosystem. It is a relatively restricted ecological unit.

Ecphoria. Refers to the establishing of a memory trace or the activation of a previously established memory trace.

Ectoderm. It is the outer layer of embryonic cellular structure which develops into the outer skin, the nervous system, the organs of special sense, the pineal gland and part of the pituitary.

Ectogenous. Refers to that which has its origins outside of the body, *exogenous*.

Ectomorphy. It is a one of the three primary dimensions of body type. An ectomorph is one whose physique is dominated by the embryonic ectodermal component, the outer skin and the nervous system.

Ectomy. Combining form meaning *removal*, particularly surgical removal.

Ectoplasm. It is the outermost layer of cell protoplasm. In *parapsychology*, a hypothesized psychic substance believed to emanate from the body of a medium in a trance during a seance.

Eczema. Refers to any of several forms of chronic dermatitis. Some cases are caused by irritating substances, of hers are considered to be due to psychological factors and are considered as *psychosomatic*.

Edge. It is a line in the vistual field at which there is a detectable difference in some aspect of the stimulus on one side of it as compared with the other.

EDR. Abbreviation for *electrodermal response*.

Education. It is the process of drawing something out, of making a connection, particularly of establishing a connection that reflects the fundamental relations between objects or events.

Educational Psychology. A branch of psychology that deals with theories and problems in education. It *includes* the application of principles of learning to the classroom, curriculum development and reform, testing and evaluation of aptitudes and abilities, socialization processes and their interaction with cognitive functioning, teacher training, etc.

Educational Quotient (EQ). It is equal to the ratio of *educational age* to *chronological age* times 100.

Effect. Refers to an event that reliably follows another event, its cause.

Effectance. It is the capacity to cope with the environment, to be competent. An effectance *motive* is that which functions by making a child feel a strong need to become competent in order to overcome feelings of inadequacy or inferiority.

Effective Reaction Potential. Refers to the *reaction potential* minus any inhibiting tendencies.

Effector. It is a muscle or gland at the terminal end of an efferent neural process that produces the observed response.

Effeminate. Means female-like. Refers to a biological male whose behavior patterns are more closely associated with females.

Efferent. Means *carry away from*. Hence, in neurophysiology it refers to the conduction of nerve impulses from the central nervous system outward toward the periphery (muscles, glands). Efferent neurons and neural pathways carry information to *effectors* and are commonly known as *motor* neurons or pathways.

Efficacy. Refers to a very primitive cognitive experience by which the young child's emotions and feelings are considered to be responsible for events in the world.

Effort. Refers to the work required to perform some action. In psychology, the subjective sense of the amount of work needed to perform some action.

E-F Scale. A scale from the Minnesota Multiphasic Personality Inventory (MMPI) consisting of 30 items and designed to measure attitudes toward ethnocentricity and authoritarianism (the "F" is for Fascism).

Ego Analysis. A psychoanalytic term for a relatively short form of analysis that focuses on the integrative, positive ego functions rather than on the deeply repressed id functions.

Ego Anxiety. In psychoanalytic theory refers to any reaction because of threats to the ego ; the anxiety caused by conflicts between id, ego and superego.

Ego, Block. Refers to anything that is seen, in psychoanalytic terms, as preventing or inhibiting the full development of the ego.

Ego Body. Refers to the belief that at its ultimate core the ego derives from the bodily sensations.

Ego Boundary. A concept according to which part of the normal ego development consists in establishing a boundary separating self from others.

Ego Cathexis. A channeling or focusing of libido on an object within the domain of the reality-oriented ego.

Egocentric. Pertaining to or characteristic of *egocentrism.*

Egocentric Speech. Speech that derives from and serves purely internal needs and thoughts.

Ego Complex. Refers to a group of emotional reactions toward or about oneself.

Ego Defense. It is the process of harboring the libidinal energies of the id in defense of the ego.

Ego Failure. Refers to "breakdown" in ego function, particularly a failure to restrain id impulses so that they conform with the strictures of the superego.

Ego Function. Refers to the primary role of the ego—to mediate between the id and the superego in ways which are responsive to society and self-protection.

Ego Integrity. The final of Erikson's *stages of man.* Full ego integrity in this conception allows the acceptance of old age and one's ultimate death without despair.

Egoism. Means *self-interest* used that such self-interest is at the base of all behavior.

Egoistic. Means conceited, self-serving, motivated by self-interest.

Ego Libido. Refers to Libido invested in the ego. It also refers to the psychic energy available for use in carrying out ego functions and sometimes used for self-love.

Egomania. Pathological preoccupation with one's ego.

Ego Neurosis. A classification in psychoanalysis which includes neuroses like paralyses, hysteria, memory loss, etc., which are hypothesized because of disruption of ego functions.

Egopathy. Refers to the tendency to bolster one's own ego by inappropriate hostility and aggression toward others.

Ego Psychology. Refers to the psychology of the ego. That is the examination of those developing structures and processes that are considered as being within the purview of the ego.

Ego Resistance. Refers to resistance on the part of the patient to give up neurotic patterns of behavior, to recognize repressed impulses and to abandon defense mechanisms.

Ego Strength. Refers to the strength of the ego in terms of its share of available psychic energy.

Ego Structure. Refers to the pattern and organization of ego traits functions, etc. Just what "structure" the ego "has" depends entirely upon the theorist under consideration.

Egotic, Pertaining to or characterizing the ego.

Egotism. Refers to the tendency to consider oneself very highly, particularly to the point of having an annoyingly overblown opinion of self.

Egotization. Refers to the process whereby some mental process becomes part of the ego or self ; *e.i.*, the process whereby it comes to be freed from id-based impulses of aggression and sexuality and becomes structured and reality-oriented.

Ego Trip. Refers to any pattern of behavior engaged in primarily for the purpose of boosting one's sense of self.

Ejaculatory Incompetence. Refers to the inability to ejaculate within the vagina during intercourse ; in a sense, the reverse of premature ejaculation.

Ekphorize. In psychiatry refers to bring back the effect of a specific psychological experience.

Elaborated Code. Refers to the speech mode adopted when one is speaking with persons from different bankgrounds from oneself. Under such conditions the discourse is relatively slow, words and phrases are carefully selected, the speech is relatively unpredictable and elaborately planned.

Elaboration. Refers to any process by which a specific memory for a stimulus is interpreted, elaborated, associated with other stimuli or in any other way "fleshed out."

Elberfeld Horses. Refers to a group of superbly trained horses in Germany popular during the early part of the century. The most startling was "der kluge" Hans who could seemingly perform complex mathematical problems, answer factual questions, spell, etc.

Elective Mutism. Means refusal to speak, psychiatrically it is considered a childhood disorder and generally associated with any of a number of other factors like abnormalities of articulation, extreme shyness, emotional trauma, social isolation, compulsiveness and functional enuresis.

Electrical Brain Stimulation (EBS). Refers to the application of a weak electrical current to a specific locale in the brain. It is used in a number of contexts from neurosurgical procedures, wherein it helps the surgeon determine the areas of the brain that need to be surgically removed and those that need to be protected, to experimental studies of the relationship between various cerebral structures and the functions they control.

Electro. Combining form meaning *electric, electrical.*

Electrocardiogram (ECG or EKG). It is a record of the activity of the heart obtained by recording the spreading electrical potential generated by the heart beat and putting it in graphic form. It has been used as a measure of emotional arousal, of physical exertion, etc., and so has served the role of dependent variable in studies of conditioning, of emotionality etc.

Electroconvulsive Shock (ECS). Refers to a brief electrical shock applied to the head which produces full-body seizure, convulsions and mostly loss of consciousness. It is used in two ways : (*a*) As a research tool to study the neurophysiology of memory and (*b*) As a therapeutic procedure for psychiatric disorders.

Electrode. Refers to any medium for transmitting an electric current to an object or for recording electrical activity from an object.

Electroencephalogram (EEG). Refers to a record of the changes in electrical potential of the brain. Electrodes are generally attached to the scalp and the wavelike potentials are amplified and transferred to paper. It has revealed that the brain undergoes systematic changes in the kinds of potential exhibited during various activities for example, *alpha wave, delta wave.*

Electrolyte. It is a substance that when in solution conducts an electrical current and decomposed by its passage. Salts, base and acids are all electrolytes.

Electromyogram (EMG). It is a graphical record of the changes in electrical potential in a muscle.

Electronarcosis. Refers to the induction of unconsciousness by passing an electrical current through brain tissue.

Electronystagmography. Refers to the recording of *nystagmus* by detection of the electrical activity of the muscles of the eye.

Electro-oculogram (EOG). It is a device used for measuring eye movements by recording the electrical potentials of the muscles that control the eye movements.

Electroretinogram (ERG). Refers to a graphic record of the changes in electrical potential of the retina.

Electrotherapy. A type of therapy which uses mild, brief electrical stimulation.

Element. It represent the basic unit of consciousness, in a way analogous with its usage in chemistry. That is, the contents of consciousness were thought to consist of combinations of a finite number of basic mental elements, in the same way as physical matter consisted of combinations of a finite number of chemical elements.

Elementarism. Refers to any atomistic philosophical position that considers that complex phenomena can be understood only by reducing them down to their most primitive parts.

Elicit. Means to draw forth, draw out. It refers to behavior which is not spontaneously produced by an organism but is "drawn out" by the presentation of the appropriate stimulus.

Ellipsis. Refers to the omission of a word or words from a spoken or written message where the missing words are predictable or determinable from the structure of the sentence or from context.

Elopement. In psychiatry refers to the unauthorized departure of a patient from a psychiatric institution.

Embryo. Refers to an organism in the earliest stages of prenatal development. In mammals, the organism during that period before it develops physical similarity to its mature form. In man, the organism during the period of about six weeks during which internal and external organs become differentiated. The embryonic period follows the *germinal*, that itself lasts about two weeks, during which time the fertilized ovum grows into a hollow sphere of approximately 5 mm. After the embryonic stage the term *fetus* is used.

Emergent. Refers to new or unexpected properties or qualities that "emerge" because of combinations or rearrangements of existing elements. For example *mind* and *consciousness*, emerging from complex neurophysiological and biochemical components.

Emesis. Vomiting.

Emission. Means a discharge, a giving out or sending forth. It broadly covers bodily discharges, specifically semen during ejaculation.

Emit. Means to produce, to send out. It is used to refer to behavior which is generated or produced by an organism within the context of an appropriate stimulus.

Emmenia. Means menstrual flow.

Emmeniopatny. Refers to any menstrual disorder.

Emmetropia. Normal vision in the sense that when the eye is at rest the light is refracted so that the focus is directly on the retina.

Emote. Means to display emotion.

Emotional. Pertaining to any aspect of emotion ; like states, processes, expressions, etc. that carry the quality of emotion.

Emotional Bias. Refers to any personal bias stemming from emotional causes.

Emotional Blocking. Refers to an individual's inability to perform complex mental tasks due to a highly intense emotional state.

Emotional Indicator. Any of a number of physiological measures that reflect the state of emotional arousal.

Emotional Instability. Refers to all tendency to be emotionally labile, to display inappropriately abrupt and unpredictably extreme emotionality.

Emotional Maturity. Refers to the state wherein one's emotional reactivity is considered appropriate and normal for an adult in a given society.

Emotional Stability. Refers to the state of one who is emotionally mature.

Emotive. Refers to a situation, event, or other stimulus that elicits emotion.

Empirical. Refers to experience in general or Descriptive of procedures carried out without explicit regard to any theory.

Empirical Test. Refers to the evaluation or assessment of a hypothesis or theory by appeal to data, facts and experimentation.

Empty-Chair Technique. A technique used in Gestalt therapy by which the client projects the image of a person about whom he or she has unresolved feelings and engages in "conversation" with the image.

Empty Organism. Refers to the system's unwillingness to make inferences about internal states or to posit hypothetical constructs.

Enantiobiosis. Refers to a relationship between organisms that is mutually antagonistic.

Enantiodromia. Refers to the view that eventually all things becomes transformed into their opposites.

Encapsulation, Psychological. Refers to behavior that avoids a person from experiencing a painful situation, like refusing to read newspaper accounts of massacres or covering one's eyes when an accident is imminent.

Encephalitis. Refers to inflammation of the membranes covering the brain or of the brain itself.

Encephalization. Refers to the gradual subsuming of the control of function by the brain.

Encephalon. Used rarely for the brain.

Encephalopathy. Refers to any disease or dysfunction of the brain.

Encopresis. Means fecal incontinence involuntary expulsion of feces.

Encryption. Within cryptography it is the act or process of converting a message into a coded form.

Enculturation. The process whereby individual adapts to a new culture, eventually assimilating in practices, customs and values.

End Brush. Refers to the delicate arborization of the ends of an axon.

Endemic. Means restricted to a particular geographical area.

Endo. Combining form meaning ***within inside*** or ***toward the inside.***

Endocathection. Refers to an inward cathection, a preoccupation with one's own feelings and thoughts.

Endocrine. Refers to glands which secrete hormones internally; that is, there secretions are distributed through the body by the bloodstream, the glands are ductless.

Endocrinology. It is the study of the body's internal secretions.

Endoderm. It is the inner layer of embryonic cellular structures which develops into the digestive tract and the viscera.

Endogomy. Refers to the limiting marriage to one's social or cultural group like caste or clan.

Endolymph. It is the liquid found in the membranous canal of the semicircular canals of the inner ear.

Endometrium. It is the mucous membrane which lines the inner surface of the uterus.

Endopsychic. Refers to that which is in the mind.

End Plate. Generally called a *motor end plate,* it is the terminus of a neuron which makes the functional contact with a muscle cell.

Engineering Psychology. It is branch of *industrial/organizational psychology* which focuses on the "man-machine interface". That is, study of the behavior of individuals using tools, working with machines, etc.

Engram. A postulated biochemical change due to external stimulation. The engram is hypothesized to be the biochemical manifestation of memory, the permanent alteration of neural tissue which represents what has been learned.

Engulfment. It is a form of anxiety which is experienced by insecure persons who view relationships with others as threats to to their identify.

Enissophobia. Refers to irrational fear of criticism.

Enrichment. Refers to some theories of perceptual learning which assume that perceptual processes go beyond a direct representing of the various aspects of the stimulus field.

Entrainment. It is a synchrony of movement between two or more persons.

Enuresis. Incontinence, the involuntary passing of urine. It is equated with bed-wetting, particularly when it takes place in young children.

Environmentalism. A general term for a class of theoretical and philosophical school which stresses the role of the environment in determining behavior.

Environmental Psychology A branch of psychology, including social psychology, sociology, ethology, political science, architecture and anthropology.

Enzygotic. Means developed from the sam envum.

Enzyme. Biological catalysts which produce chemical changes another substances without being changed themselves. Enzymes are complex proteins found in degestive process which break down complex food substances into simpler compounds.

Endyma. The membrane lining the cerebral ventricles and the central canal of the spinal cord.

Epi. Prefix designating *outside, above, apart from, in addition to.*

Epicritic. Pertaining to extreme, highly developed sensitivity, specially cutaneous sensitivity.

Epidemic. Refers to the rapid spread of an infectious disease through a population.

Epidemiology. A branch of science dealing with psychological, sociological, demographic and medical aspects that deals with the study of diseases, their distributions in populations and their environmental impact.

Epidermis. Refers to the outer layer of the skin.

Epigenesis. Refers to the belief that during development the complex morphological properties of an organism develop gradually out of an interaction between the prenatal environment and intracellular process.

Epiglottis. It is a thing valve-like structure of cartilage which covers the *glottis* and stops food and drink from entering the *larynx.*

Epilepsy. Refers to a number of disorders charcterized by different combinations of the following: periodic motor or sensory seizures with or without actual convulsions, clouding of or loss of consciousness, motor, sensory or cognitive malfunctions, and accompanied by an abnormal encephalogram (EEG).

Epileptic Equivalent. Refers to any episodic sensory or motor symptom that an epileptic may experience instead of convulsive seizures.

Epileptogenic. Refers to those factors which cause epilepsy or circumstances that produce seizures in individuals with epilepsy.

Epinephrine. It is a hormone of the adrenal medulla whose effects are similar to those brought about by stimulation of the sympathetic division of the autonomic nervous system, *e.g.*, cardiac stimulation, vasoconstriction, arousal.

Epiphenomenon. Refers to any event which takes place in the presence of or incidentally accompanies some other process or event but in fact plays on part in that process or event.

Epiphysis. In the developing infant and child refers to a bone-forming (ossification) center attached to another bone by cartilage. The degree of ossification can be used as a measure of growth.

Eplsode. Refers to a well-defined event or coordinated sequence of events that is perceived as a unit, as a whole.

Eplstemology. It is the branch of philosophy that deads with the origins, nature, method and limits of human knowledge.

Epistemophilla. Means love of knowledge, derivation of pleasure from the acquisition of knowledge.

Epithalamus. It is that part of the brain which is located just above the thalamus.

Epithelium. Refers to a thin layer of tissue which overs the surface or lines the cavity of an organ. Generally performs a secreting or protective function.

Eponym. Refers to a thing, process or function which is adapted from the name of a person.

Equated Score(s). Refers to any two sets of scores from different tests or from different parts of the same test that have been reduced to a common scale.

Equation, Empirical. It is any mathematical equation which is used to fit observed data. Empirical equations are after-the-fact attempts to characterize quantitatively a set of observations, and the value of such an equation is given by the closeness of the "fit" between it and the data.

Equation, Rational. It is a logical or mathematical expression which is based on (rational) assumptions about processes. Such equations differ from *empirical *epuations* in that their parameters are derived by deduction from theoretical assumptions and not simply from attempts to fit data.

Equi. Means *equal* or *equally.*

Equilibration. Means achieving a balance between opposing forces.

Equilibrium. It is a synonym of *balance,* with several special usages. 1. In physiology it is the point at which opposing biochemical reactions are stable, homeostasis. 2. In perception it is a point where the body maintains a stable upright posture with respect to its center of gravity also called the *equilibrium sense* or *static sense.* 3. In social psychology refers to the theoretical tendency for a social system or bring about corrective changes to maintain itself as a functionally integrated unit.

Equipotentiality of Cues. Refers to the hypothesis according to which in a perceptual situation one sensury cue may substitute for another.

Equity Theory. Refers to a class of broad social psychological theories which seek to explain behavior by reference to the concept of equity, *i.e.*, those conditions wherein the rewards to individuals in a group are in proportion to their efforts on behalf of the group.

Equivalence. Refers to a relationships between two "things" such that one may be substituted for the other in a particular setting and not alter significantly the situation..

Eremophobia. Refers to fear of solitude, of being alone.

Erethism. Refers to usually high sensitivity to sensory stimulation.

Ereuthrophobia. Refers to fear of blushing.

ERC. *electroretinogram.*

Erg. It is the work done by a force of 1 dyne acting through a displacement of 1 centimeter in the direction of the force. In psychology it is used in various combinations that are metaphoric and relate to energy, force purpose or dynamic qualities.

Ergasiophobia. Refers to fear of work or, by extension of responsibility.

Ergic. Suffix denoting *work, function, pupose.* It is used in physiology to characterize a neuron or a neural pathway in terms of the operative neurotransmitter.

Ergic. Purposive. Refers to innate drives or predispositions.

Erg(o). Combining form meaning work.

Ergodic. In probability theory, refers to any stochastic process wherein every sequence of events is statistically the same and therefore may be taken as representative of the whole.

Ergograph. Refers to device used for measuring the amount of work accomplished by a muscle or muscle group.

Ergonomics. It is the science of the "fit" between jobs and persons it deals with the study of the relationship between an individals's anatomy, physiology and psychology and the demands of particular forms of work

Ergophobia. Refers to fear of working.

Erogenous Zones. Those areas of the body whose stimulation gives rise to erotic or sexual sensation. Sometimes called *erotogenic zones.*

Eros. The Greek god of love. In Freudian theory, Eros refers to the whole complex of life-preservative instincts. 'Included among them, are the sexual instincts.

Erotic. Generally, sexual of libidinal, it may pertain to : 1. Feelings arising from the genitals particularly. 2. A more general sense of sexual arousal. 3. The stimuli that give rise to sexual arousal. 4. Any motive or need that has sexual components. 5. Love in any of its manifestations.

Eroticism. Means sexual arousal or A greater than average disposition for the sexual, a tendency to be easily aroused sexually or Sexual excitement arising from areas other than those specifically sexual, other than genitals.

Error, Average. Refers to the average error in a series of observations of judgement.

Error, Chance. Refers to an error that arises from chance factors. Since such errors are in principle random and unbiased they tend to cancel each other out and the sum of chance errors, when a sufficiently large number of cases in considered, approaches zero.

Error, Constant. An error due to some factors that affects all observations similarly so that the errors are always in one direction and do not cancel each out. Usually such an error can be detected and corrected for during statistical analysis.

Error, Experimental. Refers to a class of possible errors whose origins lie in the inadequacy of an experimental design or procedure. The history of psychology is well salted with legendary experimental errors due to improper control of some important factor. The most common are failures to control for practice effects, time errors, observer differences, experimenter biases, physiological and species differences and the abiquitious sampling error.

Error, Probable. It is used as a measure of the error of estimate or of the sampling errors.

Error, Sampling. Refers to the difference between the true value of a statistic within a popoulation and the estimated value of that statistic derived from a sample of that population.

Error, Subjective. Refers to a systematic error introduced into observation or interpretation because of individual's biases or prejudices.

Error, Variance. Refers to that proportion of the *variance,* which cannot be attributed to controlled factors.

Erythr(o). A prefix meaning *red.*

Erythrophobia. Refers to fear of blushing or Fears of red-colored objects.

Erythropia. Vision where objects are tinged. It may be due to overexposure to intense light, as snow blindness.

ESB. *Electrical brain stimulation.*

E Scale. It is an opinion scale for assessing ethnocentrism.

Escape Training. Refers to an experimental procedure wherein the subject must learn an eseape response.

Esotropia. A form of *strabismus* wherein one eye turns inward while the other fixates on an object.

ESP *extrasensory perception.*

EST. Abbreviation for *electroshock therapy:* A form of psychotherapy based on the "theories" of Werner Erhard. The procedure consists of large group sessions of rather extraordinary intensity. For up to 60 hours several hundred people are gathered in a large hall and subjected to physical privation, guided meditation and fervent diatribes on the EST way to "get in touch" with one's inner sense of personal responsibility.

Esthesiometer. It is a device used for measuring sensitivity to touch, specifically a compass-like instrument for determining the two-point threshold on the skin.

Estimate. It is a reasonable guess about the value of some factor. In statistics, it refers to a "best guess" of the value of some variable or statistic based on refined computational procedures that provide both the estimated value as well as a measure of the likelihood which that value falls within ascertainable limits of the true value.

Estradiol. The most biologically potent of the naturally occurring *estrogens.* It is produced primarily by the ovaries and, in small amounts, by the adrenal cortices.

Estriol. An estrogenic hormone that is regarded as a metabolic product of *estradiol* and *estrone.*

Estrogen. Refers to a group of related steroid hormones produced chiefly by the ovaries, but also by the adrenal cortices and, in very small amounts, by the testes. It include are *estradiol*, *estrone* and their metabolic product, *estriol.* Estrogens are responsible for the development of most of the female secondary sex characteristics, breast development, maturation of the genitalia, deposition of body fat—but not axillary and public hair.

Estrone. The less potent biologically of the primary *estrogens.*

Estrus Cycle. The ovarian cycle in female sub-primate mammals. It has four stages : proestrus, estrus, matestrus and diestrus. The second stage, *estrus,* is that associated with ovulation, swelling of the vulva, various uterine processes and receptivity copulation.

Ethics. It is a branch of philosophy that deals with that which is deemed acceptable in human behavior, with what is good or bad, right or wrong with human conduct in pursuit of goals and aims.

Ethinamate. It is a nonbarbiturate sedative which is used primarily as a sleeping pill. Its effects are similar to *chloral hydrate.*

Evolution. Refers to loosely, orderly development. More specifically, the process by which plant and animal forms developed by descent, with modification, from earlier existing forms.

Exceptional Child. Refers to both extremely talented and gifted children as well as to those having low intelligence or other learning disabilities.

Excitable. One which is capable of being aroused or excited.

Excitation. In physiology refers to a process by which some stimulus energy pattern sets up a change or pattern of changes in a receptor. In the study of learning refers to a general high level of activity in the whole nervous system. In social psychology refers to an increase in psychological tension.

Executive Area. In neurophysiology refers to any cortical area that serves integrative, organizing functions.

Executive Ego Function. In psychoanalytic theory refers to the management role that the ego plays.

Exhaustion. It is a physiological a state wherein the metabolic process has been depleted, producing fatigue, weariness and a general lack of responsiveness.

Exhaustion Delirium. Refers to acute delirium occasionally observed under conditions of extreme exhaustion brought about by intense extended physical effort or by other debilitating conditions like high fever.

Exhibitionism. Refers to a strong tendency to make oneself the constant center of attention.

Existentialism. An important 20th-century philosophical movement that carved out a domain for itself between rationalistic idealism and totally objective materialism. The emphasis is upon personal decision to be made in a world without reason and without purpose. It emphasizes subjectivity, free will and individuality and has acted as a philosophical counterbalance to theories that stress the role of society and social groups.

Existential Therapy. It is a form of psychotherapy which based upon the philosophical doctrine of existentialism. It is highly subjective and focuses on the immediate situation. It differs from most other therapies in that there is a strict avoidance of intellectual explanation and interpretation ; the focus is on the immediate reality shared by client and therapist.

Exocrine. Refers to glands that secrete hormones through a duct.

Exogamy. Refers to Marriage outside one's social or cultural group.

Exophthalmia. Refers to Abnormal protrusion of the eyeball.

Exopsychic. Refers to mental activity which has effects outside the person.

Expansive Delusion. Refers to a delusion of grandeur accompanied by feelings wealth, power, influence, etc.

Expectation. It is the anticipated outcome diprobabilistic situation.

Experimental Psychology. A brach of psychology that deals with the study of psychological issues using experimental procedures.

Explicit. Any thing which is direct and clearly specified.

Exploitive Character. Refers to one who derives satisfaction from exploiting others, who uses others to satisfy his own needs without concern for the needs of these others.

Extensor. Refers to a muscle whose action straightens out a limb.

External Rectus. It is one of the muscles controlling the eye.

Exteroceptor. Refers to sensory receptor which is stimulated by changes in the exterior world.

Extinction. It refers either to experimental procedure wherein the stimulus event that maintains the behaviour is removed, or the actual decrease in the learned response that results from this extinction procedure.

Extinguish. Means to carry out the procedure of experimental extinction, or to diminish the responsiveness of an organism by running experimental extinction.

Extinguished. Refers to a response which has been subjected to extinction procedures.

Extirpation. Refers to removal of an organ or bodily structure. Generally surgical removal. When only part of the organ or structure is removed the term *ablation* is used.

Extrafusal Fibres. Refers to muscle fibers which mediate the force extended by contraction.

Extrajection. An occasional synonym for *projection.*

Extrapolate. Means to estimate, from a series of known values, the values of a variable that are higher or lower than the known range.

Extrapunitive. Refers to the tendency to react to frustration by showing anger toward and investing blame in others.

Extrapyramidal Motor System. Refers to set of complex, diffuse neural structures both cortical and subcortical including the basal ganglia, cerebellum, parts of the reticular formation and their connections with the motor neurons of the spinal cord and nuclei of the cranial nerves.

Extraspectral Hue. Any hue which cannot be characterized by a single wavelength. *e.g.*, Purple, that requires a mixture of long wavelengths (red) and short wavelengths (blue).

Extraversion. In personality theory refers to the tendency to direct one's energies outward, to be concerned with and derive gratification from the physical and social environment.

Extravert. Refers to an individual who displays the extrovert behaviors.

Extrinsic. Refers to a property of something that derives its essential nature from relationships with outside factors.

Extro-. Variation of *extra-*.

"Eye-balling". Laboratory slang for taking a quick look at one's data to see if any obvious trends can be perceived prior to performing careful statistical analyses.

Eyewitness Testimony. Basically a legal term for the use of the eyewitness to a crime to provide testimony in court about the identity of the perpetrator.

F

F_1, F_2. In genetics refers to the first and second filial generations. F_1 represents the offspring of two unlike individuals ; F_2 represents the offspring of two individuals of the F_1 generation.

Fables Test. A test wherein the subject should interpret fables. Fable tests form a part of the Stanford-Binet intelligence scale and also used as projective techniques.

Fabulation. Refers to concocting and telling falsehoods if they were true.

Face Saving. In social psychology it refers to essentially the same meaning that is the protection of ones' public image.

Face-to-Face Group. Refers to a group whose members are so close that direct interaction between them is possible.

Facial Nerve. The VIIth *cranial nerve.* It is a mixed nerve having efferent fibers to the facial muscles, the platysmal muscle of the neck and the sublingual glands and efferent fibers from the taste buds of the front two-thirds of the tongue.

Facilitation. Means increased ease of performance, as measured by efficiency or increased case of transmission across a synapse due to practice.

Facilitator. Refers to a professional therapist or layman who serves as a leader for a group experience.

Factitious. Means characteristic of an artifact, made by humans.

Factor. Refers to a cause of antecedent condition in bringing about a phenomenon or one of the products of factor analysis, like a verbal factor.

Factor Axes. Refers to the set of coordinates representing the relationships between the various factors to each other and also to the full correlation matrix.

Factor Fixed. Refers to an independent variable in an experiment where the values that the variable may take are set naturally. For example, suppose there exist only different brands of aspirin ; an experiment evaluating and comparing them would have the "brand" variable as a fixed factor.

Factorial Validity. Refers to the validity of a test as determined by correlating the test with a factor isolated by factor analysis.

Factoring. The procees of carrying out of a factor analysis.

Factor Loading. Refers to a value which expresses the degree to which any given factor accounts for the total variability of the full set of correlations whereon the factor analysis has been carried out.

Factor Reflection. Means changing the algebraic signs among the fatctor loadings so as to maintain consistency among the factors in the matrix.

Faculty Psychology. Refers to the discredited doctrine according to which mind is constituted of a number of powers or agencies, like intellect, will, judgment, and attentiveness, which produce mental activities.

Fading. A technique in behaviorally oriented training wherein a new stimulus is presented along with an old one to which a response has already been learned. The old stimulus is then gradually diminished in size or intensity or clarity (*i.e.*, faded) and the new one gains control over the response.

Failure. Means not obtaining the anticipated result in an experiment or one who has failed a test or a course of study.

Faintness. Refers to a weakness in intensity. Or to a temporary condition bordering on loss of consciousness with dizziness, weakness, and sometimes nausea.

Faith Healing. Refers to healing accomplished through faith or belief in the power of the healer, the therapist, the therapeutic procedure, or something else.

Fallacy. Refers to an argument that involves logically invalid or improper reasoning in reaching a conclusion. Although fallacies usually lead to false conclusions they do not do so by definition.

Fall Chronometer. Refers to a device used earlier in experimental psychology for measuring short time intervals by assessing the distance a weight fell.

False. That which is not *true.*

Familial. Pertaining to the family, occuring in all members of a family.

Family Therapy. Refers to a number of therapeutic approaches all of which treat a family as a whole and not single out specific individuals for independent treatment.

Fantasm. Refers to a vivid representation of a form or person believed by the perceiver to be a disembodied spirit.

Fantastic. Refers to a product of, fantasy.

Far Point. It is the most remote point that is distinctly visible under conditions of relaxed accommodation.

Farsightedness. Refers to inability to see near objects clearly.

Fasciculus. Refers to a bundle of nerve fibers which make up a tract in the spinal cord.

Father Figure. Refers to a person who takes the place of a real father. Generally refers to a person who is unrelated but with whom another person identifies.

Fashioning Effect. It describes fact that the social role adopted by a person influences both the person's behaviour and his self-perception.

Fatigue. Refers to the decreased ability to do work or a subjective feeling or tiredness after prolonged work or nervous tension.

Fear. Any strong emotional reaction involving subjective feelings of unpleasantness, agitation, and desire to flee or hide, that is accompanied by widespread sympathetic activity.

Fachner's Paradox. Means the increase in brightness of a figure viewed binocularly when one eye is suddenly occluded.

Feeblemindedness. Previously used for mental retardation.

Feeling. Refers to any conscious state or experience. The primary dimension of feeling is pleasantness-unpleasantness.

Fallatio. Refers to sexual stimulation by introduction of the penis into the mouth.

Felt Need. Refers to any conscious need.

Femininity. Refers to the generality of the characteristics that are peculiar to the female sex.

Fenestra Ovalis. The membraneous oval window in the cochlea where the stapes articulates with the inner cochlea.

Feral Child. Any child who has been allegedly reared by animals.

Fertility. It is the capacity for bearing children.

Fertilization. Means the union of the egg and sperm.

Fetal Alcoholic Syndrome (FAS). Refers to a cluster of abnormal developmental features of a fetus which result from serve alcoholism in the mother. If includes microcephaly, growth deficiencies, mental retardation, hyperactivity, heart murmurs and skeletal malformations.

Fetish. Means the object of a fetishism.

Factor. Refers to the personality dimension of surgency-desurgency ; cheerful, social, energetic versus depressed, seclusive, subdued, dull.

FFF. Abbreviation for *ficker fusion frequency.*

FI. Abbreviation for *fixed interval.*

Fiber. Refers a single neuron or the axon of dendrite of the neuron.

Field. Refers to the psychological representation in consciousness or preception of a physical situation or the complex of social, personal, and physical forces within which an individual functions.

Field Dependent. Refers to an individual who has difficulty in ignoring factors in a perceptual field which are irrelevant to a task.

Field of Consciousness. Refers to the totality of which the individual is aware.

Figual Openness. In Gestalt psychology it refers to a condition wherein the area of a configuration is not enclosed with a figure. *e.g.*, a swastika, the area that lies between the arms is "open," while the area within the boundaries of the arms is "closed."

Figure-ground. Refers to the principles according to which perceptions are fundamentally patterned into two aspects : (*a*) the figure, that stands out, has good contour, and appears solid or three-dimensional : and (*b*) the ground that is indistinct and whose parts are not clearly shaped or patterned.

Film Color. Refers to a texture-free soft color difficult to localize, such as might be seen when looking through colored glass.

Final. Means in a series of terms or trials.

Firing. Refers to the triggering of a nervous impluse by a receptor or mechanical stimulus.

Fisher's Test. It is a test for determining the significance of an obtained correlation coefficient for a given size of sample. Coefficients not meeting the test requirements may have arisen by chance and are not considered significant.

Fissure. Refers to any of the deep grooves on the surface of the brain. The more shallow grooves are known as *sulci*.

Fit. Refers to a seizure, like an epileptic seizure. In statistics it refers to the conformity of obtained data to a predetermined standard.

Fixation. It is a persistent mode of behavior which has outlined its usefulness or has become inappropriate. It also refers to the strengthening of a learned habit, or a strong and relatively enduring emotional attachment for another person.

Fixed Idea. Refers to any strongly held and irrational idea. These are typical of obsessive neuroses and paranoiac states.

Fixated Response. Refers to a response which continues to be emitted inspite of attempts to extinguish or alter it.

Flaccid. Soft, without tone, as in flaccid paralysis in lower motor neuron disorders wherein the muscles atrophy.

Flagellation. Refers to the practice of submitting to whipping, whether for penitential purposes or for arousal sexual feelings.

Flesch Index (or Formula. It is a formula used for evaluating the reading difficulty of a passage of English prose.

Flexible. Refers to a person who is readily adaptable or one who is able to change a set or line of thinking readily.

Flexor. Refers to the muscle whose action bends of limb. Flexor and extensor muscles mostly act to form a pair of *antagonistic muscles*.

Flight of Ideas. Refers to a rapid succession of unrelated thoughts.

Floating affect or Feeling. Refers to a feeling or emotion set free from its original object.

Flowery. It refers to a class of odors which are represented by the odor of flowers.

Fluctuation. Means oscillation ; a cyclic change in a function because of chance factors or changes or variations in a species or changes in the value of statistical constants taken from successive samples.

Flaccid. Flabby, low in muscle tone.

Focal. Refers to the point at which rays of light come to a focus.

Focal Length. It is the distance from the lens to the point where parallel rays of light are brought into focus.

Focus of Attention. Refers to the object, event, idea, problem, thought, etc. upon which one is concentrating.

Folie a Deux. Refers to the occurrence of psychosis in two persons who are closely associated, such as husband and wife.

Folium. A convolution or fold on the cerebellum.

Folklore. Refers to complex of songs, legends, stories, etc. which make up the unwritten traditional literature of a culture.

Folkways. Refers to social norms or traditional ways of behavior in a culture. These are implicit and learned by successive generations through socialization and so are distinguished from *mores,* that are the explicitly presented and obligatory standards.

Follicle. Refers to a small secreting cavity.

Fontanel. Refers to the soft, unossified area in the centre of the skull of an infant.

Foot Candle. It was preciously used as the unit of illuminance and is defined as the illumination on a surface by a standard candle at a distance of 1 foot.

Foot-in-the-door Technique. A technique of inducing compliance for a larger commitment by first obtaining compliance for a small commitment.

Foraging. Refers to various activities that are involved in obtaining foodstuffs, *e.g.,* search, identification, procurement, handling, storage, etc.

Foreperiod. It is the initial period in any experiment, specially the interval between a ready signal and the presentation of a stimulus.

Foreplay. Refers to mutual sexual stimulation by two individuals as a prelude to sexual intercourse.

Form. Refers to the shape or outline of an object or the spatial arrangement of parts into a unitary whole.

Formula. It is a symbolic statement of a set of operations or relations or a set of rules, laws, or principles.

Fornix. Refers to a bundle of nerve fibers in the brain which form a tract between the thalamus and hippocampus.

Foster. Refers to persons who either provide or receive care although not related to each other by blood or marriage.

Fornication. Refers to non-coerced sexual intercourse between persons who are not married to each other.

Fourier's Law. Refers to the mathematical generalization that any complex periodic pattern, like sound waves, may be described as a particular sum of a number of sine waves.

Fovea ; Fovea Centralis. It is the small depression in the centre of the retina that is the area of fixation and the center of clearest vision.

Fractional Antedating Goal Response. A reaction which takes place progressively earlier in conditioning a series of responses and may come to serve as a conditioned stimulus for subsequent responses.

Frame of Reference. Refers to a standard or attitude against which actions or results are judged. It also refers to a perceptual schema which influences perceived meaning.

Fraternal Twins. Refers to twins who have developed from two eggs fertilized at the same time.

F Ratio. In statistics it is the ratio of the variances (σ^2) of two samples. The ratio was named in honor of the statistician Ronald A. Fisher and is given by $F=\sigma_1^2/\sigma_2^2$, where σ_2^2 is the smaller of the two variances. The size of an F ratio may be used to determine if there is homogeneity of variance between the two samples from which the two values of σ^2 were estimated.

Free Association. Refers to reporting of whatever comes to the mind of the person being analyzed, irrespective of how painful, embarrassing, or irrelevant it might appear.

Free Play. Play which is not directed by a supervisor.

Free-will Doctrine. Refers to the philosophical and religious position which behavior is ultimately directed by volition regardless of external influences.

Frequency Curve. Refers to a curve which connects the midpoints of a frequency distribution and whose height is proportional to the frequency of cases.

Frequency, Law of. According to this law other things being equal, the more an act or association is practiced, the more rapid is the learning.

Frequency Table. Refers to a statistical tally of the number of times a score or event takes place.

Freudian Slip. Refers to an error in speaking or writing which unintentionally reveals the speaker's or writer's true meaning.

Frigidity. In women it is the inability to experience sexual desire or to experience orgasm during intercourse.

Frontal. Refers to the anterior part of a body or organ.

Frontal Lobe. Refers to that portion of the cerebral cortex which lies in front of the precentral gyrus.

Frottage. A sexual perversion wherein orgasm is achieved by rubbing against the clothing of a member of the opposite sex in a crowd.

Fruity. Such odors as are typified by the fruits.

Frustration. Refers to blockage or thwarting of goal-directed behaviour or an unpleasant state of tension, anxiety, and heightened sympathetic activity due to blockage or thwarting.

F Scale (Fascism Scale). It is a scale designed to measure readiness to accept antidemocratic ideologies.

F Score. A score on the Minnesota Multiphasic Inventory of Personality which indicates if the subject has followed the directions.

F Test. It is a test of variance between two samples and is used to determine if the difference could be due to chance.

FSH. Abbreviation for *follicle-stimulating hormone.*

Fugue. Refers to an amnesiac flight The individual leaves home, changes his mode of living, and in some cases his occupation.

Functional Deafness. Refers to deafness due to malfunctioning of the auditory mechanism, without any structural defect in the ear.

Functional Pleasure. Refers to the exercise of a trait or ability for the pleasure involved.

Functional Psychosis. It is the psychosis for which no known organic basis exist. Schizophrenia, paranoia, and the manic-depressive reactions have traditionally been considered as functional. According to this point of view, they are extreme forms of maladjustment.

Functional Unity. The operation of different traits or process in such a way as to produce an integrated whole.

Function Engram. Refers to an inherited imprint upon the nervous system which gives archetypal symbols their meaning.

Function Types. Some important types are thinking, feeling, sensing, and intuitive. The attitude types may be combined with function types.

Fundamental-response Processes. Refers to the hypothetical retinal processes to underlie color fundamentals.

Funnel Technique. A technique used in interviewing and in the construction of questionnaires or inventories wherein broad, general questions are used in the beginning and gradually the scope is narrowed to specifics.

Fusion. Refers to any process wherein the several elements of a complex stimulus are blended or fused together in a whole in such a way that the component parts cannot be perceptually distinguished. In classical psychoanalytic theory refers to the balanced coordinated functioning of the life instincts and the death instincts. Fusion is considered as "normal", although different behavioral patterns are assumed to result depending on which instincts dominate.

Future Shock. Refers to the disorientation and anxiety consequent upon rapid social and technological changes.

Fuzzy Set (or restriction). The calculus of fuzzy sets is a relatively recent innovation in mathematics. It deals with domains and concepts whose boundaries are not sharply defined.

G

G. Abbreviation used for *goal,* in Hullian theory.

Gain. Refers to an increment, like an increment of learning.

Galton Bar. It is an instrument used for determing the just-noticeable difference for visual distance.

Galvanic Nystagmus. Refers to nystagmus induced when an electric current is paned through the labyrinthine region.

Galvanotropism. Refers to an orienting movement of the body toward an electric current.

Game. Refers to any pattern of social interaction or organized having well-defined rules.

Gamete. A sex cell which, when combined with another sex cell, forms the zygote or the begining of a new individual.

Gamma (γ). In psychophysics refers to the distance of any stimulus from threshold.

Gamma-aminobyturic Acid. It is a chemical which acts as an inhibitory neurotransmitter of the central nervous system.

Gam(o). Combining form used to indicate a marital relationship or a sexual union. It is typically used as prefix.

Gamophobia. Refers to irrational fear of marriage.

Gang. Social unit made up of individuals who are bound by their common intersts. Gangs may be made up of people of any age, but are very common among children.

Ganzfeld. Refers to a homogeneous visual field.

Gargalesthesis. Refers to the sensation of tickle.

Gating. Refers to the inhibition of one sensory channel by another. Gating takes places during attention, when there is a selective focusing of the sensory apparatus.

Gatophobia. Refers to fear of cats.

GAS. *General adaptation syndrome.*

Gay. Refers to homosexuals.

Gemellology. The study of twins, specially the use of twins as the primary data source for evaluating the contributions of heredity and environment on behavior.

Gender. Sex—male or female.

Gender Role. Refers the set of behaviors that are expected of each sex in any society.

Gene Frequency. The frequency of occurrence of any specific gene with population.

General Ability. Refers to cognitive ability which some presume to be basic to all the special or *specific abilities* displayed in particular situations.

General Image. Refers to an image which the subject thinks to represent any one of a class of objects.

General Semantics. It deals with the study of human responses to signs and symbols.

Generic. Refers to a biological genus.

Genetic. Pertaining to the origin and development of an organism or an entire species

Generic Name. The general chemical name for a drug, the non-proprietary name.

Genetic Drift. Refers to changes in the genetic composition of a population or, more precisely, of the gene pool of that population from generation to generation.

Geneticism. Refers to the point of view according to which behavior is inborn.

Genetic Method. Refers to explanation or understanding of behavior in terms of its hereditary origins and developmental history.

Genetic Psychology. It is the branch of psychology that studies behavior by the genetic method.

Genic. Relating to genes or to any thing which is caused by genes.

Genic. Combining form used with prefixes to characterize. The locus or point of origin of something, *e.g.*, *endogenic*=originating from within.

Genital. Any thing pertaining to the genitals, the organs of reproduction.

Genital Anomaly. Refers to *sex anomaly*.

Genital Character. Refers to the adult stage of. psychosexual development representing a fusion or synthesis of the earlier stages of oral, anal, and urethral eroticism.

Genital Eroticism. Refers sensual or sexual pleasure obtained from the genitals.

Genitals (or Genitalia). Refers to the reproductive organs.

Genital Zones. Refers to the external genitals and adjacent areas, one of the *erogenous zones.*

Genomotive. Refers to a need that results in an introspectively apparent motive.

Genome. Refers to the full collection of genes of an organism.

Genotype. Refers to the traits or characteristics common to a biological group. Also refers to any of those hereditary factors which exert a causative influence on development.

Gens. Refers to the division of an ethnic group whose line of descent runs through the male.

Genus. A biological classification embracing closely related species. The different genera make up the next higher category of family.

Geometric. Refers to the members of a series which increase by a certain constant ratio or proportion.

Geometric Series. A series that increases or decreases by a constant proportion or ratio. For example, 2, 4, 8, 16, 32,...

Geotropism. Means an orienting response to gravity.

Geriatrics. The medical specialty that deals with treatment of the aged.

Germ Cell. Refers to a reproductive cell in any stage of development.

Germinal Stage (or Period). The earliest stage of gestation. In humans, it is the period of approximately two weeks from the moment of conception.

Gesell Development Scales. Refers to inventories of development which are based on the systematic study of infants and preschool childran in the Yale Clinic of Child Development.

Gestait. Refers to form, figure, or configuration.

Gestalt Therapy. It is a form of psychotherapy and is associated with the work of Frederick (Fritz) Perls (1893-1970). It is based on the Gestalt concepts of unity and wholeness.

Gestation. Refers to the carrying of the embryo in the womb or. The period of intrauterine development from conception to birth.

Gesture. Refers to a bodily or facial movement used for communication. Gestures may accompany speech or may be used independently, as in sign language.

Geusis. It is the process or act of tasting.

G Force. It is the force needed to overcome the pull of the earth's gravity. At 3—4 G's the individual experiences "redout" due to the rush of blood to the eyes, and at 5—6 G's unconsiousness, or "blackout".

Giantism. Refers to an abnormal increase in size or stature because of malfunctioning of the anterior pituitary gland.

Gifted. One possessing a high degree of intellectual ability ; with an IQ of 140 or more or possessing some nonintellective talent, like musical talent, to a high degree.

GIGO. An acronym for "garbage in garbage out." The term is used in computer sciences for the notion that if unreliable data form the input only unreliable outcomes are possible.

Glans. Refers to the bulbous end of the clitoris and penis.

Glare. Refers to a smooth, bright surface or of strong incident light making visual discriminations difficult.

Glaucoma. It is a pathological condition of the eye that is caused by increasing intraocular pressure resulting in atrophy of the optic nerve, gradually increased visual dysfunction and, ultimately leading to blindness.

Glial. Refers to specialized glia cells.

Gliosis. The process of replacement of dead neurons with glia cells.

Glioma. It is a brain tumor.

Globus Hystericus. Refers to a feeling of a lump in the throat.

Glossosythesis. The term means to invent nonsense words.

Glottal. Pertaining to the glottis or A speech sound produced by constriction of the glottis, *e.g.*, the *h* in *hot*.

Glottis. It is the opening between the vocal cords.

Glove Anesthesia. Refers to a functional loss of sensitivity in the hand or forearm.

Glucagon. A hormone of the pancreas which functions as part of the process which converts glycogen into glucose.

Glutamic Acid. An amino acid which functions as an excitatory neurotransmitter.

Glutethimide. A non-barbiturate sedative used as a sleeping aid.

Glycine. An *amino acid* which function as an inhibitory neurotransmitter in the spinal cord and lower portions of the brain.

Goal. It is the end result toward which the organism is striving or moving or a place containing an incentive, such as the goal compartment at the end of a maze.

Goal-Directed Behavior. Behavior interpretable only in terms of the organism's seeking a goal.

Goal Object. It is the final objective as contrasted with means or subgoals.

Goal Set. Means a readiness or anticipation of a goal.

Golgi-Mazzoni Corpuscles. Bulbous encapsulated nerve endings found in the dermis.

Golgi Neurons (Type I and Type II). These are multipolar neurons in the cerebral cortex and the posterior horns of the spinal cord. Type I have long axons, Type II have short axons.

Gonad. A sex gland. The gonads in the male are the testes, that produce sperm, and in the female the ovaries, that produce eggs.

Gonadotrophic Hormone. A hormone produced by the anterior pituitary gland that stimulates activity in the gonads. Also known as *gonadotrophin*.

Gon (o). Combining form meaning *genitals, seed, generation, offspring*.

Gonococcus. It is the organism that causes gonorrhea.

Goniometer. An instrument used for measuring sway.

Gordon Personal Inventory. A self-report inventory which yields scores on cautiousness, original thinking, personal relations, and vigor for grades 8—16 and adults.

GPS. *General Problem Solver.*

Grade. Refers to a class or division in a series of measurements or on a scale.

Grain. Refers to *cumulative records.* If the record consists of relatively evenly spaced responses it is considered to have a "smooth" grain ; if there are bursts of responding with pauses in between it is considered to have a "rough" grain.

Grand Mal. A form of epilepsy that involves generalized convulsions and loss of consciousness.

Grammar, Universal. A hypothesized set of basic grammatical principles considered to be fundamental to all *natural languages.*

Graph. It is a representation by means of lines or geometric figures of the relationship between two variables.

Graphic Individuality. Refers to the fact of each of us having an idiosy cratic and unique handwriting or "graphic individuality."

Graphic Score. Refers to a score represented by a line, bar, histogram, pie chart, or other visual device.

Graphodyne. It is a device used for recording pressure in handwriting.

Gray. Refers to an achromatic visual sensation that lies between the limits of black and white.

Gray-Out. Refers to a partial or incomplete loss of consciousness.

Greek Love. Refers to homosexuality among males ; known so because of the prevalence of homosexuality among the ancient Greeks.

Green. Hue sensation elicited by lengths in the vicinity of 515nm.

Gregariousness. Refers to the tendency in certain species to congregate in herds or to live in flocks.

Grief. It an intense emotional state that is associated with the loss of someone with whom one has had a deep emotional bond.

Grooming. Refers to the removal of parasites from the fur by picking specially in monkey.

Groove. In neurophysiology refers to a narrow channel or depression *sulcus.*

Gross. Any thing dependent more on strength than on fineness coordination. The term is used to characterize muscular responses, coordination, and large anatomical parts.

Ground. Refers to the background in figureground relations.

Group Analysis. Refers to a study of the social pathology of a group.

Group Boundary. Refers to rules or regulation which determine group membership or group activities.

Grouped Distribution. A frequency distribution wherein the values are entered in ranges. For example, in tallying the weight of young adult males, the ranges in pounds might be 90-99 ; 100-109 ; 110-119 ; 120-129 ; 130-139, etc.

Group Experiment. Refers to any experiment wherein a (large) number of subjects is run together in a group.

Group Interview. The application of the interview technique to several individuals at a time.

Group Rigidity. Refers to the tendency of a group to resist change.

Group Superego. It is that portion of the superego derived from peer groups, as opposed to that portion derived by introjection from the parents.

Group Test. Refers to any test designed to be administered to more than one individual at the same time.

Growing Pains. Refers to pains in the legs experienced at bedtime or during the night generally by adolescents and may be due to overly rapid development of bones and muscles.

Group, Vertical. Refers to a group composed of persons belonging to more than one social class.

Growth. Refers to an increase in the size of bodily parts or of the organism as a whole.

Growth Curve. Refers to graphic presentation of the growth over time of some measure or variable.

Growth Differential. Refers to differences in the rate of growth or development between any two individuals.

Growth Hormone. It is a hormone secreted by the anterior pituitary which stimulates growth.

GSR. *Galvanic skin response.*

Guanine. One of the four nucleotide bases that make up *deoxyribonucle acid* and *ribonucleic acid.*

Gust. A psychophysical unit of taste. It is defined as the subjective sense of sweetness produced by a 1% sucrose solution.

Gustation. It is the sense of taste whose stimuli are substances in solution and whose receptors are on the tongue and soft palate.

Gut. Refers to the entire digestive system including the esophagus, stomach intestines and bowel.

Gyn. Combining form from the Greek, meaning *female, woman.*

Gynandromorphism. Refers to the coincidence of male and female characteristics in the one individual or organism.

Gynandry. It is the tendency of the female to possess masculine characteristics.

Gynecomastia. The development of breasts on a male. The condition may occur through hormone malfunction, or as a direct result of hormone treatments.

Gyrus. Refers to a fold on the surface of the cerebral cortex.

H

H. *Heritability* or *heritability ratio or Harmonic* *mean or *Entropy.* Or *habit strength.*

Haab's Pupillary Reflex. The process of contraction of both irises when the gaze is directed toward a source of light in a darkened room.

Habenula. Refers to a collection of fibers in the epithalamus.

Habitat. Refers to the geographical area in which conditions are well suited to the life of a particular species.

Habituation. Refers to the elimination with practice of useless, emotional responses in animal learning.

Haem (o). *hem(o)*

Hair Cells. A type of cell which acts as a receptor like the hair cells in the organ of Corti in the inner ear.

Halfway House. Refers to a self-governing facility for discharged mental patients who no longer need hospitalization but do need the support of a restricted social community to assist them in the transition back to society.

Hallucinatory Image. Refers to a mental image that is taken for reality.

Hallucinogen. Refers to any of group of psychoactive chemical pounds capable or producing hallucinations.

Halo. Refers to a band or ring of light around a stimulus.

Halo Effect. Refers to the tendency to allowing impression of a person or oners outstanding trait to influence rating of that person.

Hammer. It is one of the small bones in the middle ear.

Hampton Court Maze. The famous English garden maze which was used as a model for many early maze-learning studies with animals.

Handicapped. A person having less than normal ability or having an anatomical or functional defect which makes it difficult for him to compete with his peers.

Haphalgesia. Refers to a sensation of pain when the skin is touched by a normally nonirritating stimulus.

Hapl(o). Combining form meaning *single* or *simple.*

Haploid. Pertaining to cells having half the number of chromosomes typical of somatic cells.

Haptic. Referring to the proprioceptive and cutaneous systems of senses.

Haptics. Refers to the investigation of the cntaneous system of sensation.

Hard Colors. Refers to the yellows and red colours.

Hard Drug. Refers to any drug which produces *physiological *dependence.* Generally used for opium-based narcotics.

Hardness. A perceptual quality. In vision, it characterizes color high in saturation and brightness.

Hard of Hearing. Any one having deficient auditory acuity.

Hardware. In computer terminology refers to the physical apparatus.

Harmonic. Refers to an overtone, or partial, whose frequency is a multiple of the fundamental one.

Harria. It is a factor trait that is characterized by toughness, decisiveness, assertiveness and realism in outlook.

Harshness. It is an unpleasant quality of sounds arising out of aperiodic or irregular have forms.

Hate. Refers to a strongly aversive attitude involving anger, ill will, and the desire to inflict injury on the object of hatred.

Hawthrone Effect. It is the tendency of people to work harder when experiencing a sense of participation in something new and special.

Healy Picture Completion Test. A performance test which needs the assembling of incomplete pictures by selecting the correct parts from a large number of possibilities.

Hearing Loss. Refers to the loss of ability to hear tones at various frequencies.

Hebetic. Relating to youth generally or to occurrences particularly at the time of puberty.

Hebetude. Emotional dullness, listlessness and a withdrawn lethargy.

Hecto. Prefix denoting *multiplication by 100.*

Hedonic. Referring to feeling or to the dimension of pleasantness-unpleasantness.

Heliocotrema. Refers to the small opening at the apex of the cochlea where the scale tympani and scala vestibuli connect.

Heliophobia. Fear of the sun, particularly fear of being exposed to bright sunlight.

Helix. It is the curved portion of the outer ear.

Hemiopia. Refers to blindness in one half of the visual field.

Hemiplegia. Refers to paralysis of one side of the body.

"Here and Now" It refers, to the present.

Hereditarianism. Refers to any position stressing the role of heredity in the determination of behavior.

Heritability. Refers to that portion of the total variability in a trait which can be attributed to genetic differences.

Heritage. Refers to transmission from generation to generation. May refer to either biological heredity or to social transmission of customs and traditions.

Hermeneutics. Interpretative procedures or the science of such.

Hermetic. Airtight, used for a pure, uncontaminated process.

Heroin. It is a morphine derivative which is one of the most widely used of the addictive drugs. It has a narcotic effect.

Hertz (Hz). One cycle per second. It is the standard international term now in used and has replaced *cps* (or *cycles per second*).

Heteromorphic. Any thing deviating from the normal.

Heteromorphous Any thing differing from the normal or usual form.

Heterosexual Refers to an individual whose sexual perferences are for persons of the opposite sex.

Heterozygous. Referring to an organism possessing a triat whose genetic makeup is made up of both dominant and recessive genes.

Heuristic. A method of discovery, a procedure for solving a problem, a technique that operates as a vehicle for creative formulation. Essentially, it is any sophisticated, directed procedure which functions by reducing the range of possible solutions to a problem or the number of possible answers to a question.

Hidden-cue Test or Situation. Refers to a task wherein the learner must discover the feature of a stimulus situation which will lead to the reward.

Hex(a). Prefix meaning *six*.

Hidden Observer. Refers to a hypothesized concealed consciousness which is inferred to experience events differently from the hypnotized consciousness.

Higher-order Conditioning. Classical conditioning wherein a conditioned stimulus (CS) from an original conditioning series is used as the unconditioned stimulus (UCS) in a new experimental setting.

Higher Response Unit. Refers to integrations of simpler acts into more complex acts.

Hindbrain. During embryonic development the brain evolves three separate portions, the hindbrain, midrain and forebrain. The hindbrain is evolutionarily the oldest ; it differentiates into the metencephalon and the myelencephalon. The metencephalon gives rise to the cerebellum and the pons, the myelencephalon to the medulla.

Hippocampus. A curved nerve tract make up of gray matter in the floor of the inferior horn of the lateral ventricle. Its shape resembles a sea hours. The hippocampus is considered to function in olfactory, visceral processes and short term memory.

Hircine. Means a having a goatlike or cheeselike smell.

Histo. Prefix indicating *relating to tissue.*

Histogram. It is a graphic form of the frequency distribution wherein the number of cases within each class is represented by a vertical bar whose height is proportional to the number of cases within the class.

Hodology. Refers to the geometry of vectors, paths, and the space wherein they occur. Hodology is used as a model of behaviour. Vectors, or directed lines, are used to represent motivation and tensions, paths are the routes on which behaviour taken place in moving from one space to another; and the concept of hodological space is used in the sense of dynamic space having its psychological properties.

Holergosia. It is a psychosis which involves the entire personality.

Holergasia. Refers to any psychiatric disorder which affects the entire emotional, cognitive and behaviral repertoire of an individual.

Holmgren Test. It is a test of color blindness wherein the testee must sort a number of skeins of colored wool into three basic piles in accordance with a sample set. The test has also been used as a test of abstracting ability.

Homoerotism. Refers to sexual desire for a member of one's own sex.

Homogamy. Refers to inbreeding among members of a genetically isolated group which results in the development of similar traits among the various members.

Homologous Organs. Refers to those organs which have the same essential structure but different function—for example, the fin of a fish and the hand of a man.

Homozygous. Refers to of any organism having two like *alleles* for a particular trait.

Honi Phenomenon. Refers to failure of the well-known perceptual distortion effects of the Ames room to take place when a very familiar person like a parent or spouse is placed in the room.

Hope. Refers to an attitude which is characterized by an expectation of the favourable outcome of an event.

Horizon. In perception refers to the limit of the range of what can be perceived.

Horizontal Group. Refers to a group that draws upon only a single social class.

Horizontal Growth. It is the increase in the number of activities or skills on the same level of difficulty attained by the subject.

Horizontal Mobility. Refers to mobility within the same social or occupational class. Also known as *horizontal social mobility.*

Hospice, A specialized nursing home meant for terminally ill patients. Here patients can live out their final days in dignity.

House-Tree-Person Test. A projective test wherein the subject is asked to draw a house, a tree and a person. The drawings made are then interpreted according to a more or less standardized set of criteria.

H Scaling. Refers to the utilization of several items of equal acceptability as if they were one item, so as to increase reliability.

Human Engineering. It is an applied branch of psychology and engineering that deals with problems of machine design, working conditions, skills, learning ability and efficiency.

Human Factors. Refers to the name of the professional speciality which studies the *man-machine interface.* Its main focus is on problems of perception, psycho-physics, decision-making and other aspects of information processing.

Humanistic psychology. Refers to a theoretical and therapeutic system of psychology which emphasizes specially human processes.

Humm-Wadsworth Temperament Scale. Refers to a personality questionnaire used to measure relative standing on paranoid, hysteric, manie-depressive, and schizoid tendencies.

Hunger Pangs. Refers to the sensation associated with strong hunger contractions in the stomach.

Huntington's Chorea. Refers to a neurological disorder which is characterized by progressively more serious loss of coordination, spasmodic, jerky movements, and mental deterioration. The disease is hereditary.

Hunt-Minnesota Test. It is a test used for organic brain damage with adolescents and adults.

Hyalophobia. Refers to irrational fear of glass, of touching glass.

Hydrophobiaphobia. Means fear of hydrophobia.

Hydrotherapy. Refers to treatment using of water packs, baths, and hot water bottles.

Hypacusia. Means impaired hearing.

Hypalgesia. Means impaired sensitivity to pain.

Hyperalgia. Refers to greatly increased sensitivity to pain.

Hypercathexis. Means investing psychic energy in one process for the purposes of furthering or facilitating another.

Hypergasia. Refers to overactivity which is characteristic of the manic phase of bipolar disorder.

Hyperglycemia. Refers to increase in blood sugar.

Hypermnesia. Refers to unusual ability to remember. Hypermnesia may take place under hypnotic states or during free association.

Hyperopia. Farsightedness ; a condition wherein the rays of light entering the eye come to a focal point behind the retina due to shortness of the eyeball.

Hypermania. It is a condition of exhibiting extreme activity, rapid and erratic behavior and speech.

Hyperphagia. Refers to extreme overeating.

Hyperprosexia. Refers to a compulsive desire to attend to a stimulus, like the dripping of a faucet.

Hypersomnia. Refers to an uncontrollable urge to sleep.

Hyperosmia. Refers to extreme sensitivity odors.

Hoperphoria. Abnormal tendency for one eye to turn upward.

Hyperplasia. Refers to increase in the size of an organ due to some abnormal increase in the number of cells.

Hyperpnea. Refers to increased breathing either in frequency of respirations or in depth.

Hyperpolarization. An increase in polarization ; in neurophysiology refers to the increase in the membrane potential of a neuron.

Hyperprosexia. Refers to any exaggerated fixating on some idea to the exclusion of others.

Hypertelorism. It is an eye disease which is characterized by increased interpupillary distance.

Hyperthymia. Refers to excessive emotionality.

Hyperthyroidism. It is a condition of excessive secretion by the thyroid gland. It is associated with an elevated metabolic rate, restlessness, excessive motility, and apprehension. If neglected, the condition is fatal.

Hypertonicity. Refers to a high degree of tension in a muscle.

Hypertropy. Refers to any excessive development in an organ.

Hypesthesia ; Hypaesthesia. Refers to decreased sensitivity or raising of the threshold.

Hypnogenic. Means sleep-producing or causing or aiding hypnosis.

Hypnopaedia. Means sleep learning.

Hypnophobia. Refers to fear of falling asleep.

Hypnagogic Image. Refers to a vivid image of hallucinatory character experienced while falling asleep or during a drowsy state.

Hypochondria ; Hypochondriasis. Refers to an exaggerated concern about one's health.

Hyphochondriac. Refers to an individual who suffers from hypochondria.

Hypoergasia. It is the depressive phase of manic-depressive psychosis.

Hypofunction. Means less than the normal degree of function.

Hypoglossal Nerve. Refers to the twelfth cranial nerve. Its chief component is motor to the muscles of the tongue.

Hypoglossal Nucleus. Refers to a mass of cell bodies in the lower medulla.

Hypogeusia. Means abnormally diminished taste sensitivity.

Hypolexia. Refers to retarded reading ability, *dyslexia*, which is the more common used term here.

Hypologia. Refers to a lack of capacity for speech due to neurological or functional disorders.

Hypophrenia. Refers to mental deficiency.

Hypophrenia.. Means mental deficiency but rarely used.

Hypophysis. *Pituitary gland.*

Hypoplasia. Refers to a detective development of tissue producing a structurally diminished organ or organ part.

Hyposmia. Refers to diminished smell sensitivity.

Hyposthenia. Refers to subnormal strength, weakness.

Hypotension. Refers to diminished tension or tonus in a muscle or organ or a condition that is marked by an abnormally low blood pressure.

Hypothetical Process. An inferred process used to explain behavior.

Hypothymia. Refers a lowering of emotional responsiveness.

Hypothyroid. One who is deficient in the production of thyroxin.

Hypotonic. Means lacking in muscle tone.

Hypoxemia. Refers to a deficiency of oxygen in the bloodstream.

Hysteriform. Means resembling hysteria.

Hysteroid. Means resembling hysteria.

I

Iasis. Suffix meaning *state* or *condition.*

Iatric. Suffix meaning *healing, medical.*

Iatric. Refers to a physician or to medicine.

Iatro. Combining from used to indicate *healing* or *medical.*

Iatrotropic Stimulus. Refers to the event or symptom which causes a person to seek medical attention.

Icarus Complex. Refers to a syndrome that is characterized by fascination with fire, a history of bedwetting a desire to be immortal, narcissism and lofty but fragile ambition.

ICD. Stands for *International Classification of Diseases.*

Ideo. Combining form meaning *idea* or *mental image.*

Iconic. Refers to a pictorial representation of something, an idol.

ICS. Stands fo *intracranial stimulation.*

ICSH. Stands for *Interstitial cell-stimulating hormone.*

Ictal. Means sudden, abrupt ; ictal emotions are transitory, fleeting emotions.

Idealism. It is a philosophical doctrine which holds that the ultimate reality is mental and that this mental representation forms the basis of all experience and knowledge.

Idealiaztion. It is a defense mechanism wherein an object about which one is ambivalent is consciously split into two conceptual representations.

Ideal Observer. An observer whose sensory and perceptum systems operate without error and devoid of bias.

Ideal-Self Q Sort. A form of *Sort* designed to evaluate the difference between and individual's real, objective sense of self and his or her idealized sense of self.

Ideational. Refers to ideas or to cognitive processes.

Id-ego. In psychoanalytic theory it is the primitive unit from which the separate id and ego become differentiated.

Identical Retinal Points. Refers to any two points, use on each retina, that receive stimulation from the same objective point at infinite distance.

Identity Crisis. Refers to a lack of the normal feeling of one's historical continuity.

Identity Formation. Refers to the point of view that mature identity formation emerges when various early, more primitive identifications and influences are rejected.

deomotor Act. Refers to any overt act that is initiated by an idea.

Idio. Combining form from the Greek *idios.*

Idiocy. Refers to mental deficiency.

Ideographic. Refers to or deals with the concrete, the individual, the unique. A psychological system or theory with this orientation is labeled an idiographic approach.

Idiom. An expression having a special meaning which cannot be determined from the meanings of its component parts.

Idiopathic. Refers to a primary pathological condition. That arises within the affected organ and not as a result of external dysfunctions.

Idiot. Refers to *a person without knowledge* ; or an ignorant person.

Idiotropic. Means turning inward.

I/E Ratio. It is a ratio of the rate of inspiration to the rate of expiration.

I E. Scale. A scale of *introversion-extraversion* derived from the MMPL.

Illegitimate. Refers to those things that voliate accepted standards, especially sexual standards.

Im. Perfix meaning *not.*

Imaginal. Referring *image* or to *imagination.*

Imaginary Companion. Refers to an "invisible" friend, created by a young child and treated as real.

Imagine. Means to engage in the mental process of imagination.

Imago. In biology refers to an adult, sexally mature insect or the mature stage of insect life. In Psychology refers to unconscious representations of other persons, typically a parent with whom one identifies closely.

Imbecile. Means *weak* or *weak-minded.*

Imipramine. A *tricyclic compound* that is used as an *antidepressant.* It is a nor-adrenergic and serotonergic antagonist and functions by retarding the re-uptake of norepinephrine and serotonin.

Immature. One who is not fully developed, or one who displays less-well-developed traits and characteristics than the norm for one's age.

Immobility. Refers to a state wherein there is no visible.

Impairment. Refers to any loss of or decrement in function. When such loss or decrement is due to injury or disease.

Imperative. Refers to *speech act* wherein the speaker directly commands or orders the listener to do something.

Imperceptible. Refers to a stimulus that is too low in intensity to be perceived.

Impersonal. Refers to a point of view that is not concerned with personal feelings.

Implantation. In placental mammals refers to the attaching of the embryo to the uterine wall.

Impotence. Refers to lack of potency, weakness, powerlessness.

Impotence, Orgasmic. Refers to the inability to achieve satisfactory coitus. An orgasmically impotent person is not impotent in the sense of being incapable of coitus.

Impotence, Primary. Refers to total coital dysfunction. There is an inability to achieve or maintain an erection sufficient for coitus on the first and all subsequent attempts.

Impotence, Psychogenic. *Impotence* in the absence of any organic dysfunction.

Impulse-Control Disorder. A disorder marked by failure to resist an impulse or temptation to engage in some act which ultimately proves harmful to oneself.

Impulsion. Refers to state of great urgency wherein one is highly susceptible to performing an impulsive act.

Impulsive. Refers to acts that are carried out without reflection.

Inaccessibility. Refers to a state of psychological remoteness wherein one is unresponsive to ordinary social stimuli.

Inadequacy. Refers to any inferiority, incompetence or any such feeling.

Inanition. Refers to physical weakness because of lack of proper nutrition.

Inborn. Means innate, inherited.

Inbreeding. In genetics refers to the mating to interbreeding of those closely related.

Incidence. It is the Frequency of occurrence of an event or a condition in relation to the population under examination.

Inclusive Fitness. In evaluationary biology refers to the total measure of various strategies which an organism may use to ensure genetic success.

Incommensurable. Refers to two variables which have no common measure or standard of comparison.

Incompatible. Means incapable of existing together in harmony.

Incompetent. Refers to one lacking in qualifications, capacities or abilities.

Increment. Refers to any increase in anything can safely be called an increment.

Incubus. Refers to demon supposed to descend upon one during sleep.

Incus. It is one of the three small bones in the middle ear.

Indissociation. . In Piaget's theory refers to a very early stage of development wherein cognitive and perceptual systems are relatively undifferentiated.

Individual Differences. Refers an approach to psychological phenomena which focuses on characteristics or traits along which individual organisms may be shown to differ.

Individuality. Refers to all those characteristics which distinguish an individual from all others.

Individual Psychology. *Differential psychology* associated with the personality theory of Alfred Adler.

Individual Response. Refers to any unusual, idiosyncratic response that is given in a word-association test.

Induced Color. A perceived color or color chanse which is determined by stimulation in other parts of the visual field.

Induced Goal. Refers to goal whose attainment is induced by outside sources.

Induction Test. Refers to any test wherein the subject is asked to induce a coherent general principle on the basis of a fixed set of exemplars.

Infantile-Birth Theories. Refers to beliefs of children concerning the actual manner of birth.

Infantile Sexuality. In Freudian psychoanalytic theory, it refers to the capacity for sexual desire and experience in the infant particularly as manifested by passage through a series of stages beginning with the oral and moving through the anal and early genital.

Infantilism. It is a condition of an older child or adult who, for certain reasons, still displays cognitive and emotional behaviors which are characteristic of infancy.

Infavoidance Need. Refers to the need to avoid failure.

Infecundity. Means sterility in women, barrenness.

Inference. Any logical judgement made on the basis of a sample ot evidence, previously made judgements, prior conclusions, etc. rather than on direct observation.

Inferior. In anatomical descriptions, of a lower part of an organ or a body.

Informed Consent. Refers to permission to carry out a research or medical procedure where the subject is given information such as (*a*) the nature of the procedures ; (*b*) potential known risks and benefits ; (*c*) any other alternative procedures which are available ; and (*d*) acknowledgement that such consent is voluntary.

Infra. Combining form meaning *low.*

Infradian Rhythms. Refers to biological rhythms having cycles of considerable duration, *e.g.*, menstrual cycle.

Infrared. Pertaining to electromagnetic radiation ("light") whose wavelength is longer than that of the light to which normal human eye responds, above roughly 700 nm.

Infundibulum. Refers to any funnelshaped passage or structure.

Inherent. Meaning *sticking to* or *in*, characterizing a property or attribute of something or someone which is inseparable and permanent.

Inherit. Means to receive from one's predecessors. In biology, refers to the process of genetic transmission.

Inhibition, Central. Refers to the assumed inhibitory action that is taking place within the central nervous system.

Inhibition, External. The inhibition of a conditioned response that is produced when a novel, irrelevant stimulus is presented along with the conditioned stimulus.

Inhibition of Inhibition. Means *disinhibition.*

Injury. Refers to any damage to bodily tissue.

Inkblot Test. Refers to any of the several projective tests which make use of inkblots *e.g.*, the Rorschach Test ; Barron Movement Threshold Inkblot Test and the Holtzman Inkblot. Test.

Inner-Directed. Refers to a tendency to react according to an internalized set of goals or values.

Inner Ear. It is the innermost component of the ear containing the cochlea and the organs of balance.

Innervation Reciprocal. Refers to innervation of a pair of antagonistic muscles through which neural impulses induce flexion in one and extension in the other.

Inoculate. Means to introduce a microorganism or other substance into the body generally by means of an injection.

Inoculation Hypothesis. Refers to the hypothesis that one's belief is some point of view can be strengthened if we present weak and refutable counterarguments.

Input. Refers to any stimulus that is some form of energy that enters some system (an organism). Particularly a signal fed to an electrical circuit, a message which acts on a receiver, etc.

Insanity. In legal designation refers to the state of an individual judged to be legally irresponsible or incompetent.

Insanity Defense. A legal concept according to which person cannot be convicted to a crime if it can be shown that he or she lacked "criminal responsibility," that he or she was (legally) insane.

Insensible. Means without sensibility. Refers to an organism in a state of unresponsiveness ; *e.g.*, one who is unconscious or in a coma.

Insomnia, Rebound. Refers to insomnia taking place after withdrawal from drugs taken to relieve insomnia.

Inspection. A synonym for *introspection.*

Instant. A duration so brief that two or more (perhaps) sequential events are perceived as simultaneous.

Instigation. Means arousal, stimulation.

Instigation Therapy. It is a form of therapy wherein the therapist sets up positive models for the client and actively reinforces progress toward them.

Instinct, Closed. Refers to innate species-specific behavior patterns that are rigid and inflexible.

Instinct, Delayed. Any instinct which does not appear until some time after birth or hatching.

Institutionalize. Refers to the process of *institutionalization* of a person by either indoctrination into a system of social roles or physical placement in an institution such as a prison or a mental hospital.

Institution, Total. Refers to *institutions* where life style is sharply restricted, formalized and under the control of special staff.

Instruction(S). Means directing, teaching, imparting knowledge.

Instrumental Behavior (or Act). Refers to behavior or act which is goal directed, a means to some end.

Insulin Shock (or Coma). Refers to Hypoglycemic state produced by excess insulin, because of a lowering in blood sugar and a comatose state.

Insulin-Shock Therapy. A form of therapy utilizing a large-enough dose of insulin to induce shock and coma.

Integrate. Means to bring into a harmonious or coordinated whole by rearranging, organizing and some times adding or deleting elements or parts.

Integration, Behavioral. Means the blending, chaining or combining of many separate behaviors into a coordinated whole.

Integration, Cultural. The blending of cultural traits, that were conflicting, to form a modified, integrated system.

Intellect. Refers to the *rational* thought functions of the human mind.

Intellectualization. A defense mechanism by which problems are analyzed in remote, intellectual terms.

Intelligence, Coefficient of. It is an index of intelligence obtained by forming a ratio between the score obtained by an individual on an intelligence test and the norms for that person's age.

Intelligence, Concrete. Refers to the ability to function effectively with *concrete* problems.

Intention. Refers to any desire, plan, purpose, aim or belief which is oriented toward some goal, some end state.

Intentional. Means purposeful, goal oriented acts undertaken consciously.

Inter. Combining term meaning *between, among* or *mutual.*

Interaction. Means reciprocal effect or influence.

Interaction Variance. In statistics it is the proportion of the total variance which is not related to the action of single variables but because of the interaction between them.

Interaural Differences. These are differences in the sound arriving at the two ears.

Intercalation. Refers to any insertion in between the elements of an ordered series.

Interest Inventory (or Test). Refers to an instrument designed to evaluate a person's interests in or preferences for a variety of activities.

Interface. Refers to the circuitry in computers which connects the central processing core of a computer and is peripheral parts.

Intermarriage. Refers to a marriage between such persons who are blood relations.

Intermediate Needs. Just like physiological needs inter mediate needs are presumed to be activated by deficiencies. Such needs are safety, belongingness, self-esteem, security, etc.

Intermission. Refers to symptom-free period in a chronic disorder.

Internal Consistency. It indicates the degree to which the different parts of a test or other instrument measure the same variables.

Internal Rectus. It is one of the muscles which control the eye.

International Phonetic Alphabet (IPA). A phonetic alphabet of approximately 95 phones. It is rich and flexible enough for all of the phonemes of the world's languages to be represented.

Interneuron. A connecting neuron, which lies between sensory and motor neurons. It is found within the central nervous system and also known as *internuncial neuron* or *association neuron*.

Interoception. Refers to the perception of events within the body.

Interocular Distance. It is the distance between the pupils when the eyes are in normal position while viewing, distant objects, *i.e.*, focused on infinity.

Interpretative Therapy. Refers to any form of psychotherapy wherein the therapist interprets the significance and underlying symbolic meaning of the client's statements.

Interquartile Range. Refers to the range between the first and third quartiles (*i.e.*, between the 25th and 75th percentiles) of a distribution.

Interresponse Time (IRT). Refers to the time that elapses between responses. It is used in evaluating operant behavior.

Interrogative. Refers to *speech act* wherein the speaker requests information from the listener.

Interruption Tone. Refers to a tone produced by regular interruptions of a constant tone.

Intersexuality. It is the condition in which both male and female characteristics are present specially the secondary sex characteristics.

Interstice. Refers to gap or space in a tissue or in the structure of an organ.

Intertrial Interval (ITI). It is the time interval between two trials of an experiment.

Interval of Uncertainty (IU). In psychophysics it is the interval between the upper and lower thresholds.

Interview. It is a mode of directed conversation. In psychology, interviews aim at information-gathering or therapeutic purposes.

Interviewer Bias. Refers to the contaminating effect of the in viewer's opinions in an interview.

Intimacy Disorder. Refers to the inability to become intimate with others, to share emotions, trust others.

Intonation. Refers to the modulations of the voice, the stress patterns, and the rise and fall in pitch while speaking.

Intraception. Refers to an outlook on life that is subjective, internally motivated, imaginative.

Intrafusal Fibers. Refers to muscle fibres that function as stretch receptors. They are arranged in parallel with *extrafusal fibers* and detect the length of a muscle.

Intramural. Means within the walls ; thus it pertains to events taking place inside the boundaries of an institution.

Intraocular Modification. Refers to any change in the visual signal because of the characteristics of the eye.

Intrapsychic. Refers to anything considered to arise or occur within the mind.

Intrinsic. Meaning *inwardly* or *inward.* Refers to a property of something that reflects the nature of the thing.

Intro. Prefix meaning *moving within* or *toward the inside.*

Introjection. Refers to the process whereby aspects of the external world are absorbed into or incorporated within the self, the internal representation then taking over the psychological functions of the external objects.

Intromission. Means placing or inserting one part inside another.

Intropunitive. Refers to the tendency to react to frustration by directing anger and blame toward oneself, the internally focused emotions generally being experienced as guilt or shame.

Intrusion Response (or Error). Refers to any response in an ordered experiment that either (*a*) was not in the original list or (*b*) took place in the wrong position in the list.

Invalidate. Means to render an argument or conclusion invalid, to prove it false.

Inverse Correlation. Refers to *negative correlation.*

Inversion. It is a process of turning inside out or upside down, or the result of such a process.

Inversion or Affect. Refers to sudden switching between two emotions which are at opposite poles on a continuum, love and hatred.

Inversion, Sexual. Previously used for hermaphroditism or Transvestism or homosexuality.

Inverted-U Curve (or distribution. Refers to any distribution the curve of which is shaped like an inverted letter U, with high frequency for moderate values and low frequency for both very low and very high values.

Investment. Means *clothing*. In psychoanalysis, it is used as synonym of *cathexis*.

Involution. Means *roll into*, an occasional synonym for *menopause*.

Iophobia. It is the fear of being poisoned or fear of rusty objects.

IPA. *International Phonetic Alphabet*.

Iprindole. A tricyclic compound that is used as an *antidepressant*.

Iproniazide. A monoamine oxidase inhibitor that is used as an *antidepressant*.

Ips(a). Meaning *of one's own, of the self, the same.*

Ipsative. Means reflected or measured against the self.

Ipsilateral. Pertaining to the same side.

Iris. The pigmented muscular membrane that projects from the ciliary body of the eye.

Irradiation Theory. It is a theory of learning which makes the same assumptions as *trial-and-error learning*.

Irresponsibility. In forensic psychiatry and legal parlance it refers to the principle that an individual is not to be adjudged guilty of a crime if it can be determined that the normal conditions under which one could be held to be responsible for his or her actions do, in fact, not pertain.

Irritability. Of all living tissue it is the property of responding to stimulation.

Ism. A suffix used to denote *usage, action, practice, condition, principle, characteristic* or *doctrine.*

Iso. Combining form meaning *equal* or *the same.*

Isocoria. The normal condition, wherein both eyes show equal pupil size even when different amounts of light is falling on the two eyes.

Isolation Amentia. Refers to mental retardation observed in cases of anaclitic depression.

Isometric Contraction (or twitch). Refers to muscle contraction which causes tension but no movement.

Isomorphism. In mathematics refers to a point-by-point relationship between two systems. In psychology it is the hypothesis that there is such a relationship between excitatory fields in the cortex and conscious experience.

Isophilia. Refers to nonsexual attraction and affection toward members of one's own sex.

Isotonic. Means equal tension.

Ist. Refers to some *agent* or *actor* ; an advocate of an *ism.*

Itch. Itching is, a source of much interest and confusion. It is, a rather attention-demanding condition although little is known about the underlying physiology. The irritation may be chemical, electrical or mechanical, although itching has also been reported in the phantom limbs of amputees indicating that a central component is involved as well.

Itis. A suffix denoting *inflammation.*

ITPA. *Illinois Test of Psycholinguistic Abilities.*

IU. *Interval of uncertainty.*

IUD. *Interauterine device.*

J

Jacksonian Epilepsy. A form of epilepsy which is characterized by localized convulsions that are usually limited to one limb. The cause of the disorder gets localized irritation of the cerebral cortex.

Jackson's Law. Pertains to the manner in which memory functions are affected in mentally disturbed persons, recollection for events immediately preceding the onset being lost first.

Jactitation ; Jactation. Extreme restlessness or tossing about.

James-Lange Theory of the Emotions. A formulation that tries to integrate the conscious and behavioral aspects of the emotions. Lange, a Danish physiologist, had argued that emotional processes have been identical with changes in the circulatory system. James took this aspect of Lange's theory and incorporated it into his own theory, which holds that the emotional experience is the result of the visceral changes arising from the individual's reacting to an emotion-provoking experience. The essence of the theory has been contained in the famous argument offered by James that upon meeting a bear in the woods we do not run because we are afraid, but are afraid because we run ; that is, running stirs up a visceral reaction and this is the emotion.

J Curve. A curve describing the frequency of compliance with a rule or standard. A commonly cited example has been the manner in which automobile drivers comply with a stop sign. Some stop completely, some not at all, and some slow down to varying degrees. The curve representing the various degrees of compliance approximates the capital letter J in shape.

Jealousy. An attitude of envy toward another due to the affection that individual shows to a third person.

Job Analysis. An investigation of the ability requirements, working conditions, pay, opportunities for promotion, etc., that go with a particular job. Job analyses have been helpful in employee-selection programs.

Job Placement. The term used for the assignment of an individual to a job on the basis of his abilities, experience, interests, and the requirements of the position.

Job Specification. A description of a job and the requisite abilities which are needed for success in the work involved.

Jordan Curve. A closed, nonoverlapping curve which is used to represent various aspects of the life space.

Jost's Law. The principle that given two associations of equal strength but unequal age, practice will be of more benefit to the older. The law has been based on the empirical finding that older associations lose strength less rapidly with the passage of time.

Joy. A highly pleasant emotion which is associated with accomplishment, satisfaction, and gratification.

Judgment. Cognitive activity of bringing two ideas into an affirmation of similarity or difference, as in judging weights, lines, pictures, and the like.

Just Noticeable Difference. The minimum detectable difference between two stimuli.

Just-noticeable-differences Method. A psychophysical technique for determining the just-noticeable difference. A standard stimulus has been presented along with a variable stimulus whose magnitude is gradually increased on some trials and decreased on other trials until the just-perceptible differences is reported by the subject. The average of the ascending and descending series has been taken, and the threshold has been calculated at that point where the difference can be recognized 50 per cent of the time.

Just-world Hypothesis. The belief that people get what they deserve, and so could be held accountable for their behaviour.

Juvenile. Youth or adolescent.

Juvenile, Delinquent. From the standpoint of psychology and sociology, a youth who has been brought before police officials or presented in court, the charges having been sustained by the evidence.

K

Kallikak. Refers to a family with two lines of descendents ; one of normal and superior people, the other of delinquents, psychotics, and mental defectives.

Kappa Effect. Change in the apparent interstimulus interval when the distance between two successively presented stimuli is changed.

Katasexual. Characteristic of sexuality wherein dead partners are the sexual goals.

K Complex. Refers to a cortical response evoked by an auditory stimulus during sleep as revealed by the electroencephalogram.

Kelly's Constant Process. It is a psychophysical method used for fitting data for the normal ogive making use of the standard deviation instead of *h*. The latter measures the steepness of a distribution, where as the former measures its scatter or spread.

Kent-Rosanoff Test. It is a standardized free-association test and was devised by Grace Kent and A.J. Rosanoff. It is made up of 100 stimulus words and tables of relative frequency for responses to those words by 1,000 subjects. The results of an individual case can be compared with the tabular material for common, unusual, and doubtful responses.

Keraunophobia. Refers to fear of lightning.

Key. It is a list of the correct answers used in scoring a test or a devise for coding or decoding information.

Kinephantom. An illusion of movement, specially in a shadow movement, like that which takes place when the shadows of the spokes of a wheel are seen moving in the opposite direction from that of the wheel.

Kinesics. Refers to the study of bodily language or communications by gestures and bodily positions and movements.

Kinesimeter. It is a device used for measuring the threshold of the sensation for movement.

Kinesthesis. Refers to the muscle, tendon and joint sense. This combination of senses provides information about the position of the limbs and body in space. The receptors for the muscle sense are known as muscle spindles, that take the form of microscopic fibrils which wrap around muscle fibers.

Kinesthetic Method. It is a technique used for treating speech and writing disabilities by having the patient attend to the muscular sensations involved.

Kinesthetic Response. It is a response category for projecting action into the blots.

Kinetic Information. Refers to gestures, expressive movements, posture, and tension patterns which are used in making judgments about peasons.

Kjersted-Robinson Law. Accoraing to this principle the amount of material learned during equal portions of the learning time is relatively constant for different lengths of material.

Kleptolagnia. Refers to sexual excitement associated with stealing.

Kleptomania. Refers to an obsessive impulse or compulsion to steal.

Klinefelder's Syndrome. Refers to a genetic abnormality where the sex chromosome pattern is XXY. It is characterized by retarded gonadal development, mental retardation, and a tendency toward femininity.

Kluver-Bucy Syndrome. It is a behaviour pattern observed in those monkeys whose temporal regions have been removed with involvement of the tissues deep in the frontolateral region. They display "psychic blindness," or the inability to recognize objects, are aggressive, and suffer from hypersexuality.

Knee-jerk Reflex. Refers to the reflexive extension of the lower leg upon a sharp tap to the tendon just below the patella, or kneecap.

Knowledge of Results. Refers to any information given to a subject about the correctness of his response.

Knox Cube Test. It is a performance test wherein the subject must tap a series of four cubes in different sequences according to a pattern presented by the experimenter.

Kohs Block Design Test. It is a performance test of intelligence and makes use of a set of one-inch colored cubes whose sides are painted red, blue, yellow, white, yellow and blue, and red and white respectively. Colored designs presented to the subject on seventeen test cards must be reproduced using the blocks. It is a part of the Arthur Performance Scale.

Korsakov's Psychosis ; Korsakov's Syndrome. Refers to a mental disorder brought on by alcoholism and marked by neural irritation, disturbances of memory and orientation.

Korte's Law. Laws of apparent movement which state for the optimal movement of phi : (1) if intensity is held constant, the time interval for optimal movement changes directly with the distance between stimuli ; (2) if time is held constant, the distance for optimal movement changes directly with intensity : and (3) if distance between stimuli is held constant, then intensity for optimal movement changes inversely with time interval.

Krause end Bulb. Refers to an encapsulated neuronal ending considered by some authorities to be a receptor for cold.

K Scale. A special scoring key for the Minnesota Multiphasic Inventory of Personality that detects malingering.

Kuder Form E General Interest Survey. Grades 6 12. A vocational interest survey similar to the Kuder Preference Record.

Kuder Occupational Interest Survey. Grades 11-12 and adults. An interest inventory which yields 114 occupational scores reported in terms of the relationship between the examinee's responses and those of successful groups in the occupations recorded.

Kuder Preference Record—Vocational. An early interest inventory which gives the subject's relative standing on ten broad areas of vocational interest, like social service, science, art, etc.

Kuder-Richardson Coefficient of Equivalence. Formulas used to estimate the correlation between comparable forms of a test on the basis of one administration.

Kuhlmann-Anderson Test. It consists of a series of tests of general intelligence ranging from kindergarten to adulthood.

Kundt's Rule. According to this principle the divided or graduated lines or distances appear greater than nongraduated or undivided distances.

Kurtosis. Refers to the degree of flatness or peakedness of a frequency curve in the region of the mode.

Kwashiorkor. Refers to a protein deficiency disease of infants and children that is characterized by edema, pot belly, and skin lesions. Found chiefly in Africa.

Kymograph. It is an instrument used for tracing records of temporal variations in any variable on a smoked or lightly waxed drum.

L

L. Stands for *lambert, lumen,* or *limen,*

$L_{1, 2}$. In the study of bi- and multilingualism, L_1 is used to denote the first language learned, L_2 the second, etc.

$_SL_R$. Stands for reaction threshold in Hullian theory.

Labia. Refers to the folds surrounding the opening of the vagina.

Labial. Refers to lips in general, but most commonly with reference to the oral lips.

Labia Majora. Refers to the outer fatty folds which surround the vulva.

Labia Minora. Refers to the inner, richly vascular folds that surround the vulva.

Labile. Means flexible, free in expression.

Labiodental. It is a class of speech sounds which are produced by using the lower lip and the upper teeth ; *e.g., f* and *v* in *five.*

Labyrinth. Refers to the portion of the inner ear. It contains the receptors for hearing and those for the static sense.

Lacrimal. Any thing relating to tears.

Lacrimal Gland. The tear gland that lies beneath the upper eyelid and secretes tears than moisten the cornea.

Lactate. Means to produce milk. It also refers to salt of lactic acid.

Lactation. Refers to the process of milk production in mammals.

Lacuna. Refers to a gap or a temporary lapse in memory.

LAD (or LAS). An acronym for *language-acquisition device.* The status of LAD is highly equivocal and most psycholinguists and cognitive psychologists find the idea fascinating but doubtful.

Ladder Scale. It is a self-anchoring scale used to measure the individual's attitude toward the real world as contrasted with his attitude toward his ideal world.

Ladd-Franklin Theory. A theory of color vision which is not generally accepted now a days, that assumes a complex photosensitive molecule which responds differentially to red, green, blue and yellow light by releasing substances which stimulate respective nerve endings.

Lag. Refers to a time delay between stimulus and response or a brief period after the removal of a stimulus, when it is still perceived.

Lagnia. Combining form meaning ***lust***.

Laissez Faire. It is a kind or leadership wherein a minimum of control is exerted.

Laissez Faire Atmosphere. Refers to general socio-political climate established when the nominal leader of a group maintains a "hands off" policy and there is little or no guidance or direction imposed.

Lalia. Combining form used in reference to speech, specifically disorders of speech.

Lallation. Refers to an unintelligible, infantile babbling.

lalopathy. Refers to any speech disorder.

Lalophobia. Refers to fear of speaking.

Laloplegia. It is the inability to speak because of paralysis of all those muscles which are used for speech except the tongue.

Lamarckism ; Lamarckianism. According to this theory structural changes acquired by an organism through use or disuse can be transmitted to the offspring.

Lamaze Method. It is a method of psychological preparation for childbirth wherein the expectant mother is trained in breathing exercises and muscle relaxation techniques which facilitate delivery.

Lambda (λ). Symbol for wavelength of different waves.

Lambert. A unit of luminance or brightness. It is equal to the brightness of a perfectly diffusing surface emitting one lumen per square centimeter.

Lambert's Law. This law states the interrelation of incidence, emission, and reflection of light, to the effect that these factors change directly as the cosine of the angle of the rays perpendicular to the surface.

Land Effect. This effect produces the perception of color from black and white photographs.

Landolt Ring(s). Refers to doughnut-shaped figure having an opening in it which is used for measuring visual acuity.

Landolt Circles. These are the circles having gaps of different degree and are used in the determination of visual acuity.

Language Acquisition Device (LAD). The Innate mechanism which operates on linguistic data supplied by parents to produce a given language structure.

Language Behavior. Refers to behavior that involves the use of language whether oral, written, or in the form of gestures.

Language Centers. A number of areas of the cerebral cortex which function in different aspects of spoken and written language and in music.

Language Disability. Refers to any non-normal language function.

Lanugo. Refers to fine, infant-like hair, or such fine hair which briefly covers the body of the fetus during the later stage of gestation.

Lapse. Means a slip or error or a brief period of forgetfulness.

Lapsus Linguae. Refers to a slip of the tongue.

Laryngeal Reflex. Refers to coughing that is caused by irritation of the larynx.

Larynx. It is a cartilaginous structure which sits atop the windpipe. It has a "valve" made up of a double set of muscular folds which is covered with a layer of mucous membrane.

Lashley Jumping Stand. Refers to a device used for experimenting on small animals. The animal is placed on a stand and must jump toward one of two or more stimuli placed in front of it. The device finds wide use in studies of discrimination and choice behavior.

Latah Syndrome. Refers to psychiatric syndrome that is characterized by symptoms of excitement, echolalia, echopraxia, coprolalia and often fugue and hallucinations.

Latency. Refers to a condition of inactivity between the application of a stimulus and the onset of a response.

Latency Period. In classical psychoanalytic theory it is the period from roughly age 4 or 5 to the beginning of puberty during which sexual interest is considered to be sublimated.

Latency, Response. It is the time between the onset of a stimulus and the occurrence of the overt response to that stimulus.

Latent. Means hidden ; not manifest. Sexual behavior in young children may be said to be latent in this sense.

Latent Content. Refers to the hidden content of a dream which must be brought out during analysis by means of free association.

Latent Homosexual. A latent homosexual is merely a heterosexual.

Latent Learning. Refers to learning which is not manifested in performance.

Latent Period. It is a time interval between the reception of a stimulus and the onset of a response.

Latent Process. Refers to a process that is *latent*. Generally in psychoanalytic theory an infant's ego processes are said to be latent.

Latent Social Identity. Refers to social role which, though not a factor in functioning in a society, but has significant impact upon an individual's behavior in a social organization.

Latent Traits. Refers to those genetically determined traits which do not manifest themselves in the phenotype of an individual but which can be passed on to future generations.

Lateral. Pertaining to the side of an organ or of the body.

Lateral Fissure. Refers to a deep fissure in the temporal cortex that divides the temporal lobe from the parietal and frontal lobes.

Lateral Inhibition. Refers to a set of conditions established when two or more neural cells are interconnected in such a way that excitation of one produces inhibition in the other.

Laterality. Refers to any preference for one side of the body over the other, like having a preferred hand or eye.

Lateralization. It is the process whereby different functions and processes become associated with one or the other side of the brain.

Lateral Lemniscus. Refers to a bundle of nerve fibers in the medulla and pons that carry auditory impulses.

Lateral Thalamic Nucleus. Refers to a large mass of cell bodies on the lateral aspect of the thalamus.

Lateral Thinking. Refers to heuristic for solving problems wherein the individual attempts to look at the problem from many angles instead of making a search for a direct, head-on solution.

Latin Square. It is a type of experimental design which provides for as many trials as there are experimental conditions.

Latitude. Means freedom from narrow restrictions.

Law. Refers to a statement of a uniformity found in nature. Scientific laws are broad generalizations which describe cause-and effect relations among variables and their antecedent conditions.

Law, Empirical. Refers to principle or generalization which relates variables to each other and based on observations or experimental findings.

Law Analysis. Refers to psycho analysis as practiced by some one who does not possess a medical degree but who has undergone special training in the theory and technique of psychoanalysis.

Lax. In phonetics, a *distinctive feature* descriptive of speech sounds produced when the vocal tract is in its normal resting position.

Lay. Refers to a nonprofessional ; *e.g.*, a layman.

Lay Analyst. Refers to one who has received psychoanalytic training and is recognized to practice but who has not taken a degree in medicine.

LD. Stands for *Learning disability* or *Language disability.*

Layman. Refers to an individual who is not professionally trained in a given area.

L Data. Stands for life record data that is obtained by rating the individual as he reacts to life situations.

Leader. Refers to one who guides, directs, or controls the actions of others or one who possesses the personality traits and other qualifications for leadership.

Leadership. Means the exercise of authority; the control, guidance, and direction of the conduct of others or the qualities of personality and training that make for success in guiding and controlling the conduct of others.

Leading Eye. Refers to the eye which first turns toward an object of attention.

Learned Helplessness. Refers to a condition that follow a number of bad experiences, where the individual thinks he is helpless to control events.

Learning, Laws of. Three are the principles that attempt to formulate the conditions under which learning takes place.

Learning Set. Means an intention to learn or the acquisition of a certain method or approach in learning.

Learning. S-R. Stands for *stimulus-response learniag.* It refers to any and all kinds of learning which are assumed to be fundamentally governed by the forming of some link or bond between a particular stimulus and a specific response.

Learning, S-S. Learning based on the association between two stimuli.

Learning Theory. Refers to formulation of laws and conditions of learning.

Learning to Learn. Refers to the fact that with successive presentations of problems of a similar form the subjects become increasingly successful in learning how to solve them.

Least-effort Principle. Refers to the generalization that an animal tends to follow that route to a goal which involves a minimum of effort.

Least Preferred Co-Worker Test. It is a test used to measure if a leader is people-centered or task-centered.

Least Square. Law of. It is the assumption that the best estimate of a value is that for which the sum of the squares of the deviations is at a minimum.

Leboyer Method. It is a natural childbirth method developed around the assumption that child bearing can be made less "violent" for the infant. Delivery takes place in a darkened room, the infant is bathed in warm water and then placed on the mother's abdomen and the severing of the umbilical cord is delayed.

Legend. Refers to a traditional belief about a person, place, or important event which is not supported by adequate historical evidence.

Leiter International Performance Test. It is a nonverbal test of intelligence and makes use of matching pictures and forms, color designs, number series, and concealed figures.

Lemma. In logic refers to a proposition which is accepted as true for use in the proof of another proposition.

Lemniscal System. It is a polysynaptic pathway which ascends through the reticular formation. It is made up of the *lateral lemniscus,* that runs rostrally through the medulla and pons carrying fibers of the auditory system.

Lens. Refers to the transparent structure attached to the body of the eye by the ciliary muscle. The lens is capable of accommodation or adjustment for near and far vision and so it makes focusing possible.

Lentiform or Lenticular Nucleus. It is the outermost of two large nuclei of the corpus striatum.

Leptokurtic. In a frequency curve refers to possessing peaks.

Leptosome. Refers to a person of slender build.

Lerema. Refers to the tendency of some types of psychotics to be talkative.

Lesbianism. Female *homosexuality.*

Lesion. Refers to an injury to tissue from disease or surgical procedures.

Lethargy. Drowsiness. It is on apathetic condition of extremely low motivation and activity level.

Lethologica. Refers to temporary inability to recall a proper noun or a name.

Leuk(O). Combining form which means *white, colorless.*

Leukocyte. Refers to a white blood cell.

Level. Refers to a position or rank attained on a test or a mental age or point score that all persons of a given chronological age should reach.

Leveling. In memory refers to the tendency to reduce irregularities, to make drawings or stories less sharp, to leave out details.

Leveling Effect. Refers to the tendency for repeated series of measurements to group or cluster about the mean, because of the reduction of extreme differences due to practice effects.

Levophobia. It is the fear of things being on the left side of the body.

Lewinian. Pertaining to Lewin's system of psychology.

Lexicon. Refers to an alphabetic listing of the words of a language, a dictionary.

Lexicostatistics. It is a technique for estimating the historical connection between two languages.

Libidinal. Relating to the sexual energy obtained from the id ; highly sexual.

Libidinal Development. Refers to the growth and differentiation of the libido through different infantile stages of oral, anal, and early genital eroticism.

Libidinal Object. Refers to the object (person or thing) wherein libido is invested.

Libidinization. It is the process of becoming the object of libidinal attachment.

Libido. Refers to the sex instinct or erotic desire or erotic pleasure or more generally, the combination of the life instincts (eros) and death instincts (thanatos).

Librium. It is a tranquilizing or anti-anxiety drug.

Library. In cognitive psychology, refers to the totality of information about the world which a person carries about.

Lie Detector. Refers to a collection of instruments used to measure minute changes in emotionality which accompany the telling of lies.

Life. It is the collective total of those properties that differentiate the living from the nonliving.

Life Age. It is the age of the individual since birth ; chronological age ; calendar age.

Life Cycle. Refers to the typical pattern of birth, development, maturity, reproduction, and death which characterizes a given species.

Life Goal. Refers to the fundamental aim of achieving the particular form of superiority which will allow one to compensate for one's primary, felt inferiority.

Life Lie. Refers to the individual's rationalization that he cannot succeed due to obstacles or personal defects.

Life Plan. Refers to the individual's style of life, including his guiding fiction, his attempts to achieve superiority, and to rationalize or explain failures.

Life Span. It is the actual duration of life of an individual organism from inception to death.

Light. The stimulus for vision, electromagnetic radiation of wavelengths between approximately 400 and 700 nanometers. Light may be either particle or wave ; the latter is most useful for work in psychology.

Lightness. Refers to that attribute of an object color which allows it to be classified along the series of grays which runs from black to white,

Light Reflex. Refers to the pupillary response ; it includes both dilation when light levels drop and constriction when they are raised.

Likert Scale. It is a type of attitude scale whereon the subject is asked to indicate his degree of agreement or disagreement with stated attitudes on a three or five-point scale.

Limbic System. It is a complex set of evolutionarily old structures of the forebrain lying in an area below the corpus callosum. The individual structures probably are involved in behaviors which are emotional and motivational.

Limen. Means *threshold*.

Liminal Stimulus. Refers to a stimulus that is just at the threshold or that barely evokes a response.

Limit. Refers to the terminal value of a series or the end(s) of some continuum.

Limulus. The horseshoe crab. Important in psychology due to a very large compound eye which lends itself nicely to experimental study.

Linear. Pertaining to a straight line or pertaining to continuous, as opposed to discrete, functions.

Linear Perspective. Refers to the relative differences in size of an object at different distances from the eye.

Linear Regression. Refers to a regression whose equation develops a straight line.

Lingual. Pertaining to the tongue, or pertaining to languages.

Linguistic Relativity. The theory according to which cultural differences are created by linguistic differences ; hence individuals in different cultures perceive and think about the world differently.

Linguistics. It is the study of the origins, evolution and structure of language(s).

Linkage. In genetics refers to two or more genes which are said to be linked if they tend to be passed from generation to generation as a unit.

Lip Eroticism. Refers to a tendency to seek sexual satisfaction through stimulation of the lips.

Lip Key. It is a device used for measuring the reaction time of speaking as detected by lip movements.

Lip Reading. It is a technique used by the deaf to understand spoken speech by watching the speaker's lips.

Listing's Law. It is a principle of eye movement stating that if the eye moves from one primary position to another, the rotation of the eyeball in the new position is the same as if the eye had turned in a fixed axis that is at right angles to the initial and the final lines of regard.

Lisp. Refers to articulatory speech disorder wherein sibilant sounds (*s*, *z*, *sh*, *ch*) are mispronounced. generally by substituting a *th* sound.

Lissajou's Figures. Refers to revolving abstract designs which are produced either by reflections from vibrating mirrors or on an oscilloscope screen. When watched closely for a time the direction of apparent rotation reverses.

Literacy Test. Refers to a test of the ability to read and write.

Lithium Carbonate. It is a compound of the element lithium which has been found useful in treating manic-depressive disorders.

Load. Refers to a weight or factor loading or a caseload, or the number of patients or clients being cared for by a social worker or therapist.

Lobe. Refers to any reasonably well-defined part of an organ.

Lobectomy. Refers to the surgical removal of the preforental region of the frontal lobes.

Location Chart. Refers to reproductions of the Rorschach inkblots includen in the record blank so that the examiner may record the location of the subject's response.

Locomotion. Refers to the movement of a person through his or her *life space*.

Locomotor Behavior. It is the behavior involved in traveling -from place to place.

Locus of Control. It is the degree to which the individual attributes the cause of his behavior to environmental factors or to his own decisions.

Logagnosia. Refers to a condition wherein the patient can see and read words but not identify them in terms of their meanings.

Logamnesia. Condition wherein the patient is unable to recognize spoken or written words.

Logic. It is a branch of philosophy that deals with the criteria of validity in thought, the canons of correct predication and the principles of reasoning and demonstration.

Logical. Pertaining to logic ; characterized by sound or correct reasoning.

Logomania. It is a pathological state of volubility or incoherent wordiness. Characteristic of mental disorders.

Logography. Refers to any writing system which is based on the use of signs to represent words or morphemes.

Logopathy. Refers to any speech disorder.

Logorrhea. Refers to incoherent bursts of talking ; pathological volubility.

Long-Term Memory (LTM). Refers to permanent memory or memory which endures for long periods may be for life.

Looking-Glass Self. Refers to a person's perception of himself or herself as a reflection of the perception which the person has of how he or she appears to others.

Looming. Refers to the complex of gradient transformations produced as one rapidly approaches some object, or vice versa.

Loose Construct. Refers to a construct which permits variable, even contradictory, predictions.

Loudness. It is the psychological attribute of an auditory stimulus corresponding to the physical dimension of intensity.

Love, Romantic. Refers to that kind of love which is hypothesized to exist between opposite-sexed peers.

Low-Grade Defective. Refers to an individual of subnormal ability needing institutionalization and close supervision.

Lucidity. Means clarity, particularly of mind.

Lues. Means syphilis.

Lumen. The unit of luminous flux it is defined as the amount of light within a solid angle of a unit size originating from a source of one candlepower.

Luminance. It is the *luminous flux* emitted, reflected or transmitted by a surface and measured in foot-lamberts.

Luria Technique. It is used in the measuring of emotional tensions. It this method the subject presses the fingers of one hand on a sensitive tremor recorder as he responds in a free-association test.

Luteinizing Hormone (LH). A hormone which in the female, regulates progesterone production during the latter stages of the menstrual cycle and, in the male, regulates the production of androgen. Also known as *interstitial-cell-stimulating hormone.*

Luster. Refers to the brightness of highly polished surfaces.

Lutenizing Normone It is a tropic hormone produced by the anterior pituitary that stimulates ovulation, the growth of the corpus luteum, and the testes to produce androgen.

Lux. A unit of *illuminance* which is equal to the amount of light falling on a surface 1 meter from a source of 1 international candle or candela.

Lycanthropy. It is the delusion that one is or can change into a wolf.

Lymph. Refers to the alkaline fluid of the lymphatic vessels. Lymph differs from blood in that red corpuscles are absent and the protein content is lower. It is found in tissue spaces all over the body ; it is gathered into small vessels and carried centrally, eventually entering the blood stream at junctions with the large veins near the heart.

Lymphocyte. It is a white blood cell found in the lymph.

Lysergic Acid Diethylamide (LSD). It is one of a group of psychomimetic drugs which product psychological changes resembling a psychosis.

M

M. Abbreviation for the *mean.*

Machiavellianism. According to this belief people can be manipulated through flattery, threats, and deceit.

Mach Scale. It is a test used to measure the extent of Machiavellianism in an individual.

Macrocephalic. One having an abnormally large head.

Macromania. Refers to a pathological tendency to overevaluate the self.

Macropsia. Refers to an increase in the apparent size of visual objects because of pathology of the visual apparatus.

Magenta. A purplish red colour having a wavelength of about 515 nanometers. It is the complement of green.

Magnetotropism. Refers to an orienting response to a magnetic force.

Magnitude. Refers to the characteristic of objects, spatial extents, temporal durations, etc.

Maler's Law. It states that, "if the data do not fit the theory, the data must be disposed of."

Main Score. Refers to a score which is based on responses given during the test proper.

Maintenance Schedule. Means the provision of food and water in large enough quantity to keep an animal in good physical condition and to avoid undue weight loss.

Major Hemisphere. In most individuals it is the left hemisphere of the cerebrum, controlling speech and logical functions.

Make-a-Picture-Story Test. It is a projective technique and makes use of a miniature theater, backgrounds and characters. The subject is given a background and left to select figures and make up a story, that is then analyzed.

Mal. Prefix meaning *faulty, ill, imperfect.*

Malapropism. The wrong substitution of one word for another similar in sound.

Maleness. The condition of having such physiological and anatomical characteristics of a male which relate to his reproductive capacity.

Malergy. Refers to a condition of the organism which is characterized by maladaptive, inefficient, or subnormal functioning.

Malign. Tending to harm, damaging, malignant, or to speak about a person in an injurious manner that denigrates or causes harm.

Malignant. Characteristic of a condition that is growing worse; virulent, harmful, ultimately fatal.

Malleus. Refers to one of the three small bones of the middle ear.

Malpractice. Refers to incorrect or negligent treatment by a physician, psychologist or other health practitioner.

Mammal. Any member of the Mammalia class of vertebrates.

Mammary Gland. These are the gland that secretes milk in the female, the breast.

Mammillary Bodies. Refers to two small rounded projections in the medial area of the hypothalamus which have been implicated in emotional behavior and sexual motivation.

Mania. Refers to violent, uncontrollable behavior that is characterized excessive motor activity, by excitement, and impulsiveness.

Maniacal. Pertaining to mania.

Manifest Anxiety. Refers to overt, displayed anxiety. This over-anxiety is a symptom of a deeper, represented conflict.

Manifest Anxiety Scale. It is a questionnaire used to measure anxiety as a general drive.

Manifold. Refers to a collection of things having something in common, or a classification which includes two or more subdivisions.

Manipulanda. Refers to those characteristics of objects which support motor activity.

Manometer. It is a device used for measuring pressure in a liquid or gas. In physiological experiments it is used to measure blood pressure directly from an artery or vein.

Manoptoscope. It is a device used for testing eye dominance. The apparatus consists of a simple hollow cone through which the subject sights.

Mantle Layer. Refers to the embryonic layer of the neural plate which ultimately develops into the gray matter of the cerebral cortex.

Marasmus. Refers to the deterioration of tissue in the young caused by poor nutrition.

Marathon Group. It is a group-therapy technique wherein a group of individuals, generally with a fairly singular focus or purpose, meets for an extended period of time ranging anywhere from roughly 6 hours up to 48 hours.

Marbe's Law. Refers to the generalization that in word-association tasks the more frequently a response takes place the more rapidly it tends to take place latency is inversely related to frequency.

Marfan's Syndrome. Refers to a genetic condition consisting of large, bony fingers, hyperextensible joints and a gaunt, angular face.

Marijuana (or Marihuana. Refers to any part of the hemp plant.

Marker. In linguistics refers to a signal which indicates (*i.e. marks*) a function or a feature.

Masculinity ; Masculinism. It is a state or condition of any organism which has male characteristics.

Masculinity-Femininity Scale (MF Scale). A scale used to measure the degree of masculinity and femininity in a person. The scale is gender-free ; that is, one's sex does not limit one to scoring on either extreme.

Mass Contagion. Refers to the fast spread of behavior patterns among groups of people not essentially in direct contact.

Massed Practice. The learning of material without any periods of rest between blocks of practice.

Mass Media. Refers to any means of communication to the masses.

Masson Disk. A white disk whereon black squares or rectangles are placed in such a way that when it is rotated, a series of concentric rings of diminishing grayness is seen. The first ring from within, which becomes indistinguishable from the background, measures the difference threshold of brightness vision.

Mass Pyschology. Deals with the study of crowd behaviour or of the behaviour of loosely organized groups.

Masturbation. It is the induction of a state of erection of the genital organs and the achievement of orgasm by manual or mechanical stimulation.

Matched Sample. Refers to any sample found to be identical with another sample for all known variables under consideration.

* **Matching Law.** According to it organism will select each of several alternatives with a probability which matches the overall probability that each of the alternatives actually takes place

Matching Test. A test wherein the subject is asked to select the appropriate item from one list and match it with an item in a second list.

Mate. Means to copulate, or to enter into a durable relationship with a member of the opposite sex, typically by marriage.

Mathematical Psychology. Refers to any systematic effort to frame psychological ideas, hypotheses and theories in formal mathematical terms.

Maturation-Degeneration Hypothesis. According to this theory developmental is best described as a trajectory having functions reaching an optimal state sometime after birth and thereafter gradually declining.

MAVA Techniquea. The multiple abstract variance analysis method used for determining the relative contribution of heredity and environment to various personality traits.

Maxim. A type of *heuristic* or a general principle considered as somewhat less compelling than a *canon.*

Maxwell Disks. Slotted colored disks which can be mounted on a rapidly rotating spindle. By controlling the quantity of overlapping of disks of different hues the basic principles of color mixture can be shown.

Maze. Refers to any experimental apparatus made up of pathways and culs-de-sac (blind alleys) leading from a start box to an outlet or goal box. The most common form is the multiple T-maze (and its progeny, the Y-mazes).

MBD. Stands for *minimal brain dysfunction* or *damage.*

Means Object ; Means Situation. Refers to an object or situation which results in bringing the animal closer to the goal. It may be thought of as a sign, or cue, which arouses an expectancy.

Mean Square. The average of a set of squared deviations from the mean.

Meatus. Refers to a passageway or an opening.

Mechanical-Aptitude Test. A test used to evaluate the individual's ability to deal with mechanical devices and to understand mechanical relationships.

Medea Complex. Refers to a compulsion to kill one's own children.

Medial. Pertaining to or situated in the middle.

Median Gray. A gray halfway along the scale of brightness values from pure white to pure black.

Medial Syllable. Refers to a syllable in the middle of a word.

Mediate. Refers to a stimuli, responses, items or events which are in between other stimuli, responses, items or events.

Mediation Theory. Refers to any approach to the study of learning which assumes that some event(s) intervene between the stimulus and the response and that explanations of behavior need explication of these processes.

Medium. Refers to any intervening substance through that forces act or events are produced.

Mediator. In information theory refers to the system which intervenes between a receiver and a transmitter. The organism may be thought of as a mediator between stimuli and responses.

Medical Model. Refers to the conceptualization of behavior disorders and psychological abnormalities as diseases analogous to organic diseases.

Mediation. Any sustained effort at thinking generally of a contemplative variety.

Medulla. It is the central portion of an organ, such as the medulla of the adrenal gland or the medulla oblongata.

Medulla Oblongata. It is the lowest or hind-most part of the brain, continuous with the spinal cord and containing nuclei that control vital bodily functions like breathing, circulation, etc.

Medullary Sheath. It is a thin fatty layer which covers peripheral sensory and motor neurons. It is considered to have an insulating function.

Medullated. Means covered with a medullary or myelin sheath.

Megalomania. Refers to an exaggerated self-evaluation or sense of self-worth.

Megalopsia. An increase in the apparent size of visual objects due to retinal pathology or distortion of the lens.

Meiosis. Refers to the cell division found in the gametes or sperm and ova, where the number of chromosomes is reduced by one half.

Meissner's Corpuscles. These are the nerve endings found in the papillae of hairless skin. These are considered as one of the sets of receptors for the sensing of pressure and, are referred to as tactile receptors.

Melancholia. Means *black bile*. Now a days it refers to a pronounced depression with feelings of foreboding and a general insensitivitv to stimulation.

Melatonin. An *indoleamine* produced mainly by the pineal gland. Its secretion during childhood serves to inhibit the development of sexual maturation. It also plays a role in sleep.

Melancholy. Refers to a mood that is characterized by sadness, loss of interest in one's pursuits, and underreactivity to stimulation.

Melioristic. Pertaining to that which improves or makes better.

Membrane. Refers to any thin, flexible layer of tissue.

Memorial. Pertaining to memory or to that which is in memory.

Memorizing. It is the process of committing verbal material to memory by repetition.

Memory Drum. A common laboratory equipment which presents a series of stimuli to a subject for memory experiments.

Memory Trace. The supposed neurological event(s) which are responsible for any relatively permanent memory.

Menarche. Refers to the first menstrual period.

Meninges. Refers to all the three membranes (dura, pia and arachnoid) covering the spinal cord and the brain.

Menopause. Refers to that period which marks the permanent cessation of menstrual activity, the period during which menstruation gradually ceases.

Menses. It is the period of menstruation.

Menstruation. Refers to the cycle discharge of blood and sloughed-off uterine material which takes place in mature females.

Mental Development. Refers to the progressive changes in the mental process which go on from birth to death.

Mental Disease. Refers to any disabling psychological maladjustment or behavioral disorder.

Mental Element. Refers to a psychological process which cannot be resolved into anything simpler.

Mental Healing. Refers to the healing of mental disorders and physical diseases by suggestions or faith.

Mental Health. It is a state of good adjustment with a subjective state of well-being.

Mental Hygiene. Refers to the art of developing and maintaining mental health.

Mentalism. According to this doctrine an adequate characterization of human behavior is not possible without invoking mental phenomena as explanatory devices.

Mentality Refers to mental or intellectual activity or the quality of mind that is taken as characteristic of a specific individual or class of individuals.

Mental Measurement. Refers to quantitative methods of measurement or psychological processes, such as intelligence.

Mental Organization. Refers to the individual's pattern of mental processes taken as a whole.

Mental Process. Refers to an activity on the part of an organism which is of a psychological nature or involves the mind.

Mental Paper-folding Test. Refers to a test of spatial and configurational skills.

Mental Structure. Refers to a hypothetical construct used to account for behavior.

Mental Test. Refers to any *test* which is designed to evaluate a specified mental ability or performance.

Menticide. Means mind-murder ; brainwashing ; the systematic attempt to break down one's beliefs, attitudes, and allegiances, in favor of the ultimate adoption of those of another.

Meprobamate. It is a mild tranquilizing drug sold under the trade name Miltown.

Merit Rating. It is the appraisal of an individual's performance on a particular job.

Merkel Corpuscle. Refers to an encapsulated sense receptor that is located in the mouth and tongue and considered to be associated with touch and pressure.

Merkel's Law. It states that equal supraliminal (above-threshold) sense differences correspond to equal stimulus differences.

Mescaline. It is a hallucinogenic drug obtained from the peyote cactus. The effects are similar to those of LSD but of lesser intensity.

Mesencephalon. Refers to the midbrain, made up of the corpora quadrigemina, the cerebral peduncles, the tegmentum, and the nerve tracts known as the crura cerebri. The mesencephalon is the middle portion of the embryonic brain.

Mesial. Medial.

Mesmerism. An old name for *hypnotism*.

Mes(o). Combining form meaning, *middle, moderate* or *intermediate*.

Mesocephalic. Refers to a head having a median ratio of length to breadth.

Mesoderm. Refers to middle layer of embryonic cellular strcture which develops into the muscles and bones.

Mesomorphy. It is one of the three primary dimensions of body type. A mesomorph is one whose physique is dominated by the embryonic mesodermal component : muscles, skeleton, circulatory system. Thus, mesodermic persons are strong, well-muscled and have moderate skin-surface-to-weight ratios.

Mesopic Vision. Refers to the vision which occurs in the vaguely defined region between *scotopic* and *photopic.*

Mesokurtosis. Refers to the peakedness of a distribution curve characteristic of one found in the normal distribution curve.

Messenger RNA. The ribonucleic acid molecule which is assembled on the DNA molecules in the cell nucleus which migrates to the ribosomes of the cell cytoplasm and forms a pattern for transfer RNA.

Meta. A prefix meaning *about, beyond, among, after, between, behind* or *change in.*

Metabolism. Refers to the physico-chemical change in living organisms.

Metacontrast. A kind of backward masking wherein the original stimulus and masking stimulus are presented in adjacent retinal areas.

Metallic Color. Refers to color sensation evoked by the reflecting surfaces of certain metals and of paints containing particles of metal, like aluminium.

Metamers. Color stimuli which produces *metameric matches.*

Metamorphosis. Refers to a rapid and radical change of form, like one observed in the development of the frog from a tadpole.

Metaneeds. Refers to the higher human needs, including justice, beauty, order, honor and self-actualization.

Metaphysics. That branch of philosophy which seeks out first principles and must go beyond what can be learned by mechanical or physical analyses.

Metapsychics. Refers to the study of super-normal phenomena, spiritual manifestations, clairvoyance, telepahty, etc.

Metapsychoanalysis. Refers to an analysis or analytical approach which goes beyond traditional psychoanalysis.

Metapsychology. Refers to any branch of psychology that deals with phenomena which lie outside the province of empirical psychology, like telepathy, clairvoyance, and psychokinesis.

Methadone. A synthetic narcotic which blocks the effects of other narcotics. It is often used for the treatment of heroin addiction in *methadone maintenance* programs.

Methamphetamine. It is a powerful amphetamine which is addictive if taken intravenously.

Metonymy. It is a language disturbance in schizophrenia wherein approximate or related terms are used instead of direct terms.

Metric Methods. Refers to the psychophysical methods or any quantitative method.

Micro. Combining term meaning ***very small, minute.***

Micron. It is equal to a thousandth of a millimeter or a millionth of a meter.

Micropsia. Refers to a decrease in the apparent size of objects because of disease of the retina or a functional disorder.

Microtome. It is an instrument used for cutting thin sections of tissue for the preparation of microscopic slides.

Midbrain. The mesencephalon, made up of the corpora quadrigemina, cerebral peduncles, and the tegmentum.

Middle Ear. Refers to the air-filled space of the ear between the ear-drum and the cochlea containing the ***auditory ossicles.***

Midparent. Refers to any measure expressing the average for the two parents in respect to any characteristic, like height, weight, intelligence, etc.

Migraine. A syndrome that is characterized by extremely severe headaches, generally unilateral and accompanied by nausea, vomiting and visual disturbances.

Milieu. The environment, mostly external, if not qualified.

Military Psychology. It is the branch of applied psychology which investigates the selection and assignment of military personnel, training procedures, morale, the design of equipment, and other problems bearing on life in the armed forces which may have psychological aspects.

Miller Analogies Test (MAT). It is a test of the ability to formulate analogies. The MAT is used as a screening device for selecting students for graduate schools in the USA Examination.

Mimetic. Characterized by mimicry ; imitative.

Mimetic Response. Means responding by imitation ; copying the response of another organism.

Mimicry. Refers to process whereby one species takes on the phenotypic characteristics of another as a defensive ploy.

Mind-dust Theory. Refers to the assumption that mind is made of particles or atoms which exist everywhere in the universe and coalesce to form the individual mind.

Mind Reading. It is the alleged paranormal ability to know what is going on in the mind of another, a type of telepathy.

Mineralocorticoids. Refers to group of hormones of the adrenal cortices which effect metabolism of potassium and sodium.

Mind-twist Hypothesis. According to this theory mental disorders are functional in nature, or are the result of severe maladjustments.

Minnesota Clerical Aptitude Test. A test of aptitude for clerlcal work, involving number-and-name comparisons, spelling, computation, and speed of checking.

Minnesota Spatial Relations Test. A mechanical aptitude test which is based on spatial relations.

Minnesota Rate of Manipulation Test. It is a test of motor or manual aptitude made up of pegboards into which multi-colored cylindrical disks must be filled in a prescribed order.

Minor Hemisphere. In most individuals refers to the right cerebral hemisphere which controls spatial activities and musical functions.

Mirror Writing. Refers to a writing which, when held up to a mirror, looks in the proper orientation.

Misandry. Refers to hatred of males.

Misanthropy. Refers to hatred of males or human beings.

Misogyny. Refers to hatred of females.

Miss. Refers to an inaccurate judgement by a subject that there was no signal present on a trial when one was, in fact, presented.

Mixoscopia. Refers to sexual arousal obtained through watching others engaged in sexual acst.

Mneme. It is a memory trace.

Mnemonic System. It is a scheme for remembering specially verbal or numerical materials.

Mnemonics. It is the art of improving the memory with the aid of artificial systems.

Mnemonist. Refers to one who is expert in the use of various mnemonic devices and capable of feats of memory which seem to most of us to be evidence of extraordinary mental functions.

Mob. Refers to a crowd of individuals who act under strong emotional conditions mostly leading to violence or illegal acts.

Mobility. Refers to physical movement of a stimulus, an object or an organism, or a metaphysical movement through strata which are social, occupational or even cognitive.

Modal. Relating to the *mode*, to the most common score or occurrence.

Modality. Refers to a sensory system.

Mode Interval. It is the class interval which contains the mode.

Mode Pleasure. Refers to satisfaction derived from carrying out some activity.

Modification. Refers to any change in structure or function because of internal, external, or hereditary influences.

Modulator. Any of retinal ganglion cells which have relatively narrow ranges of responsiveness across the visible spectrum.

Modulus. Refers to a standard stimulus used as the basis of comparison in studies of scaling of sensory magnitudes.

Molar. Referring to the entire mass of material, to large units, or to relatively unanalyzable units.

Molarism. It is a preference for a molar approach to the study of behavior.

Molecular. Refers to that which is small or pertaining to that which can be analyzed into units or divisions which are small.

Monad. These are indestructible, uncreatable, immutable but quite active entities that constitute the fundamental units of all reality.

Monaural. Pertaining to one ear or to the use of only one ear.

Monism. The point of view according to which there is basically only one kind of reality.

Monitor. Means to scan or watch; the monitoring may be of a machine to detect malfunction, of persons to oversee their behavior or of oneself to evaluate personal, internal processes of a cognitive or affective kind.

Monogamy. It is a system of marriage in which each party has only a single mate. That is, a marriage of two (opposite sexed) persons.

Monogony. Refers to asexual reproduction.

Monoptic. Any one having one eye, *monocular*.

Monorchid. Refers to male having only one testicle.

Monorhinic. Pertaining to smelling with only one nostril.

Mood. Refers to a transitory emotion.

Mooney Problem Check List. It is a personality inventory made up of a list of items each describing some problem in a variety of areas, personal, social, family, school, work, health, etc.

Morale. Refers to the attitude or spirit characterized by the presence of confidence, strong motivation to continue, cheerfulness, and good organization

Morbid. Pertaining to a diseased or pathological condition or relating to attitudes which result in excessive interest in pathological conditions.

Morpheme. It is the minimal linguistic unit with meaning.

Morphine. It is a powerful narcotic obtained from the opium; poppy. It is the principal alkaloid of opium; its primary action is as a depressant producing euphoria, drowsiness and relief of pain.

Morphogenesis. Refers to the development of the organism's form and structure.

Mortality Rate. Refers to the death rate, given as number of deaths per unit of population (typically 100,000) in a specific time period (usually 1 year) and generally expressed as an age-specific rate.

Mortido. It is the death instinct.

Mosaic. Refers to a design made up of small parts. Mosaic tests may be used on individual intelligence scales or in projective techniques.

Mosaic Test. A projective test wherein the subject is given several hundred differently shaped and colored pieces and told to make anything they wish.

Moses Test. A nonparametric test which assesses the difference between two sets of scores by comparing the number of extreme scores from one sample with the number from the other.

Motivate. Means to incite to action or to serve as an incentive or goal.

Motivation. Refers to an intervening variable that is used to account for factors within the organism which arouse, maintain, and channel behavior toward a goal.

Motion, Epsilon. Refers to apparent motion produced when a white line on a black background is abruptly changed into a black line on a white background.

Motive. Refers to a state of arousal which impels an organism to action or a rationalization, justification or excuse which a person gives as the reason for his or her behavior.

Motone. Refers to a muscular-motor action pattern.

Motoneuron. It is a nerve cell or neuron which supplies a muscle or gland.

Motor Unit. Refers to the neuron and its connected muscular or glandular terminal.

Movement. Means *motion* or any change in the position of an organism or of one or more of its parts.

Movement Determinant. Refers to the quality of the inkblot which causes the subject to see either human or animal movement.

Movement Disturbances. Refers to a large array of abnormal patterns of bodily movement.

Mullerian Ducts. Refers to the structures in the embryo which develop into the female internal sex organs.

Mullerian System. In the embryo, the primitive sexual structures which will develop into female reproductive organs provided testes are not present.

Multimodal. Pertaining to a distribution which has more than one mode or peak.

Multipolar Cell (or Neuron). Refers to neuron having more than two neural processes rising from the soma. One of these is the axon and the others are "trunks" of dendritic "trees" which undergo multiple branchings.

Multitrait Measurement. Measurement in which no attempt has been made to single out the effect of any one trait but in which the combined effect of all traits is measured.

Multivariate. Pertaining to a measuring scale or technique which attempts to measure the effect of several variables or to demonstrate their effect in behavior.

Muscle Sensation. Refers to that aspect of kinesthesis which provides an awareness of muscle movement and muscle position.

Muscle Tonus. It is the slight degree of contraction muscles maintain when inactive. Tonus keeps muscles in good condition and makes it possible for them to respond more readily than would otherwise be possible.

Muscular Imbalance. Refers to inequality in the tension exerted by a muscle group, by which the organ of movement may be adversely affected. Muscular imbalance generally affects the eyes, a condition called *heterophoria.*

Musculature. Refers to the totality of the striped muscles.

Mutation. Refers to a sudden, inheritable genetic variation. Mutations are the chief reasons for the evolution of the species.

Mute. Refers to an individual suffering from mutism or pertaining to an inability to speak due to mutism.

Mutagen. Refers to any substance or grant that causes genetic mutations.

Myasthenia. It is a muscular weakness because of disease.

Mydriasis. It is abnormal dilation of the pupil of the eye.

Myelencephalon. Refers to that portion of the embryonic hindbrain which develops into the medulla oblongata.

Myograph. Refers to any instrument used for measuring muscular strength.

Myelination. Refers to the formation of the myelin sheath during embryonic development.

Myelitis. Refers to inflammation of the spinal cord.

Myelon. Means the spinal cord.

Myoclonus. Refers to muscular spasms that is characterized by alternating periods of rigidity and relaxation.

Myogram. Refers to any graphic representation of muscular activity.

Myogenic. Any thing having its origin in muscle tissue.

Myopia. Nearsightedness ; Vision is indistinct for far objects.

Myotonia. Refers to abnormal rigidity of the muscles.

Mysophilia. Refers to a pathological interest in filth or dirt.

Mysophobia. Refers to an obsessive fear of dirt or contamination. It is associated with a hand-washing compulsion.

Mysticism. According to this belief knowledge can be obtained by avenues other than the senses.

Myth. Means *tale* or *speech* ; a story that is of unknown or unverifiable origin but is part of the traditions of a culture or a group.

Mythology. Refers to the body of myths in a given culture.

Mythomania. Refers to a tendency to give exaggerated reports of imaginary adventures.

Myxedema. Refers to a condition of severe depression of nervous-system activity having symptoms of lethargy, low basal-metabolism rate and general weakness. It takes place in adults with thyroxin deficits.

N

N. On abbreviation for *number e.g.*, the number of scores in a distribution, a population, a sample, an experimental condition, the number of reinforcements, a number factor, etc.

Nail Biting. It is a nervous habit, generally observed in children, wherein the fingernails are chewed down to the quick.

Naive. Any one lacking sophistication or experience.

Nalorphine. Refers to narcotic antagonist which blocks the primary pharmacological effects of opium-based drugs.

Naloxone. It is a drug which inhibits the action of opiates and blocks the painrelieving effect of endorphins.

Nancy School. It is a school of hypnotism. It held that hypnosis was a normal phenomenon induced by suggestion.

Nanism. Means dwarfism.

Nano. Prefix meaning *one-billionth.*

Narcissism ; Narcism. Means self-love ; exaggerated concern with the self.

Narcissistic Neurosis. Refers to a neurosis wherein the libido regresses to a very early phase of development.

Narcissistic Object-Choice. Refers to the object which is chosen for narcissistic reasons. The choice is either the self or one very much like oneself.

Narcissistic Wound. Refers to rather clumsy phrase which means any blow to or attack upon one's self-esteem.

Narc(O). A prefix meaning *sleep, numbness* or *stupor.*

Narcolepsy. Refers to a pathological desire for sleep.

Narcomania. Refers to extreme desire for narcotic drugs.

Narcosis. Refers to a state of markedly reduced responsiveness, both in behavior and in normal physiological functioning, induced by narcotic drugs.

Narcosynthesis. The interpretation of the patient's verbal productions obtained under the influence of narcotic drugs.

Narcotherapy. Refers to any therapy which makes use of narcotic drugs.

Narcotic. In psychopharmacology refers to any drug which has both *sedative* and *analgesic* properties.

Narcotism. It is the state of being under the influence of narcotic drugs or drug addiction.

Nares. Refers to the nasal passages.

Nascent. Means incipient, beginning, just born.

Naso. Combining form meaning *nasal, pertaining to the nose.*

National Character. Refers to characteristic behavior patterns, attitudes,values, etc., that are found in a nation.

National Norm. Refers to a norm based on a representative sample drawn from an entire nation.

Native. Means innate, inherited.

Nativism. According to this point of view the role of heredity is important as opposed to environment, in the development of mental and behavioral processes.

Naturalism. According to this point of view mental processes, attitudes, and other psychological processes are part of the system of natural phenomena and so interpretable according to natural laws.

Naturalistic Observation. Refers to the collection of data by careful observation of events in their natural setting.

Natural Law. Refers to a statement, generally in mathematical form, of a consistently observed and predictable phenomenon of nature.

Natural Monism. According to this point of view all sciences are ultimately reducible to physics and chemistry. Thus, psychology would be reducible to physiology, physiology to physics and chemistry.

Natural Sciences. Those sciences which deal with physical and biological objects and processes. Psychology may be considered as a natural science or as a social science, depending upon the definer's point of view.

Natural Selection. It is evolutionary process of "survival of the fittest".

Nature. Refers to the innate or inherited characteristics of an individual or the phenomena of the universe taken as a totality.

Nature-Nurture Problem or Controversy. The problem of deciding the relative contribution of heredity and environment to the development of individual differences.

Nausea. Refers to a complex disturbance of the gastric, vasomotor, and sebaceous systems involving dizziness, sweating, a tendency toward vomiting, and feelings of weakness.

Near Effect. It is the degree of excitation of a neuron depending upon how close the neuronal system is to the point of application of the stimulus and how appropriate that stimulus is for the system in question.

Near Point. In visual accommodation it is the nearest point where an object can be seen clearly.

Near Vision. Means the visual discrimination of objects at about two feet of less from the eye.

Necker Cube. An ambiguous figure made up of a cube whose edges fluctuate in perspective.

Necro. Combining form meanina *dead*.

Necromania. Refers to morbid desire, mostly sexual, for a dead body.

Necrophilia Necrophilism. Means sexual attraction to corpses.

Necrophobia. Means a fear of corpses.

Necropsy. Refers to an examination after death to know its cause, an autopsy.

Necrosis. Refers to localized tissue death along with degeneration while still in contact with living tissue ; *e.g.*, as takes place at the site of a wound.

Need. Refers to any cellular substance which organisms must have so as to remain healthy.

Need-Drive-Incentive Model. A model of motivation which considers that basic, physiological needs are produced by states of deprivation, that such needs produce drives which are the true instigators of action and that the action is directed toward the incentive components of the goal state.

Need Gratification. Refers to the reduction of a need by consummatory behavior at a goal.

Need Reduction. Refers to any event or behavior which diminishes a need.

Need State. It is the hypothetical condition of the organism because of a need of period of deprivation.

Need Tension. Refers to the tension or emotional feeling which accompanies a need.

Need, Tissue. The primary physiological need(s) of tissue for substances essential for life like oxygen, food, water, etc.

Neencephalon. Refers to the new brain or cerebral cortex.

Negation. Means the disproof or denial of a statement or suggestion.

Negative. In mathematics, characteristic of a quantity less than zero or pertaining to denial, negation, disputatiousness, and attitudes or hostility.

Negative Induction. Refers to the intensification of inhibition in a system due to the influence of preceding excitation.

Negative Narcissism. Means underevaluation of the self.

Negative Phase. Refers to any period that is marked by withdrawal of the individual or negativism during development or during the course of a disease.

Negative Practice. Deliberately practicing an error so as to overcome it.

Negative Reward. Refers to a stimulus, situation, or verbal statement that leads to dissatisfaction, withdrawal or a decreased probability of response.

Negative Sensation. Refers to a stimulus whose intensity is below threshold.

Negative Suggestion. Refers to a suggestion designed to prevent or inhibit another's behavior.

Negative Transference. It is a state of hostility toward the psychoanalyst which commonly follows the stage of positive transference.

Negativism. It is an attitude of resistance to the suggestions or commands of another.

Neobehaviorism. A derivative of the older school of behaviorism, that retains the point of view that behavioral responses are the fundamental data of psychology but lacks the militant objections to certain molar concepts which are characteristic of the parent school and is more tolerant of verbal reports and the use of intervening variables.

Neo-Freudian. Refers to a psychoanalyst who follows Freud's major doctrines but has added theoretical formulations which depart significantly from Freud's original premises.

Neolalia. Refers to speech made up of many neologisms or words coined by the speaker.

Neologism. Refers to a new word or phrase or a new meaning attached to an existing word or phrase.

Neology. Means the coining of new words or terms or the use of existing word or terms in novel ways.

Neonate. Means a newborn infant.

Neopallium. Refers to all of the tissues of the cerebral cortex except the olfactory area.

Neophasta. The elaborate language developed by schizophrenics.

Neophilia. Means a desire for the new or novel.

Neophobia. Means fear of the new or novel.

Neoteny. Refers to the retention of immature characteristics in adulthood.

Nerve. A bundle of neurons. Nerves may be made up of sensory or motor components or be a mixture of both.

Nerve Block. Refers to temporary inhibition of neural transmission by either chemical or mechanical means.

Nerve Cell. Refers to the cell called neuron, the elementary unit of the nervous system.

Nerve Deafness. Deafness due to malfunctioning or damage to the auditory nerve.

Nerve Ending. It is the end process of a neuron in an effector.

Nerve Fiber. Refers to an elongated process of a *neuron* which carries neural impulses.

Nerve Pathway. It is the path or route through the nervous system of a specific neural impulse.

Nerve Plexus. Refers to a complex mass of neurons closely associated with each other in a functional network.

Nerve Root. Refers to a nerve that is connected directly with the brain or spinal cord.

Nerve Tissue. Refers to all the neurons, the cells which comprise the nervous system.

Nerve Trunk. Refers to the main stem of a peripheral nerve.

Nervism. According to this hypothesis all bodily functions are controlled by the nervous system.

Nervous. Pertaining to nerves or their functions or characterizing individuals in a state of heightened emotionality.

Nervous Breakdown. Refers to a severe emotional disorder.

Nervous Disease or Disorder. Refers to an organic disease of the nervous system or a functional disorder.

Nervous Energy. Refers to a high state of drive and activity.

Nervous Habit. Refers to an oft-repeated set of movements (*e.g.*, nailbiting, finger-tapping, facial and bodily mannerisms) which take place when one is under tension.

Nervousness. It is a state of restlessness with heightened emotionality and visible signs of muscular tremor, tenseness, and overactivity.

Nervous System. Refers to the full-system of structures and organs composed of neural tissue.

Neural. Pertaining to the structure or functioning of nerves or neurons.

Neural Arc. Refers to any network or path of afferent, interneural and efferent neurous which forms a functional unit from a receptor through the central nervous system interconnections to an effector.

Neural Bond. It is a hypothetical functional association between two neurons.

Neural Circuit. Refers to a neural arc or the functional passage of a nervous impulse from one center within the nervous system to another.

Neural Conduction. Refers to the transmission of neural excitation along a nerve fiber or between two neurons.

Neural Crest. Refers to a band of cells arranged longitudinally along the *neural tube* of a vertebrate embryo which gives rise to the cells which form the cranial spinal and autonomic ganglia.

Neural Discharge. Refers to the excitation and propagation of a localized disturbance in a neuron or nervous center.

Neural Fold. Refers to one of two longitudinal elevations of the embryonic *neural plate,* that in vertebrates, unite to form the *neural tube.*

Neuralgia. It is a nervous disorder which is characterized by bursts of sharp pain generally localized to the field of innervation of one nerve.

Neural Groove. It is the groove along the *neural plate* in the vertebrate embryo which ultimately forms the *neural tube.*

Neural Parallelism. According to this theory for every mental event there is a corresponding neural activity.

Neural Plate. Refers to the layer of ectodermal tissue which forms the beginning of the embryonic nervous system.

Neural Reinforcement. Refers to strengthening of one response by the simultaneous operation of another response.

Neural Tube. It is the tube produced by the fusing of the *neural folds* in the vertebrate embryo from which the central nervous system develops.

Neuraminic Acid. An acid of unknown structure which can be isolated from the brain. It is said to be deficient in schizophrenics.

Neurasthenia. It is a form of psychoneurosis that is characterized by excessive weakness, fatigue, complaints of visceral malfunction, and anxiety.

Neuraxis. The spinal cord and brain represented as a line of reference along the vertical axis of the body.

Neurilemma. Refers to the thin membraneous covering of the *myelin sheath* of the axons of peripheral neurons. Neurilemma consists of *Schwann cells.*

Neurin. It is a protein found coating the membrane of presynaptic vesicles.

Neuritis. Means inflammation of a nerve.

Neuroanatomy. It is the study of the structures and functions of the nervous system.

Neurobiotaxis. It is the phenomenon in which the dendrites of neurons are stimulated to grow toward the axon endings of active neurons.

Neuroblast. Refers to an embryonic neuron.

Neuroeffector Junction. Refers to a junction between an efferent neurons and an effector like a smooth muscle or a gland.

Neurofibrillae. Refers to the fine filaments which form the axis cylinder of the neuron.

Neurogenesis. Means growth and development of nerve tissue or growth and development of structures originating *from* nerve tissue.

Neuroglia. These are the supporting tissues of the cerebrospinal axis.

Neurogram. It is synonym of *engram.*

Neurohumors. Refers to chemical agents, like acetylcholine or norepinephrine, which serve as mediators of nervous activity.

Neurology. It is the science of the structure and functioning of the nervous system.

Neuromuscular. Pertaining to any process which is a joint function of the muscles and nerves.

Neuron. It is a nerve cell which is the basic structural and functional unit of the nervous system.

Neuronal. Pertaining to a *neuron.*

Neuropathic. Refers to either organic or functional nervous disabilities. It is generally restricted to the organic.

Neuropathology. It is the branch of medicine that deals with diseases of the nervous system.

Neurophypophis. Refers to the posterior pituitary gland.

Neuropsychiatry. It is a branch of medicine which deals with the relationship between neural processes and psychiatric disorders.

Neuropile or Neuropil. Refers to a network of nonmyelinated fibrils found at the synapse of a neuron.

Neuroplexus. Refers to a network of peripheral nerve fibers. These common in the autonomic nervous system.

Neuropsychiatry. It is a medical specialty which deals with neurological and psychiatric disorders.

Neurosis. Refers to a benign mental disorder that is characterized by (*a*) incomplete insight into the nature of the difficulty ; (*b*) conflicts ; (*c*) anxiety reactions ; (*d*) partial impairment of personality.

Neurosyphilis. Refers to syphilis of the nervous system.

Neurotic. Pertaining to an individual suffering from a neurosis or characterizing behavior or traits symptomatic of a neurosis.

Neurotic Fiction. Refers to a guiding fiction far removed from the possibility of real accomplishment thus unachievable and to keep the individual pursuing unrealistic selfish goals.

Neurotic Inventory. Refers to a questionnaire used to reveal tendencies toward neuroticism.

Neuronal Periodicity. Refers to the tendency for neurons to fluctuate in their susceptibility to stimulation.

Neurotic Process. Refers to the central inner conflict in the neurotic between the idealized self and the real self.

Neurovegetative System. Refers to the autonomic nervous system, specially the parasympathetic division.

Neutral. indifferent ; characterizing values which are not categorized as reflecting properties of specific classes.

Neutral Color. Refers to any achromatic color, one along the black-white continuum.

Neutral Gray. A gray which lies at the midpoint of the continuum of brightness, one which is intermediate between black and white.

Neutralization. In psychoanalysis it is the process whereby the sexual and aggressive impulses of infancy are softened.

Neutral Stimulus. Refers to a stimulus which produces an indifferent response ; a stimulus which does not ordinarily elicit the response is made to elicit after conditioning, when it has become a conditioned stimulus.

Nevus. Refers to congenital discoloration of an area of the skin.

Newborn. Refers to an infant less than one month of age.

Nialamide. It is an *antidepressant drug* belonging to the monoamine oxidase inhibitor class.

Nicotinic. Refers to characterizing receptors which mediate the excitatory effects of acetylcholine.

Night Vision. Refers to vision under greatly reduced conditions of illumination.

Nigro-Striatal Bundle. Refers to an axon bundle that originate in the substantia nigra of the pons and terminate in the caudate nucleus and putamen.

Nihilistic Delusion. Refers to the delusion that is characteristic of some psychotics that the existing order of things has disappeared.

Nissl Bodies. Refers to granular bodies found in the cell body of the neuron and in the dendrites.

Nirvana. It is the Buddhist notion of liberation from the cycle of death and rebirth.

Nit. It is a measure of luminance of a surface and is equal to *lux* times 1 *k*. Nit (symbol : nt) is a relatively new term in photometry. It has replaced the *meter-candle* or *foot-candle.* Multiplying it by 0.292 gives *foot-lamberts.*

Nitrazepam. It is a *minor tranquilizer* that is used mainly as a sleeping drug.

NM. Abbreviation for *nanometer.*

Noctambulation. Means sleepwalking ; somnambulism.

Nociceptive. Pertaining to *pain.*

Noctambulation. Means walking at night ; sleepwalking.

Nocturnal. Pertaining to night.

Nocturnal Emission. Refers to loss of semen in the male during sleep.

Nodal Points. These are two points in an optical system which are located along the axis of a lens in such a way that a ray of light sent through one will produce a parallel emergent ray through the other.

Node. It is a point in a wave, like a sound wave, which has zero amplitude.

Noesis. Means the intellective function, or cognition ; particularly cognition or knowledge that is self-evident.

Noise. The auditory experience which arises upon stimulation with aperiodic sound waves or any undesirable or undesired sound.

Nomadism. Refers to a tendency to wander or change occupation or residence frequently.

Nominal. Pertaining to names or naming ; classifying, designating.

Nominal Aphasia. Refers to the inability to utter or recognize the name of an object or person.

Nominalism. It is the tendency to believe that by naming things they are made real.

Nominating Technique. Refers to a sociometric technique used for the exploration of the structure of a group wherein each member nominates the person who best satisfies some criterion.

Nomogram ; Nomograph. It is a chart made up of three parallel line representing values of related variables in such a way that a straight lines drawn through the first two will intercept the related third value.

Nomological. Pertaining to general laws of nature.

Nomothetic. Pertaining to the formulation of general laws and principles.

Non. A prefix meaning *not, without*.

Nonadditive. Pertaining to objects or variables which cannot be combined due to heterogeneity. Thus, IQ's and income cannot be added.

Nonadjustive. Pertaining to behavior which fails to bring the individual into harmony with his social or physical environment

Non Compos Mentis. Used to characterize an individual legally not responsible for his conduct.

Nonconscious. Means without consciousness, specially in reference to inanimate objects.

Nondirective. Pertaining to counseling or therapeutic procedures wherein a minimum of direction is given by the counselor or therapuetician.

Noneducable. Refers to persons who cannot be educated in the conventional sense.

Nonlanguage Test. It is a test which makes use of concrete, non-verbal materials, like a series of mazes of increasing difficulty.

Nonlinear. Means not falling along a straight line.

Nonliterate. Refers to cultures or societies having no written language.

Nonmetric. Refers to that which is not measured in a quantitative manner.

Nonparametric Statistics. It is the branch of statistics that deals with distributions which are not normal.

Nonrational. Refers to considerations where rational arguments do not apply.

Nonsense Syllable. Refers to a pronounceable combination of letters which do not make meaningful words, *e.g.*, *lor*, *zuk*, *rul*.

Non Sequitur. Refers to a ranacy in logic ; an invalid conclusion drawn from established premises.

Nonsocial. Refers to one who is indifferent to or actively avoids social groups.

Nonverbal. Refers to those characteristics of a task, a process or a situation which exclude the specifically linguistic.

Noradrenaline ; Norepinephrine. It is a hormone that is believed to be the chemical transmitter in some sympathetic synapses. Its action is similar to that of adrenaline or epinephrine.

Noradrenergic. Refers to neurons and neural fibers and pathways that when stimulated, release *norepinephrine*.

Norm. Refers to a representative standard or valve for a given group. A norm may be a single value or a range of values expressing the typical performance of a group against which any individual can be compared.

Normal. Anything which does not deviate markedly from the average, or the norm. Some psychologists prefer the statistical definition. That is, the individual who does not differ widely from the norm or average is considered normal.

Normality. It is the state or condition of being adjudged *normal*.

Normalize. Means to adjust or alter a set of measures in such a way that they will conform to the normal frequency curve.

Normative. Relating to norms or standards.

Normative Science. Any of those sciences, like ethics, mental hygiene, logic, etc., which attempt to discover correct patterns of behavior.

Norm Line. It is a curve representing the mean (or median) scores of successive age groups. Such norm lines are generally furnished with group tests for use in school systems.

Nose. It is the structure containing the organs for olfaction. The receptors are high up inside the nose, in the olfactory epithelium.

Nos(o)e. Combining form meaning *disease*.

Nosology. It is the branch of medicine that deals with the classification of diseases.

Nosophobia. Refers to a fear of disease, particularly of a specific disease.

Notation. A system of representation making use of symbols.

Nous. Refers to the intellect or highest faculty.

Noxious. Means painful, injurious.

NREM Sleep. Refers to those stages of sleep which are not characterized by rapid eye movements (REM). Also known as *non-REM sleep*.

Nuclear Complex (or Conflict. Within a number of psychoanalytic or psychodynamic theories refers to a fundamental conflict taking place during infancy or early childhood which is considered to be a root cause of a number of psychoneurotic disorders which may only emerge later in life.

Nucleus. It is the central, dark-staining portion of a cell generally containing a nucleus, or small, darkened mass, or the central portion, or mass, around which material is gathered, or a mass of cell bodies within the brain.

Nucleus Gracilis. Refers to a nucleus in the medulla where fibers of *fasciculus gracillis* and *fasciculus cuneatus* terminate.

Nucleolus. It is a small, spherical body present within the nucleus of a cell.

Nucleic Acids. It is a group of complex acids found in the cells of all living things. They are involved in the self-duplication mechanisms which are fundamental to life and form the core of the processes whereby hereditary characteristics are transmitted.

Nucleo Combining form meaning *pertaining to a nucleus.*

Null Hypothesis. A statistical statement about a set of data to be obtained and formulated in such a way that the facts to be elicited by the experiment may disprove the statement.

Null Result. Refers to any experimental outcome which was not significant. Mostly null results tend not to be reported in the scientific literature—that is occasionally unfortunate because the knowledge that such and such an effect does not obtain is often of considerable importance.

Number Factor. In factor-analysis studies of intelligence, an ability revealed by competence at manipulating numbers and carrying out simple numerical operations. *Symbol* N.

Numerical Value. Refers to any value expressed as an absolute number irrespective of its sign.

Nurturance. Refers to the provision of food, shelter, and care for the young.

Nurture. Refers to the collective impact of all environmental factors which affect growth and behavior.

Nurturance Need. Refers to the need to protect, aid, and nourish a helpless organism.

Nutrient. Refers to any substance which can be taken into the body and converted into food for the tissues.

Nyctalopia. Refers to abnormally poor vision under low illumination conditions.

Nyctophobia. It is the patnological fear of the dark.

Nymphomania. Refers to a pathotogically exaggerated state of sexual desire in women.

Nystagmus. Refers to a rapid sideways snap of the eye followed by a slow return to normal fixation or rapid oscillatory movements. Nystagmus may take place in pursuit movements of the eye, as in following a moving target, in blindness, or after-rotation of the body.

O

Object. It is a part of the environment—a material thing, a person, or an abstraction.

Object-assembly Test. It is a test wherein the subject is asked to put together disassembled objects.

Object Attitude. It is used in structuralistic psychology for the attitude wherein the observer attends to the stimulus or object instead of attending to experience.

Object Blindness. A disorder wherein one is unable to recognize visually presented objects due to brain injury.

Object Cathexis. Refers to the investment of the libido in a non-sexual object.

Object Choice. Refers to the selection of an object or person as the object of love.

Object Finding. Refers to the process of directing the libido away from the body from the objects or persons in the environment.

Objectifying Attitude. Refers to the attitude of reacting to the properties of an object while disregarding one's personal feelings toward it.

Objectivation. Means attributing one's own feelings to another who, in fact, has such feelings.

Objective Anxiety. Refers to any anxiety for which there is an external and identifiable cause.

Objective Examination. It consists of tests of true-false or multiple-choice type in whose scoring standards no latitude of choice among examiners in permissible.

Objective Psychology. That psychology which would restrict psychological observation to behavioral processes open to public inspection to the exclusion introspective or subjective data.

Objective Scoring. Scoring method based on a formula, key, or rule such that the same score is obtained at by a number of different scorers.

Objective Set. Perception whose frame of reference is directed toward the external world.

Objective Type. Refers to a class of individuals who are characterized by a tendency to view events and objects as things in themselves and not in relation to the viewer.

Object Libido. Refers to the libido as attached to persons or objects except the self. *Contr.*

Object Loss. Refers to the loss of love from an individual who had at one time bestowed it.

Object of Instinct. It may be a person, object, or situation that elicits instinctive action.

Object Permanence. Refers to the child's ability to recognize an object which continue to exist even when object is hidden from view.

Oblique. Something characterizing the relationship between factors which are not at right angles to each other and are therefore correlated.

Oblique Rotation. Means the rotation of the axes in a factor analysis in such a way that the axes meet at acute angles.

Oblique Solution. Refers to a set of factors not at right angles and therefore correlated.

Obliviscence. Means forgetfulness.

Obsession. Refers to a persistent and generally irrational idea which may be accompanied by a compulsion to carry out an act.

Obsessional Neurosis. A neurosis that is characterized primarily by the presence of obsessive ideas and compulsive actions.

Obstacle Sense. It is the ability of the blind to avoid objects in their path. It primarily dependents upon echolocation, or hearing sounds bounced off from such objects.

Obstruction Method. A technique used for measuring the relative strength of animal drives by pitting one against another. The thirst, sex, and maternal drives can also be studied using this technique.

Occam's Razor. It is a scientific principle for interpretation according to it the simplest possible explanation for a phenomenon is to be preferred to complex explanations.

Occipital. Referring to the back part of the brain, the occipital lobe.

Occipital Lobe. Refers to the rear portion of the cerebrum which contains centers for vision.

Occlusion. Refers to the stopping of a passage-way or the manifestation of less than the expected number of motor units responses, because overlapping neuronal fields.

Occupational Test. It is a test designed to measure achievement or aptitude for a given occupation.

Occupational Therapy. It is the treatment of mental disorders by giving the individual useful work to do.

Ocular. Referring to the eye.

Ocular Dominance. Refers to preferential use of one eye in reading, sighting, etc.

Oculogyral Illusion or Movement. Refers to the illusory movement of a faint light in a dark room following rotation of the body.

Oculomotor. Referring to eye movements.

Odd-even Technique. It is a technique used for estimating of the reliability of a test by finding the correlation between the odd- and even-numbered items.

Odorivector. Refers to any substance which emits such particles which, in contact with olfactory receptors, stimulate olfactory sensations.

Off-Fibers. Fibers in the optic nerve which respond to the cessation of stimulation.

Ogive. A mathematical function which takes an S shape.

Olfactie. It is a unit of smell intensity and is equal to the threshold strength of a stimulus when measured by the Zwaardemaker olfactometer.

Olfaction. It is the sense of smell whose receptors are in the upper part of the nose and are made up of hair cells in a specialized tissue known as the olfactory epithelium. The stimulus for smell is generally a substance in gaseous state.

Olfactometer. A device used for regulating the amount and intensity of olfactory stimuli in threshold experiments.

Olfactory. Referring to olfaction, or the sense of smell.

Olfactory Lobe. It is the region of the brain under the frontal lobe and includes the olfactory bulbs and their associated structures.

Oligergasia. Means intellectual deficiency ; feeblemindedness.

Oliogophrenic Detail. Refers to an extremely low-level response which indicates mental deficiency.

Olivary Nucleus. Refers to a mass of nerve cells shaped like an olive, a complex structure in the medulla.

Omnibus Test. It is a test wherein the different types of tasks are randomly distributed instead of being grouped in accordance with the nature of the task involved.

Omnipotence of the id. The infantile conviction that wishes must and will be fulfilled.

Onanism. Refers to coitus interruptus withdrawal on the part of the male prior to ejaculation.

Oneiric. Referring to dreamlike states.

Onomatopoeic. Referring to the formation of such words which sound like their referents.

Ontogenesis, Ontogency. The origin of individual organisms.

Ontology. It is a branch of philosophy that deals with the nature of being.

Open-cue Situation. Refers to those learning, tasks wherein all cues or means essential to achieve the goal are presented to the animal.

Open-ended Question. Any question in questionnaires or public-opinion polls, which a subject is allowed to answer in his own way.

Operating Characteristic. In tests of significance it refers to the probability of accepting the null hypothesis in a specific situation.

Operation. It is one of three basic dimensions of intelligence, the other two are content and products.

Operator. In statistical equations refers to the symbol which indicates an operation to be performed on a number or other symbol.

Ophidiphobia. Refers to fear of snakes.

Opthalmia. It is an inflammation of the conjunctiva or other outer tissues of the eye.

Opthalmic. Referring to the eye.

Opthalmotrope. It is a model used for demonstrating the movement of the eyes through the action of the six extrinsic eye muscles.

Opthalmology. It is the branch of medicine specializing in diseases of the eye and their correction.

Opiate. Any drug of the opium class or any agent that tends to quiet or soothe.

Opinionaire. A questionnaire that is designed to measure opinions.

Opposites Test. A test wherein the subject's task is to give the opposite of the stimulus word.

Opsin. It is a metabolic breakdown product of rhodopsin in rod vision.

Optacon. It is a device used for converting light intensities into vibratory patterns on the fingertips thus enabling the blind to read.

Optic Chiasm. It is the point where the optic fibers from the eye join and diverge again at the base of the brain.

Optic Disk. It is the area in the retina in which the neurons are gathered just before leaving the eyeball.

Optogram. The image of an object on the retina of the eye.

Oral Dependence. Refers to the desire to return to the early [oral stage of development.

Oral Eroticism. Means the derivation of pleasure from oral activities—sucking, biting, talking, chewing, smoking etc.

Oral Incorporation. Refers to the tendency on the part of the young child to put things into the mouth.

Orality. Refers to the oral component in eroticism or neuroticism.

Oral Neurosis. Refers to stuttering, stammering, and speech defects as manifestations of psychic disorders associated with oral eroticism.

Oral Sadism. It is the desire to hurt or destroy by biting or chewing.

Oral Stage. Refers to the stage of infantile development when the infant obtains satisfaction from nursing, biting, and chewing.

Orbital. Referring to the bony cavity surrounding the eye.

Orestes Complex. Refers to the desire on the part of the son to kill his mother.

Orexis. Refers to the affective and conative aspects of behavior in contrast to its cognitive aspect.

Organ Eroticism. Refers to the sexual attachment for a specified organ, or sexual arousal associated with a specified organ.

Organicism. The philosophical point of view according to which life is the end product of organization.

Organic Psychosis. Refers to a psychosis that is caused by pathological changes in the brain, like general paresis and alcoholic psychosis.

Organic Sensations. Refers to those sensations which arise from within the body.

Organismic Psychology. A branch of psychology that places emphasis on the study of the biological organism.

Organization. Refers to a structure or grouping composed of units which function in an interrelated manner in order to form a unified whole.

Organ Libido. Refers to eroticism that is associated with a specific bodily organ.

Organ Pleasure. It is the pleasure associated with a particular organ.

Orgastic Impotence. Refers to the inability to achieve orgasm during the sex act.

Orgone Theory. This theory formulated by Wilhelm Reich considers that all space is filled with a specific form of energy known as orgone energy, that accounts for life and living functions.

Orthogenic. Characterizing development from a nondifferentiated or global state to a differentiated and hierarchically integrated state.

Orthogenesis. It is the doctrine according to which evolution has a certain direction and that in successive generations an organism will follow a certain line irrespective of natural selection.

Orthogenital. Referring to sexual patterns which are normal and, hence, closely, related to sexual intercourse with members of the opposite sex.

Orthopsychiatry. It is a branch of psychiatry that places emphasis on the early treatment and prevention of mental disorders.

Osmometric Thirst. Refers to the thirst produced by cellular dehydration because of increased osmotic pressure from the intracellular fluids.

Osmoreceptor. It is a complex of cells in the hypothalamus which respond to changes in osmotic pressure in the blood.

Osphresis. Refers to the sense of smell olfaction.

Osseous. Referring to bones, bonelike.

Ossification Ratio. It is an anatomical index made up of the ratio of the ossified area of the wrist bones as shown by X-ray plates to a certain selected area of the wrist.

Ossify. Means to harden and to become bonelike.

Ostwald Colors. Refers to a series of chromatic and achromatic sample colors which are based on a mixture of pigments, with black and white added for tints and shades.

Otoliths. Refers to small calcium deposits in the endolymph of the inner ear which, when the head moves, activate neuronal endings to aid in maintaining equilibrium.

Otology. It is the science of the ear—its anatomy, physiology, functions, and disorders.

Outbreeding. Means mating outside a designated social group.

Oval Window. Refers to an oval opening in the wall of the bony laborinth that is covered by a membrane against which the stirrup vibrates, communicating vibrations to the inner ear.

Ovary. It is a glandular organ in the female which produces the egg, or ovum, and the estrogens, or female sex hormones. The ovaries are paired bodies located in the abdominal cavity and are connected to the uterus by means of the Fallopian tubes.

Overlapping Factor. Refers to any factor which is common to two or more tests.

Overt. Means open to public observation ; not concealed.

Overtone. Refers to a partial tone created by partial vibrations of the sounding body.

Ovum (plural ova). It is the female sex cell.

Oxytocin. It is a hormone produced by the hypothalamus which is stored and released by the pituitary gland. It causes contractions of the uterus and the release of milk from the mammary glands.

P

Pacemaker. Refers to region in the heart which functions as an integral part of the system and is rhythmically active and controls the rate of cardiac contraction.

Pacing. Means controlling the speed (*i.e.*, "pace") of an act or structuring a learning program or educational curriculum in such that materials are introduced gradually over time in order to correspond with the developmental level of the learner.

Pain Principle. In Freud's early psychoanalytic formulatiops this notion is only hinted at ; later it was made explicit in the form of Thanatos, the death instinct, that was conceived of as operating along with Eros, the life instinct.

Pair-bond. In ethology refers to a lasting male-female union.

Palatability. Anything that is agreeable to the palate, and pleasant-testing.

Palate. Refers to the roof of the mouth ; it is furthur divided into the anterior hard palate and the posterior soft palate.

Paleopsychology. A branch of psychology wherein processes suspected of having been carried over from earlier evolutionary eras are studied.

Palilalia. A condition wherein the patient continuously repeats words and phrases.

Palin. Combining form that means *backward* or *repetitive.*

Palindrome. Any word, phrase or sentence which reads the same forward and backward.

Palliative. Anything that eases pain.

Pallidum. It is one of the large subcortical nuclei which make up the *basal ganglia.* Also known as *globus pollidus* and *paleostria tum.*

Palpitation(s). Refers to rapid heartbeat. It generally accompanies anxiety attacks and can be quite frightening.

Palsy. Refers to paralysis. Generally used in combined form to specify the nature, location or type of disability.

Panpsychism. A philosophical position which holds that the ultimate, meaningful (or perhaps *only*) reality is psychic or mental ; that all that exists is "mindlike."

Pansexualism. A sobriquet thrust mostly upon the classical Freudian point of view by its critics, who argue that the strong emphasis on sexual determinants that view embodies is unwarranted.

Pantheism. According to this doctrine God and the cosmic totality are coterminous.

Paradoxical Cold. Refers to sensation of coldness when an actually rather warm object of about 113°F (45°C) or above stimulates a *cold spot* on the skin.

Paradoxical Warmth. It is sensation of warmth experienced them an object of roughly 84° to 48°F. (29°-31°C.), stimulates the skin.

Parafovea. It is the area of the retina that immediately surrounding the fovea.

Paraldehyde. A quick-acting, nonbarbiturate sedative having anticonvulsive effects. It is administered by injection as it is foul-testing and leaves a distinctly unpleasant odor on the patient's breath and irritates the stomach.

Paranoia. In the standard psychiatric nosology refers to a functional disorder wherein the symptoms of delusions of jealousy, and delusions of either grandeur and persecution, cannot be explained, by other disorders like schizophrenia, organic mental disorder or organic brain syndrome.

Paranoiac (and Parauoid). Refer to a person suffering from a diagnosed paranoia and *paranoid.*

Paranoid Anxiety. Refers to anxiety produced by fear of attack from hostile others. Also known as *persecutory anxiety.*

Paraphasia. Refers to any habitual inappropriate use of words in speech.

Paraphobia. It is a mild form of a phobia.

Paraphonia. Refers to a weakness or other abnormal change in voice quality.

Parasexuality. Means perverted sexuality.

Parasomnia. Refers to sleep disorders including sleepwalking (*somnambulism*), night terrors (*pavor nocturnus*) and bed-wetting (*enuresis*).

Paraxial. Means on either side of the axis of the body or of an organ.

Parkinsonism, Drug-induced. A parkinsonian syndrome with many of the classic symptoms of *Parkinson's disease*, produced as a side-effect of many of the antipsychotic drugs.

Parkinson's Disease. A paralytic syndrome. The primary symptoms are a rapid, coarse tremor, masklike facial expression, loss of sensory-motor coordination, loss of the ability to initiate action and a general tendency toward exhaustion.

Parous. Refers to females who have borne at least one viable offspring.

Partial Aim. Refers to any means for deriving sexual gratification prior to the development of the genital stage.

Particularism. It is an approach to social theory wherein standards of conduct are developed with a recognition of the role of individual circumstances and possible mitigating contexts.

Parturiphobia. Refers to fear of childbirth.

Pastoral Counseling. Psychological counseling given by members of the clergy who have been trained to work with members of their congregation who seek help with emotional problems.

Patella. The kneecap.

Pathic. Refening to disease, diseaselike.

Peak-clipping. Refers to the elimination or "elipping" off of the high-amplitude portions of a speech wave. Peakclipping produces strange sounding speech but surprisingly little reduction in its intelligibility, specially when compared with *center-clipping.*

Peak Experience. Refers to a profound moment in a person's life, when they feel in harmony with all things, clear spontaneous, independent and alert and generally with relatively little awareness of time and space.

Pearson Chi-square (χ^2) Tests. Refers to several statistical tests based on variations of the basic *chi-square* statistic. They are used as tests of *goodness-of-fit* between a large sample and a population and as tests of association between two samples.

Peccatophobia. Refers to an irrational fear of committing a sin.

Pecking Order. Refers to the order of dominance and its attendant privileges and priorities in terms of which chicken pecks which chicken.

PEC Scale. A scale used to measure tendencies toward politico-economic-conservatism, that is considered by many as a component of *authoritarianism.*

Pedagogy. Refers to the science and art of teaching.

Pederasty. Refers to anal intercourse with a young boy.

Pediatrics. It is that medical specialization the concerned with the diseases of childhood.

Pedigree. Refers to schematic representation of the structure of a family showing marriages, offspring, etc.

Peduncle. Refers to any of several stalk-like bundles of nerve fibers in the brain.

Pegboard Test. Refers to one of tests of manual dexterity wherein pegs must be placed in holes as quickly as possible.

Penile. Referring to the penis.

Penis. The copulatory (and, in mammals, urinary) organ.

Penis Captivus. A set of circumstances wherein the penis is held within the vagina and cannot be withdrawn. It does exist as a momentary normal component in the copulatory behavior of some species but it is clinically unknown in humans.

Penis Envy. Refers to the hypothesized envy of the penis.

Pentatonic. Refers to a musical scale that is based on five tones.

Pepsin. An enzyme that is secreted by the stomach which breaks peptide bonds and therefore initiates the process of breaking the proteins in food into their constituent amino acids.

Peptic. Referring to the stomach and to digestion.

Perimeter. Refers to a device used for mapping the sensitivity of the retinal field.

Personal Equation. Refers to a procedure for correcting for differences in reaction time between two observes of stellar transit.

Personal Fitness. In evolutionary biology refers to an individual organism's reproductive success.

Personalism. It is an approach to psychological science which maintains that the individual personality is the central construct against which all else must be considered.

Personalistic Psychology. The orientation which argues that psychological principles only have meaning when they are mapped into or shown to be reflections of personal life and personal experience.

Personality Dynamics. Refers to the study of the complex, interactive, dynamic aspects of motivation, emotion and behavior.

Personality Problem. Refers to any minor, persistent or recurring behavioral, motivational or emotional pattern which makes a person unhappy.

Personality Syndrome. Refers to a set of maladaptive behavioral characteristics which have been shown to be common to many persons.

Personality Test. Refers to a device or instrument that is used for assessing or evaluating personality.

Personality Trait. Refers to *trait* of personality, or characteristic of a person that, can be used as an explanation of the regularities and consistencies of behavior.

Personality Type. Refers to any label that is used for classifying an individual's personality. There are many different typologies, each with its own categorization system.

Personalized Instruction. Refers to any educational program with sufficient flexibility to be adapted to individual students of differing capabilities.

Personnel Psychology. It refers to that aspect of industrial/organizational psychology which in concerned with (*a*) the selecting, supervising and evaluating of personnel, and (*b*) a variety of job-related factors lik morale, personal satisfaction, management-worker relations, counseling etc.

Persuasion. It is a process of inducing a person to adopt a particular set of values, beliefs or attitudes.

Perversion. Refers to any turning away from the right course, any distortion from the proper path to the proper end.

PGR. Abbreviation for *psychogalvanic response*.

Phacoscope. An instrument used for observing the changes in the images reflected from the lens of the eye during accommodation.

Phallic Primacy. Refers to the focusing of erotic interest upon the penis or the clitories during the early *genital stage*.

Phallic Woman. Refers to a female with phallic traits. The idea of a phallic woman is also commonly found in folklore and myth and, according to some interpretations, is manifested in the conception of women in masochistic, submissive men.

Phallus. While *penis* is used as an anatomical term, the connotations of *phallus* are primarily symbolic. The reference then is the image or representation of the penis as a symbol of power.

Phantom Limb. Refers to subjective experience of sensations arising from a limb which has been amputated.

Pharmacology. It is the science of the study of drugs:

Pharmacopeia. It is an authoritative treatise on drugs, their preparation, chemical make-up, properties and recommended dosages and manner of administration.

Pharynx. If the part of the oral cavity, including the surrounding muscles and membranes, connecting the mouth and nose with the larynx and esophagus.

Pheromone. A chemical substance that is used for communication between members of a species.

Phobia. Means *fear* or *dread*.

Phobic Character. Refers to an individual who tends to deal with difficult or anxiety-provoking situations by avoiding them, generally by restricting his or her activities in life and seeking a protective environment.

Phone. Refers to discrete speech sound whose characteristics can be specified independently of that sound's role in any specific language.

Phonography. Refers to a writing system that is based on the sounds of the spoken language.

Phonoscope. It is a device that converts sound energy into a visible form.

Phorometry. Measurement of the balance of the muscles which turn the eyeballs.

Phot. It is unit of illuminance.

Photic. Referring to light.

Phylaxis. Refers to the body's active defense against infection.

Phylum. A primary division in the classification of animals and plants.

Physiodynamic Therapy. Refers to a number of psychotherapeutic procedures such as *electroconvulsive therapy, insulin-shock therapy, narcotherapy* and *psychosurgery* etc.

Physiogenetic. Characterizing that which originates in the body or in a part of thereof.

Physiological Limit. Refers to the theoretical asymptote or upper limit of performance as dictated by biological factors.

Physiological Motive. Refers to a motive based on body needs or tissue needs, *e.g.*, food, water, avoidance of noxious stimulation, etc.

Physiological Psychology. A branch of psychology that is oriented toward description and explanation of psychological phenomena based on physiological and neurological processes.

Physiological Zero. Refers to the temperature to which a response neither of warm nor of cold is experienced.

Physiology. It is a branch of biology that studies the functions of cells, tissues and organs or living organisms.

Pia Mater. Refers to the intermost of the three meanings covering the brain and spinal cord.

Pidgin. A verbal communication system which develops when two different language communities make occasional contact with each other.

Pigment Layer. Refers to the first layer of the retina containing the pigmented cells.

Pilo. Combining form meaning *hair*.

Piloerection. The state when one's hair stand on end.

Pinna. Refers to the fleshy outer part of the external ear. It serves some sound-gathering functions.

Placenta. In mammals it is an organ consisting of embryonic and maternal tissue to which the fetus is attached via the umbilical cord. The placenta is the "life support system" for the fetus; oxygen, food substances and antibodies enter through it, metabolic waste products leave through it.

Planophrasia. Means erratic flight of ideas.

Plantar Reflex. Refers to a stroking of the sole of the foot.

Pleiotropic. Refers to a gene which influences more than one phenotypic trait.

Plethysmograph. It is a device used for measuring volume, generally that of blood supply, in a part of the body.

Plexus. Refers to a network of nerves or of blood or lymphatic vessels.

Pneumograph. It is an instrument used for recording breathing.

Poetzl Effect. Refers to the later appearance in dreams and waking imagery of parts of tachistoscopically presented pictures which were not reported as being perceived when actually presented.

Polydactyl. Means possessing more than the usual complement of fingers.

Polydipsia. Refers to excessive drinking.

Polydipsia, Psychogenic. A psychological disorder characterized by the drinking of extreme amounts of water.

Polyglot. Refers to one who speaks many languages.

Polygyny. A marriage system wherein a single male may have two or more wives simultaneously.

Posterior. In human anatomical terminology, *posterior* is generally found as a synonym for *dorsal*, *anterior* as a synonym for *ventral*.

Postremity (Principle). Refers to the principle according to which the most probable response an organism will make in a particular situation is the last one it made in that situation.

Postural Set. Refers to a body position which is preparatory for a particular response.

Posturology. Refers to the study of the ways in which different psychological states, wishes, conflicts, emotions, etc. are reflected in one's posture.

Power Spectrum. In acoustics refers to a graph of the mean square amplitude of a sound wave.

Power Test. Refers to a test which measures ability by determining the degree of difficulty of material which can be mastered with no time pressures on the test taker

Prandial. Concerning meal ; *e.g.*, prandial drinking is drinking associated with eating.

Preconscious. Refers to knowledge, emotions, images, etc. which are not momentarily in consciousness but which are easily accessible.

Predication. In logic and linguistics refers to a formal linking between a subject and a predicate.

Preference. Means a liking of one thing more than another thing.

Premack Principle. Refers to the generalization according to which if any two behaviors differ in their momentary probability of occurrence, the opportunity to engage in the more probable will serve to reinforce the less probable.

Prenubile. Concerning the period from birth to the onset of puberty.

Priapism. A chronically erect penis.

Primal Trauma. Refers to some painful childhood experience. The experience of birth, an severe punishment, the death of a parent, witnessing parental coitus etc.

Primary Amentia, It is mental deficiency assumed to because of genetie factors.

Primary Object. Refers to the initial or first *object* to which the infant relates, generally the mother or the breast.

Primary Zone. Refers to the zone which provides maximum libidinal satisfaction at each particular stage of psychosexual development.

Primate. Refers to any member of the Primates, the highest order of mammals.

Primipara. Refers to female who has borne offspring but once.

Proband. Refers to an individual who first comes to the attention of investigators and, due to his or her mental or physical disorder, leads to a detailed study of the genetic-transmission pattern within the family to determine if there is a pattern of disorders which might be genotypic in nature.

Probe. Means to penetrate with intent to explore.

Problem. Refers to a situation wherein some of the attendant components are known and additional components must be ascertained or determined.

Progesterone. Refers to hormone that produced by the corpus luteum following ovulation and, during pregnancy, by the placenta.

Progestin. It is synthetic hormone having progesterone-like, effects.

Prosthesis. It is an artificial device that is used in addition to or in place of a dysfunctional or missing body part.

Prolactin. It is a hormone secreted by the anterior pituitary and is responsible for the onset and maintenance of lactation in mammals after birth of the young.

Prosocial. Refers to those social behaviors which are cooperative in nature.

Protensity. Refers to the direct experience of the duration of sensation.

Protocol. Refers to the original record of an experiment or other investigation made during or immediately after the event.

Pseudocyesis. Refers to false pregnancy. This can be a most compelling functional syndrome which may include abdominal swelling and cessation of the menses.

Pseudophone. Refers to device that transposes the spatial location of sounds so that those that normally would enter the right ear enter the left and vice versa.

Pseudopsychology. Means fake or false psychology. The term has two common uses : 1. To characterize those unscientific endeavors which are clearly fraudulent and whose practitioners are thus quacks, *e.g.*, graphology, palmistry, phrenology. 2. To characterize one's scientific foes who insist on adhering to theoretical points of view which one knows are clearly unscientific. Here everything from psychoanalysis to behaviorism to parapsychology has been called a pseudopsychology at one time or another.

Pseudoscope. It is an optical device which transposes the images to the two eyes in such a way that light that would fall on the right retina falls on the left and vice versa.

Psi (ψ). The Greek letter. When the letter itself is used it serves as an abbreviation for *psychology* ; when spelled out in English it refers to the parapsychologist's *psi processes*.

Psi-missing. In parapsychology refers to a situation wherein a paranormal "process" seems to be working in a negative fashion.

Psi Process. Refers to any individual paranormal ability, *e.g.*, telepathy.

Psyche. Refers to one who envisioned the psyche as the soul or the very essence of life.

Psychiatric Social Work. It is a specialization within social work wherein the social worker is trained for collaborative work with psychiatrists and clinical psychologists.

Psychiatrist. Refers to person trained in medicine who specializes in the prevention.

Psychical Research. Research into paranormal phenomena.

Psychic Determinism. It is a form of *determinism* reflecting the point of view that all psychological processes are causally determined by antecedent factors.

Psychic Impotence. Refers to *impotence* which is psychogenic.

Psychic Secretion. Refers to those first few drops of saliva elicited by a once-neutral stimulus.

Psychic Trauma. Refers to any painful psychological experience.

Psycho. Combining form meaning pertaining to *mind*, *psyche* or *psychology*.

Psychoacoustics. A branch of psychology concerned with sound, its perception and the physiological foundations of hearing.

Psychoactive Drug. Refers to any drug which affects consciousness, mood and awareness.

Psychoanalyst. Refers to one who practices *psychoanalysis*. They may have had any of a number of different forms of training prior to the psychoanalytical, *e.g.*, an MD degree with a psychiatric residency, a doctorate or other advanced degree in psychology or even a master's degree in social work or counseling.

Psychoasthenia. Means mental deficiency, mental retardation.

Psychoasthenics. Refers to the study of mental retardation.

Psychobiology. Refers to the study of psychological process from a biological point of view.

Psychogalvanometer. It is a device used for measuring the *galvanic skin response.*

Psychohistory. Refers to any literary work which attempts to understand historical events by providing a detailed psychological analysis of the characters involved.

Psychokinesis. It is a hypothesized para-psychological phenomenon by which an individual supposedly influences a physical event without direct intervention.

Psycholagny. Means sexual excitement brought about by the use of one's imagination, generally by forming mental images.

Psycholepsy. Refers to sudden loss of mental alertness, a feeling of hopelessness, helplessness, depression.

Psychological. Concerning psychology in any and all of its manifestations.

Psychological Environment. Refers to all aspects of the environment which are psychologically relevant to an individual at any point in time.

Psychological Test. Refers to all tests of a psychological nature *test* and related entries for discussion and definitions of various kinds of tests.

Psychological Warfare. Refers to the use of psychological manipulations in the waging of wars.

Psychologism. Refers to the point of view that psychology is *the* fundamental science and to treat the events of the world from that perspective.

Psycholytic. Means mind-loosening.

Psycholytic Therapy. A radical form of psychotherapy that is based, in part, on the administration of psychedelic drugs.

Psychometrics. Includes the branches of psychology concerned with measurement.

Psychomotor. Concerning to mental events that have motor effect or vice versa.

Psychosexual Disorder. A functional sexual disorders wherein psychological factors are considered to be of major significance, *i.e.*, it specifically excludes those of organic origin.

Psychosexual Dysfunction. Refers to psychosexual disorders all of which reveal an inhibition of some aspect of the appetitive and physiological changes which normally characterize the complete sexual response cycle and wherein the dysfunction is not because of known organic factors.

Psychosocial. Refers to any situation where both psychological and social factors are considered to play a role.

Psychotherapist. Refers to one who practices psychotherapy.

Pubescence. Refers to the process of first reaching puberty.

Pubescent. It is one in the early period of puberty.

Purposive Psychology. An orientation of psychological science which stresses the role of purpose in the determination of behavior.

Pursuitmeter. Refers to any device used for measuring a subject's ability to follow an erratically moving target.

Pyramids. These are compact elevated bundles of nerve fibers in the medulla.

Pyrophobia. Refers to an exaggerated fear of fire.

Pyrosis. Means heartburn.

Q

Q. Stands for *Quartile deviation.* When subscripted stands for *quartile.*

Q. It represents the proportion of events in a population failing to show a particular characteristic and thus distinguishable from a mutually exclusive proportion of events, p, such that $p+q=1$.

Q Data. It is the information, or *data,* collected through questionnaries.

Q Metbod. Refers to the use of questionnaries for obtaining psychological data.

Q Sort. It a technique used in personality assessment that is based on a series of statements and trait names that the subject sorts into categories from "most characteristic of me" to "least characteristic of me".

Q Technique. It is the correlation of the scores of two persons on a series of tests.

Quadrant. It is one of the four cells in a 2×2 table or one of the four equal-sized areas of a plane obtained by subdividing it with intersecting prependicular lines.

Quardriplegia. Refers to paralysis of all four limbs.

Quale. Refers to a sensation that is thought to be simple bit of experience, without any considerations or significance.

Quality. It is a basic aspect of a sensation by means of which it is distinguished from all other sensations. It emphasises difference in kind and not in degree, and represents the relative level of goodness or excellence of anything.

Quality Scale. It is a scale wherein the steps are shown by a series of items of increasing worth or value.

Quantal. Refers to that which takes place. Changes in small discrete steps, or takes place in small elemental units.

Quantal Hypothesis. Refers to the assumption that changes in sensation occur by discrete steps and not along a continuum.

Quantity. Refers to an aspect or property of a thing that renders it countable or measurable in numerical terms.

Quantum. It is a specific or discrete amount of anything.

Quartile. It is one of the three points which divide an ordered distribution into four parts each containing one quarter of the scores, or one of the four parts of the distribution so divided.

Quartile Deviation. A measure of variability which is equal to one half the difference between the 25th and 75th percentiles. In a normal distribution, the deviation quartile is equal to the probable error.

Quasi. A combining from whose usual connotation is that the thing has a resemblance of or only superfically similar to some other thing.

Quasi-experimental Research. Refers to any research carried out without full control over the independent variables. Much naturalistic social psychological research falls within this category, like analysis of people's reactions to natural disorders when the subjects are those who just happen to fall victim to the disorder and are not selected by any controlled sampling procedure.

Quasi Group. Refers to an aggregate of persons with the, which has not yet been utilised potential for forming into a true, *group*.

Quasi Need. Refers to a purpose which excites and directs behavior toward a goal but does not originate in changing psysiological rhythms.

Questionnaire. Refers to a set of questions dealing with any topic or group of related topics designed to be answered by a respondent.

Quick and Dirty. Refers to a laboratory technique for making a rough estimate. For example, "eye-balling" a regression line, using the quartile deviation as a measure of variability, etc.

Quickening. Refers to the first fetal movements *in utero*. Such a movement is felt between the 18th and 20th weeks, although earlier movements are also common.

Quota Control. Refers to a technique used for population sampling wherein the elements chosen for the sample are proportionate in numbers to the number of elements in the population as a whole.

Quota Sampling. Refers to the selecting a certain proportion of elements from a set of subgroups which make up the population from which the sample is drawn.

Quotidian. Occurring daily.

Quotidian Variability. Day-to-day variability.

Quotient. The result obtained by dividing one number by another. Quotients are commonly used to express data in psychology, *e.g*, IQ=*intelligence quotient*. Their mathematical status as such is often misunderstood.

R

R_c. It is sometimes used as an abbreviation for *conditioned response* *CR* is more common.

RG. In Hull's theory refers to any goal-attaining response, *e.g.*, eating, drinking.

Racism. It is a *prejudice* that is based on race and characterized by attitudes and beliefs about the inferior nature of persons of other races. It also refers to social/political doctrine which argues for differential social, economic, educational and legal treatment of persons based on their race.

Radiance. *Radiant energy* as measured by the rate of emission and the area of the source.

Radical. *Pertaining to a root.* Thus in social/political terms, descriptive of any point of view or proposal which argues for basic, fundamental change.

Radicalism. Refers to any sociopolitical point of view which propagates extreme, rapid and fundamental change.

Radiometer. It is a device used for measuring radiant energy.

Rage. Refers to the extreme end of the domain of emotionality denoted by *anger*.

Ramus. Refers to any branch of a nerve or vein or any of the many branches of each of the spinal nerves.

Random. It indicates words or phrases like *haphazard, by chance, occurring without voluntary control, aimless, purposeless,* etc.

Randomization Test. It is one of the more powerful nonparametric statistical tests and is based on the determination of the exact probabilities of an observed set of differences in scores between two matched samples and the assessment of just how likely such a difference would be under the null hypothesis of no difference in the underlying distributions.

Randomize. Means to select or choose objects, events. experimental subjects, etc. in a manner that there are no detectible biases or systematic patterns.

Range. Refers to the extent to or the limits between which variation can take place. Thus, : 1. The interval or "distance" between the highest and lowest scores in a distribution. 2. In sociology and ethology, the physical area over which a particular group lives or a particular species is found.

Rank. In statistics, it is the position in an ordered series of scores. The rank of a score on some measure tells only where that score is relative to all others (*i.e.*, 1st, 2nd, 3rd, ..., *n*th).

Rank Order. Refers to ordering of scores according to their *ranks*.

Ranschburg Effect. Refers to the generalization that under tachistoscopic viewing conditions more individual stimuli can be recognized if all are different than if some are identical.

Ranvier's Nodes. Refers to small gaps in the myelin sheath of nerve fibers.

Raphe. In anatomy refers to a crease or seam marking the joining of two halves. Particularly, a complex of nuclei in the core of the brainstem which plays a part in the brain's complex sleep mechanism.

Rapport. Refers to a comfortable, relaxed, unconstrained, mutually accepting interaction between persons, particularly when the persons are a tester and a subject in psychological testing, a client and a therapist in therapy.

Rationality. Refers to a state that is characterized by reasonableness, a wiilingness to accept that which is well reasoned.

Rational Learning. Refers to any learning that is based on logical, conscious reasoning.

Rational Psychology. Refers to any approach to psychology wherein the overall theoretical structure for interpretation and understanding of psychological phenomena is grounded in a theological and philosophical framework.

Rayleigh Equation. It is a quantitative relationship between the proportions of red and green needed to match a given yellow.

Reactance, Psychological. Refers to an unpleasant drive state brought about by a threat to one's perceived freedom.

Reaction Potential. In Hull's learning theory refers to the likelihood of occurrence of a particular response.

Reaction Process. Refers to the full sequence of acts involved in *reaction time* experiments.

Reactive Psychosis. Refers to a psychosis which stems from strong environmental pressures and stresses.

Reality Adaptation. In psychoanalytic theory it is the process through which the infant gradually brings its perceptions, desires, needs, etc. into line with the external reality.

Reason. Means logical thought or a justification offered as an explanation for one's actions, expressed in terms of one's motivations.

Reasoning. Means thinking, with the implication that the process is logical and coherent.

Reber's Law. It states, that the closer anything is examined, the more complex it is seen to be.

Rebirth Fantasy. In psychoanalysis it is a fantasy of being born.

Rebus. A writing format that is based on the notion that two words that are homophones can be expressed using the same sign.

Receptive Character. Refers to an individual who is excessively passive and needs a great deal of support and guidance from those about.

Recognition. Refers to the awareness that an object or event is one that has been previously seen, experienced or learned.

Recognition Procedure (or Method). An experimental procedure used in the study of memory wherein the subject is asked to respond to a series of test stimuli by stating whether or not they were among those stimuli presented in a learning session held earlier.

Recognition Test. Refers to a test which relies on differentiating old, previously seen material from new material. Most multiple-choice exams are of this type.

Red Nucleus. It is a group of nerve cells in the tegmentum which forms part of the extrapyramidal motor system. It is an important link in the transmission of information along the corticorubrospinal system which runs from the cortex through the red nucleus to the spinal cord.

Reflection of Feeling. Refers to a technique that is used in non-directive therapy wherein the therapist rephrases what the client has said with an emphasis on the emotional aspects.

Reflectivity-impulsivity. A hypothesized dimension of *cognitive style* based on the observation that in the solving of problems some people tend to be rather "impulsive" and react quickly on the basis of the first thing that comes to mind while others are more "reflective", more systematic and tend to think the problem through before acting.

Reflex. Refers to any relatively simple, "mechanical" response. Reflexes are generally considered as species-specific, innate behaviors which are largely outside of volition and choice and show little variability from instance to instance.

Reflex Arc. Refers to the hypothesized neural unit representing the functioning of a reflex.

Reflex Facilitation. Refers to the increase in the magnitude of a reflex by presentation of another stimulus which would not, by itself, produce the reflex.

Reflex Inhibition. Refers to the inhibition of one reflex by a mutually incompatible one.

Reflex Latency. It is the time between the presentation of the eliciting stimulus and the appearance of a reflex.

Reflexology. It is a mechanistic, behavioristic point of view which argues that all psychological processes may be represented as reflexes and combinations of reflexes.

Reflex Reserve. Refers to the hypothetical reservoir of responsiveness remaining after reinforcement had terminated.

Refractory. Means stubborn, unmanageable, unresponsive.

Regnancy. Refers to "totality of brain processes taking place during a single moment".

Regression Neurosis. Refers to a neurosis that has ***regression*** as its dominant symptom.

Regret. Refers to the feeling that, in retrospect, one might have behaved differently in the past or that things might have turned out better had events gone differently.

Reissner's Membrane. It is the delicate membrane in the cochlea which separates the cochlear canal from the scala vestibuli.

Reiz. German for *stimulus*.

Rejection. Means a failure or refusal to assimilate or to accept.

Relaxation. Refers to the state of low tension wherein emotional level is diminished, particularly the level of emotions like anxiety, fear, anger etc.

Relaxation Therapy. Refers to any psychotherapy which places emphasis on techniques for teaching the client how to relax, to control tensions.

Release Therapy. Refers to, any therapeutic procedure which is based on the assumption that there is therapeutic value in the releasing of deep, pent-up, emotional conflicts.

Reliability. Means dependability. In personality assessment, a characteristic trustworthiness; a reliable person is a responsible person, one who can be counted upon. In psychological testing it refers to all aspects relating to the dependability of a measurement device or test.

Religion. Refers to a system of beliefs with either an institutionalized or a traditionally defined pattern of ceremony. Religion is considered by many as a cultural universal which emerges invariably as an outcome of the need to understand the human condition.

Religiosity. Refers to involvement, interest or participation in religion.

Religious Instinct. Refers to an assumed *instinct* in *Homo sapiens* for religious beliefs.

Reminiscence. It is the unconscious recall of information or a rambling, sequential recalling of information about some earlier experience.

Remission. Refers to cessation of the symptoms of a disorder or disease.

Renin. It is hormone of the kidney. Release of renin is produced by sympathetic stimulation or by reduction in blood flow in the kidneys. When released, it causes angiotensinogen in the blood to convert to angiotensin which, in turn, produces thirst as well as stimulating the adrenal cortex, resulting ultimately in sodium retention.

Renshaw Cell. It is a small neuron with a short axon which functions as an inhibitor of motor neurons.

Renunciation. Means a surrendering of self, will, title, inheritance, etc. or the surrendering of one's personal will or desires to what one perceives to be the will of one's God.

Reparation. In psychoanalysis refers to the reduction of guilt by the doing of good works.

Repertoire. Refers to the full compendium of behaviors of an organism or a species.

Repress. Means to hold or put down, to suppress, keep from occurring.

Reproduction Theory. It is a theory of mental imagery or ideation which maintains that an image is a copy or point-by-point reproduction of the original stimulus.

Rep Test. It is personality-assessment test designed by George Kelly to facilitate the process of coming to know how an individual views his or her world. The full name of the instrument is *Role Construct Repertory Test* and it is used for diagnosing or assessing one's *personal-role constructs* which, in Kelly's theory, are essential components of personality.

Reserpine. An alkaloid obtained from the Indian shrub R*auwolfia serpentina*, this was the first *antipsychotic* drug to be used widely.

Response Rate. It is the number of responses per unit time. It is used as a measure of learning in operant-conditioning experiments.

Retinex (Theory). Edwin Land's theoretical model of color vision. He hypothesized three separate visual systems (retinexes), one responsive primarily to long-wavelength light, one to moderate, and the third to short-wavelength light. Each is represented as an analog to a black-and-white picture taken through a particular filter, with each one producing maximum activity in response to red, green and blue light for the long-, moderate-, and short-wavelength retinexes respectively.

Retinol. Vitamin A ; it is an essential precursor for the synthesis of *retinal.*

Retrograde. Means moving backward, retreating, retiring.

Retrospection. Means inspecting and reporting on that which has passed.

Retrospective Falsification. Means unconscious modification and distortion of previous experiences in order to make them conform with present needs.

Reverie. Refers to relatively purposeless mental state, which is characterized by aimless mental meanderings and fantasies.

Reversal. In psychoanalysis refers to the turning about of an instinct, *e.g.*, sadism changes to masochism.

Revival. Means bringing back to life. In the study of memory, the process of recall in the sense that a dormant memory has been triggered or "revived".

RGB System. A system for specifying colors.

Rh Blood Group. A blood group found in roughly 80% of all humans ; the name is derived from the rhesus monkey, where it was first discovered. Its presence is noted as Rh+ (or Rh positive), its absence as Rh− (or Rh negative). If the factor is introduced in those who are Rh− it causes the production of antibodiee (anti-Rh agglutinin) and subsequent transfusions of Rh+ blood will cause serious reactions. During pregnancy, an Rh− woman may become sensitized if the fetus is Rh+ and subsequent pregnancies with Rh+ fetuses are potentially dangerous because the Rh antibodies in maternal blood may cross the placenta and destroy fetal blood cells.

Rheobase. In neurophysiology refers to the threshold of excitability of neural tissue ; it is given as the minimum direct current which when applied indefinitely would be sufficient to produce excitation.

Rho (ρ). The symbol for a correlation coefficient resulting from an analysis of rank-order data on two variables.

Rhypophobia. Refers to extreme sense of aversion and disgust at the act of defecation or its products.

Ribonucleic Acid (RNA). It is a large, complex molecule consisting of a sequence of four nucleotide bases (*adenine, guanine, cytosine* and *uracil*) attached to a sugar-phosphate "backbone" *Messenger RNA* (*mRNA*) is copied from one strand of *deoxyribonucleic acid* (*DNA*) and delivers genetic information from part of a chromosome to a ribosome where *transfer RNA* (*tRNA*) coordinates the assembling of the proper amino acids into enzymes for cell specialization.

Ribosome. It is small structure that is found in all cells that functions as a site for protein synthesis.

Rod and Frame Test. It is test used primarily in measuring *field dependence.* The subject is presented with a rectangular frame and a rod within the frame, The orientation of the frame is changed from trial to trial and the subject attempts to set the position of the rod to the true vertical.

Role Conflict. Refers to a situation wherein a person is expected to perform in two or more roles that conflict in fundamental ways with each other.

Role Rehearsal. Refers to the preliminary playing out of an adult role by a child.

Romberg's Sign. Refers to the inability to maintain body balance when standing with eyes shut and feet close together. It is indicative of neurological damage.

Romeo and Juliet Effect. Refers to the increase in the attractiveness between two people resulting from an attempt on the part of their parents or others to keep them apart.

Rorschach Ranking Test. It is simplified variation on the *Rorschach test* wherein the subject is given each of the ten inkblots along with a list of nine possible responses and asked to rank them as to their values as adequate descriptions of each inkblot.

Rosenthal Effect. Refers to the manner in which one's beliefs, biases and expectations can have an impace on the phenomena under investigation.

Round Window. Refers to small, round, membrane-covered opening in the *cochlea* of the inner ear that vibrates back and forth, functioning to alleviate the pressures set up by the vibrations of the *oval window.*

R-R Conditioning. Conditioning of a series of responses wherein each response is the precondition for the next response.

R-R Laws. Conditioning principles based on underlying response relationships.

R Strategy. It is a type of reproductive breeding used by many species wherein many offspring are born at a time. The *r* strategy involves the expenditure of little or no energy or effort in the rearing of the offspring and is generally accompanied by relatively short periods between one birthing and the next.

Rubella. A relatively mild disease with one serious complication. In a pregnant woman during the first two or three months of pregnancy, it can produce a number of fetal anomalies including mental retardation, cataracts, heart disease and deafness.

Rubin's Figure. The common ambiguous figure that is seen as either a vase or as two faces in profile.

Rubrospinal Tract. Refers to the efferent nerve tract running from the red nucleus to the spinal cord.

Ruffini Corpuscle. Encapsulated, branching nerve ending in subcutaneous tissue ; suspected of mediating the sense of warmth. Also known as *Ruffini cylinder.*

Ruffini End Organ. Refers to branching nerve ending found in subcutaneous tissue and suspected of functioning as a mediator of constant skin indentation and hence playing a role in the sense of pressure.

Rumination Disorder of Infancy. Refers to a serious eating disorder which is characterized by repeated regurgitation of food.

Rumor-intensity Formula. A formula proposed by G. Allport and L. Postman which captures the generalization that the intensity of rumors tends to be a function of the importance of the subject and its ambiguity, *i.e.*, $R=ia$, where R is the intensity of the rumor, i=importance and a=ambiguity.

Runs Test. A nonparametric statistical test which determines if a single data sample is significantly different from random by analyzing the pattern of *runs*.

Rut. In lower animals, a seasonal period of sexual excitement, *estrus, heat.* In animals, copulation.

S

Sacral. Refers to the sacrum or back of the pelvis.

Sacrum. It is the triangular bone near the base of the spinal column that forms the dorsal part of the pelvis.

Sado-masochism. Refers to the tendency toward both sadism and masochism.

Sagittal Axis. It is the line which runs from the center of the retina outward through the eye of the center of the object in view.

Salpetriere. Refers to a French asylum for the insane where Charcot practiced hypnotism and founded the so-called Salpetriere school of psychopathology based on hypnotic phenomena.

Sampling. It is the process of selecting a sample.

Sapid. Means capable of being tasted.

Sapphism. Refers to homosexuality among women also called Lesbianism.

Satyriasis. Refer to pathologically strong sexual desire in men.

Savings Method. It is a technique used for measuring retention by comparing the time of trials necessary for relearning something which has already been learnt.

Scalability. Refers to the characteristic of being represented in a quantitative series.

Scale Valus. It is the number assigned to a point on a psychological scale.

Scalogram Board. Refers to a device to facilitate the selection of items for a cumulative scale.

Scan. Means to examine quickly or superficially or to look over something for the presence of certain items or to traverse any area with a device, like a camera, for recording what is present.

Scatological. It is characterized by interest in filth or excrement or refers to obscene speech.

Scedasticity. Means the variability of the rows and column of a sectar diagram.

Schotastic Test. Refers to any test in a school subject.

School Psychologist. Refers to a psychologist who specializes in the problems associated with elementary and secondary educational systems. He may counsel or advise children, may help to plan curricular units, administers tests, and assists in the interpretation of test results to children and parents.

Schwann Cell. Refers to a cell that is wrapped around peripheral neurons which forms the neurilemma, providing one layer of the myelin sheath.

Scientific Attitude. Refers to the attitude characteristic of the sciences—involving chiefly the search for objective facts by empirical methods.

Scientific Method. Refers to the techniques used scientists in the search knowledge. The scientist may utilize either naturalistic observation or experimentation.

Scientific Psychology. Refers to any system of psychology or body or psychological facts which are based on the scientific method.

Scintillating Scotoma. Refers to the appearance of bright flashes before the eyes.

Scopic. Refers to systems of measurement wherein the scores or data are directly observed.

Sphilia. Refers to the sexual pleasure derived from looking at the naked human form or at sexual acts.

Screen. Refers to a device used for blacking out part of the visual field. The common form is a reduction screen, that is essentially a tube which limits vision to the central portion of the field, thereby blocking out the background.

Seashore Tests of Musical Talent. Refers to a series of recorded tests of pitch discrimination, tonal memory, loudness, discrimination, rhythm, time, and timbre. These are useful in identifying the relative standing of an individual on the components of musical aptitude.

Seclusion Need. Refers to the need for privacy : the need to be alone.

Secondary Integration. The process of the unification of the pregenital psychic components into an integrated psychosexual unity.

Secondary Mental Deficiency. Refers to sub-normality in intelligence because of brain injury or disease.

Secondary Motivation. Refers to learned motives which are not universal in a culture and for which the bodily basis is not known.

Secondary Narcissism. Refers to the withdrawal of the libido from the body and its investment in the ego.

Secondary Repression. Refers to the repression of psychic contents associated with primary repression that would remind the individual of the primary material.

Segregation. Means the isolation of mental processes into compartments having relatively little interaction between them.

Self-denial. Refers to an act or practice of forgoing satisfactions or desires.

Self-desensitization. It is technique used in behavior therapy, wherein the patient in instructed to carry out muscle relaxation when anxiety-arousing stimuli are present in the everyday environment.

Self-determination. Refers to the regulation of one's own behaviour by inner-directed controls and not because of social pressure.

Self-discipline. Means the regulation of one's own conduct or the self-application of punishment.

Self-Evaluation. Refers to a rating or judgment made by the individual about himself.

Self-love. Refers to extreme self-regard ; narcissism ; the centering of love or erotic processes on one's own body.

Self-Marking Test. Refers to a test that is designed in such a way that the testee's response is immediately scored by one of several devices, a like carbon backing sheet which transmits the subject's response to "right" or "wrong" spaces.

Self-Psychology. Refers to any system of psychology stating that the self should be the central fact of psychology and that all behavior must be interpreted in reference to the self.

Semantics. It is the science that deals with the meanings of words.

Semantic Therapy. It is a system of psychotherapy which tries to readjust individuals by reinterpreting the distorted meanings which such individuals have associated with words.

Semeiology. It is the science of signs and signs language or the investigation of symptoms of diseases or the science of symptomology.

Semen. These are the male sperm cells and the fluid vehicle secreted by the testes and prostate gland respectively.

Senile Psychosis. Refers to a disorder of old age that is characterized by deterioration of cerebral tissue with accompanying loss of memory, irritability, narrowing of outlook, and stubbornness.

Senilism. Refers to the presence of symptoms of senility with or without old age.

Senium. Means old age.

Sensing. It is the process of apprehending the activities of a receptor ; who is aware of sense data.

Sensitive. Referring to sensitivity, or describing an individual whose threshold of emotionality is low and so can be easily hurt.

Sensitization. Refers to the process of becoming sensitive to a stimulus.

Sensory Cortex. Refers to those parts of the cerebral cortex which are the terminal points for incoming sensory neurons.

Sensual. Refers to gratification, specially excessive gratification, obtained from the senses.

Septum. It is a partition or division in the brain or other organ.

Sequela (Plural Sequelae). Refers to the lingering or more or less chronic aftermath of a disease.

Serialization. It is the tendency to arrange objects along a quantified dimension, like size or weight.

Serial Memorization. Refers to memorizing a sequence of items in a predetermined order.

Seriatim. Means sequential ; in a series.

Seriation. Refers to the arrangement of data into a series.

Sex Chromosome. Refers to the chromosome, or dark staining body bearing the genes, which are responsible for determining the sex of the individual. In the human being sex is determined by a special pair called the XX chromosomes in the female and the XY in the male. The female chromosomes make a true pair, whereas in the male the Y chromosome is smaller than the X chromosome.

Sex Determination. Refers to the genetic mechanism which determines the sex of the offspring.

Sex Education. Refers to instruction in the physiology of reproduction, or instruction in the physiology of reproduction and in attitudes promoting good sexual adjustment toward sexuality in general and marriage in particular.

Sex Feeling. Refers to the distinctive, pleasurable feeling or emotion associated with stimulation of the sexual organs or with sexual intercourse.

Sex Hygiene. It is the science of maintenance of health and prevention of disease, through proper conduct and sanitary techniques, in the area of sexual activity.

Sex-influenced Character. Refers to a trait transmitted as dominant in one sex but recessive in the other. Thus, baldness in men may be transmitted by either parent but must be transmitted by both if it is to appear in the offspring.

Sex Perversion. Refers to sexual behavior which differs widely from normal standards and is typically prohibited by law in most states.

Sexual. Refers to reproduction by the union of two different individuals who produce an egg and sperm respectively, or refers to behavior, feelings, or emotions associated with stimulations of the genital organs, erogenous zones, or with the process of reproduction.

Sexual Aim. Refers to the goal of sexual satisfaction or pleasure ; the release of sexual tension.

Sexual Anesthesia. Refers to the inability to enjoy sexual activities ; a lack of sexual feeling.

Sexual Congress. Means sexual intercourse ; coition.

Sexual Intercourse. Refers to the introduction of the penis or male sexual organ into the vagina of the female with accompanying rhythmic pelvic movements to the point of orgasm, or the introduction of the penis into the body of another male ; technically known as anal intercourse.

Sexual Maturation. Refers to the development of the reproductive organs to such a level that sexual intercourse and reproduction are possible.

Sexual Object. Refers to an individual or an object toward which sexual desire and behavior are directed.

Sexual Reflex. Refers to the erection of sexual tissue.

Sexual Reproduction. Refers to the production of a new individual by the union of sex cells.

Shame. Refers to an emotion that is characterized by feelings of guilt, embarrassment, and avoidance.

Sheltered Workshop. It is a professionally designed and managed workshop wherein retardates or handicapped persons can attain useful skills.

Shock. Refers to a sudden, often fatal, depression of physiological process induced by an accident, surgery, or a powerful emotion, or the condition resulting when a strong electric current is passed through the body.

Shock Therapy. Refers to the treatment of mental disorders by passing an electric current through the brain or by the administration of such drugs which induce convulsions.

Short-answer Test. Refers to any objective test utilizing multiple choice, fill-in, matching alternatives, and the like, which do not require lengthy or complex answers.

Shyness. Refers to a condition of discomfort, embarrassment, and inhibition in the presence of others.

Sign Test. Refers to a nonparametric test for significance of differences; it is quite useful where an experiment can be devised as a series of events following a binomial distribution.

Simulator. Refers to a training device which resembles the equipment to be used in the final performance.

Sinistral. Refers to the left side of the body.

Sixteen D Scale ; 16-D Scale. It is an intelligence-measuring score obtained from a multiple of the standard deviation from the mean score at the sixteen on a member of standardized tests.

Sixteen Personality Factor Questionnaire. Refers to a questionnaire which designed to yield scores on 16 first-order factors and 8 second-order factors according to Cattell's system of personality analysis.

Skeletal Muscle. Refers to the straited or striped muscles which are under voluntary control.

Skelic Index. It is the ratio of leg length to length of trunk.

Skiascope. It is an instrument for measuring the refractive condition of the eye.

Skin. It is the external covering of animals, and consists of two distinct portions or layers, the epidermis (outer covering) and the dermis (deeper tissue).

Skin Eroticism. Refers to the of sexual or erotic pleasure obtained from stroking or rubbing the skin.

Skinner Box. It is an enclosed boxlike structure in which the correct operation of a mechanism brings the animal a reward. In some boxes elaborate controls on temperature, humidity, external sounds, lights, and odors are maintained.

Snake Symbol. It is the male sex organ.

Snellen Chart. It is a card containing printed letters ranging from very large to very small, to be read by the subject at a specified distance as a test of visual acuity.

Social Atom. Refers to the psychological relations of the individual to the smallest social structure.

Social Attitude. Refers to a predisposition to behave in a particular manner toward people.

Social Code. Refers to any system of social regulations, whether formal or informal.

Social Control. Refers to the regulation of individual behavior by means of group or institutional decisions.

Social Instinct. It is the tendency of the individuals to form groups ; gregariousness.

Social Integration. It is the process whereby the individual fits into a social group, or the unification of diverse elements in a society.

Sociality. Refers to the characteristic of being co-operative, of adapting to social demands, or gregariousness or the tendency to form groups.

Social Psychiatry. Refers to a viewpoint in psychiatry which places emphases on social factors in the causation of the mental disorders.

Social Psychology. It is the branch of psychology that deals with psychological processes which occur in groups. It deals with the behavioral interaction of individuals within groups and the interaction between groups.

Social Scale. These are the social classes and the criteria for assigning individuals to those classes.

Social Sciences. Refers to those sciences which are concerned primarily with man as living in relation to his fellowmen. These include anthropology, psychology, sociology, economics, history, political science, and economic geography.

Social Selection. Refers to biological selection by social means, giving certain individuals a better chance of survival in the struggle for existence.

Society. It is the group of individuals of a given species, specially the human species, who live together, or mankind as a whole, or any formally organized social group.

Sociocenter. Refers to the individual most frequently chosen in a sociometric test.

Sociocentrism. Refers to the tendency to take one's own social group as a standard.

Sociology. It is a branch of science that deals with the organization and functions of groups and institutions.

Sociometry. It is a technique used for mapping the relationships of attraction and rejection among members of a group.

Socionomics. Refers to the study of nonsocial influences, like the effects of weather, on the group or society as a whole.

Sodomy. Refers to sexual intercourse between males by way of the anus, or sexual intercourse with animals, or any kind of illegal or socially disapproved sexual behavior.

Solipsism. It is the philosophical position according to which only one's own experience can be known.

Somatic Nerves. Refers to the nerves serving the striated or skeletal muscles.

Somatist. Refers to some one who attributes all mental disorders to organic causes.

Somatopsychic. Means psychosomatic or characterizing psychological symptoms or disorders having physical or organic origin.

Somatopsychosis. Refers to a mental disorder wherein the delusional symptoms are primarily centered around the individual's own body.

Somatosexuality. Sexaulity expressed in bodily activity.

Sonant. Refers to a voiced speech sound.

Sone. It is a unit on the ratio scale of loudness. The standard is a loudness of 40 decibels above the mean threshold at a frequency level of 1,000 Hz.

Sonometer. It is an instrument made up of one or more strings stretched over a resonating box. It is used in auditory research and demonstrations.

Soporific. Refers to a sleep-inducing agent.

Sorting Test. Refers to a test involving the classification of objects, colors, etc., into certain categories. Such tests are used to measure the individual's ability to conceptualize, abstract, or generalize.

Soul. In theology refers to an entity hypothesized to have real and permanent existence beyond mortal life.

Sound Spectograph. It is a device used for indicating change in intensity and frequency of sounds as a function of time.

Source. Refers to any system which emits a sound wave, a light, or any type of electronic signal.

Spasm. Refers to a localized, involuntary muscular contraction.

Spay. Means to remove the ovaries or sex glands of a female animal.

Spearman-Brown Prophecy Formula. It is a formula for estimating the reliability of an entire test from the reliability of the two halves of the tests. Mathematically it is

$$r_{AA} = \frac{A^{r}II}{1+(A-1)\ ^{r}II}$$

where $A^{r}II$ is the reliability of the single length and A is the number of times the test is lengthened.

Specific Thalamic Projection System. Refers to the anatomically distinct and direct sensory pathways for vision, hearing and somesthesis.

Spectrophobia. Refers to fear of seeing oneself in a mirror, or fear of specters or phantoms.

Speculation. Means thinking without any significant or convincing evidence.

Speech Therapy. It is a therapy that is directed to the correction of speech disorders.

Sphincter Morality. Refers to attitudes of prudishness, pettiness, overconcern with detail, and other attributes of the anal character, considered to be induced by overly harsh toilet training.

Sphygmomanometer. It is an instrument used for measuring arterial blood pressure.

Spinal. Refers to the backbone or the spinal cord.

Spiral Test. It is a test wherein items in different categories keep repeating at higher and higher levels of difficulty. The test might contain a vocabulary item, followed by an arithmetic reasoning problem and a perceptual task. The entire cycle would then be repeated with each item in the sequence being more difficult.

Spirograph. It is a device used to measure the rate and magnitude of breathing.

Split-Brain Technique. Refers to the separation of the brain it the corpus callosum and, in some cases, at the optic chiasma, so as to study the different functions of the two cerebral hemispheres.

Spontaneity Test. It is a part of the general process of psychodrama where the individual is placed in a real-life situation wherein he acts our his feelings and typical behavior patterns toward other individuals.

Spontaneity Therapy or Training. Refers to psychodrama or role-playing that is directed toward acting out one's problems for discovering more adaptive modes of behavior.

Stabilimeter. It is a device used for measuring the degree of bodily sway under conditions where the subject stands erect, blindfolded or with eyes closed, and attempts to remain immobile.

Standardized Test. Refers to a test subjected to thorough empirical tryout and analysis and which provides time limits, instructions, scoring standards, reliability and validity coefficients, and norms.

Stanford Achievement Test. Refers to a test that is designed to measure a pupil's progress in paragraph meaning, word meaning, and grammatical usage.

Stanine. It is a statistical measure equal to one ninth of the range of the standard scores of a distribution. The statistic was the United States Air Force during World War II and was used in their testing program.

Stapes. Refers to one of the three auditory ossicles. The stapes is attached to the oval window of the cochlea.

Startle Reflex or Pattern or Response. Refers to a complex response to a loud and unexpected sound. It is made up of a general flexion of the muscles of the body accompanied by visceral changes. It is considered as a kind of primitive emotional response.

Statistical Psychology. It is the branch of psychology that makes use of statistical models and techniques to obtain explanatory constructs.

Statistics. It is a branch of mathematics that deals with a data either *descriptively*, in terms of summaries, like the measures of central tendency, dispersion, and relationship, or *inferentially*, in terms of sampling the significance of data and errors of observation.

Staves Scale. Refers to a scale exactly like the sten scale except that the units are fives.

Sten Scale. It is a standard seale of 10 units or scores, each step being one-half of a standard deviation.

Stereochemical Theory. In olfaction refers to the position according to which odors can be classified into seven primary groups on the basis of their molecular shape.

Stereognosis. Refers to perception of objects or forms through the modality of touch.

Stereogram. Refers to a picture which is placed in a stereoscope to give striking depth effects.

Stereoscope. It is a device used for viewing stereograms or two-dimensional pictures taken with a double-lens camera whose openings are set apart the same distance as the eyes. When the images are brought together in the stereoscope, the effect is one of depth.

Sterility. Refers to the inability, due to physiological or psychological deficiencies, to reproduce.

Sterilization. It is the process of rendering the indivisual incapable of reproduction by castration or vasectomy in the male or by salpingectomy or ovariectomy in the female.

Sthenia. Means strength.

Stilling Test. It is a test made up of a chart with numerous colored dots of different hues, saturations, and intensities, for the detection of color weakness. Some of the dots are arranged to form numbers visible to the normal eye but invisible to the color-blind or color-weak eye.

Stimulant. Refers to a drug which accelerates physiological or psychological functions or more generally, any agent which increases physiological or psychological activity.

Stimulation. It is the application of any form of energy (stimulus) to a receptor or the arousal of an organism by any change in energy, whether external or internal.

Stimulus. Refers any change in physical which energy activates a receptor or any change in external or internal energy alerts or activates an organism.

Stimulus Object. Refers to an object or an individual which serves as a stimulus.

Stimulus-Response Psychology. It believes that psychologist task is to discover the functional relationships between stimuli and responses.

Stroboscope. It is a device used for exposing a series of related visual stimuli rapidly. Under such conditions the stimuli give rise to an illusion of continuous movement.

Strong-Campbell Interest Inventory. An interest inventory made up of 325 items referring to occupations, activities, school subjects, amusements, etc., for which the examinee expresses like, dislike or indifference. Scores are reported for the degree to which the examinee's interests are similar to those for men and women in some 50 different occupations.

Stroop Effect. Refers to the finding that subjects have difficulty in eliminating irrelevant information from a task.

Stylus. It is a pointed device which is used for recording on smoked drums, graphic recording paper, etc.

Stylus Maze. A modification of the finger maze wherein individual traces the path by means of a stylus.

Subception. Refers to the ability to react to an emotion-provoking stimulus which is not perceived to the point of being reported correctly, although it may be detected by means of the psychogalvanometer or from reaction time to such stimuli as compared with reaction time to neutral stimuli.

Subcutaneous. Means below the surface of the skin or the receptors located under the surface of the skin.

Subjective Psychology. Branch of psychology which uses the method of introspection or phenomenological reporting.

Subjective Test. Refers to a test which does not have objective scoring standards.

Sublimation. Refers to an unconscious process by which the libido, or sex instinct, is directed or transformed into a more acceptable form of outlet.

Submission. It is a state of conforming to the wishes of another.

Submissiviness. It is that trait which leads one to seek and accept the domination of others.

Substitution Test. Refers to a test wherein the subject's task is to substitute one set of symbols by another. The code test is a substitution test and on a simple level may be made up of the substitution of numbers for letters in accordance with a prearranged plan.

Successive-Reproductions Method. Refers to a technique used for studying changes in long-term memory by having the individual reproduce material at relatively long intervals of time.

Superior Intelligence. Refers a to level of general mental ability exceeded by only 15 per cent of the population. Such persons have an IQ equivalent of 120 or better.

Supernormal. Some one beyond the normal range yet within the scope of natural law.

Supination. Refers to a movement of the hand which brings the palm upward.

Supportive Therapy. It is a form of therapy wherein the therapist tenders advice and encouragement and assists the individual, particularly during painful periods in the course of therapy.

Suppression. Refers to a stoppage of any neurological or physiological activity, or voluntary inhibition of activities on the part of an individual. It also refers to a conscious inhibition of impulses or ideas which are incompatible with the individual's evaluation of himself according to his ego ideal.

Superanominal Difference. Refers to any difference between stimuli above the difference threshold.

Surdity. Refers to deafness.

Surgency. It is a personality trait which is characterized by cheerfulness, sociability, trustworthiness, and social responsiveness.

Surrogate. Refers to one who functions in the place of another's parent.

Symonds' Picture Study Test. It is a projective technique made up of a set of twenty pictures showing various interpersonal situations. The subject is asked to tell a story about each. The stories are analyzed in terms of the psychological force which gave rise to them.

Sympathin. It is an adrenalinelike hormone secreted by the nerve endings of the sympathetic division of the autonomic nervous system.

Symptom. In medical and psychological pathology refers to an indicator of the presence of a disease or disorder.

Symptomatic Epilepsy. Refers to a condition wherein epileptoid convulsions represent a symptom of some underlying organic disease.

Synapse. It is the junction between two neurons. It is considered that the junction takes the form of a close contact between the fibrils of the end brush of one neuron and the dendrites and cell body of the next.

Synchronicity. Refers to those events whice take place simultaneously or are coincidental but have no known causal relation ship to each other.

Syncope. Refers to a temporary cessation of consciousness; a fainting spell.

Syncretism. It is an attempt to combine unresolved elements of a group of propositions or doctrines into a system without any regard for contradictions.

Syndrome. Refers to a collection of related symptoms. The syndrome for influenza is made up of the separate symptoms of sore throat, cough, high fever, and muscular aches.

Synergic. Means exerting a force together, as synergic muscles work together to move a limb.

Synonym-Antonym Test. It is a test wherein pairs of words are presented and the subject must indicate whether they are the same or opposite.

Syntaxic. Refers to those experiences which can be communicated by means of concepts having definite objective referents.

Systematized Delusions. Refers to a set of false beliefs which are internally consistent.

Systemic. Refers to the organs of the body as an interrelated whole.

Systole. It is a phase of the cardiac contraction cycle during which the heart is in contraction.

Szondi Test. It is a projective test wherein the subject must choose from among pictures of psychiatric patients those he likes best and those he likes least.

T

T. Stands for temperature, or Time.

sTR In Hull's notational system, *reaction time* generally *RT* is used.

Taboo. Refer any banned or prohibited act, object or behavior.

Tabula Rasa. Means *blank tablet.*

Tachistoscope. It is an instrument which presents visual materials under conditions of very brief exposures.

Tactile. Relating to touch, tactual.

Tadoma Method. A method used for communicating by the deaf and the deafblind by placing the fingers on the speaker's lips and cheeks.

Tag Question. Any interrogative formed by appending a "tag" onto a declarative sentence. For example, in "It's raining out, isn't it?" the "isn't it?" is a *tag.*

Talbot-Plateau Law. Refers to the generalization according to which when the rate of a flickering light is high enough so that a steady light is seen is well have a perceived brightness that is the mean of the periodic impressions.

Talion Principle. The principle of retribution, "an eye for an eye and a tooth for a tooth."

Tangentially. Refers to a manner of speaking wherein questions are answered in inappropriately oblique and irrelevant ways.

Target. Refers to the item which the subject searches for in an array of items. If more than one item is searched for, the several are collectively called the *target set.*

Tartinal's Tone. *Difference tone.* The term honors an 18th century Italian violinist who first noted the existence of difference tones during double-stopping of a violin string ; he used them as a cue to assist in the tuning of his instrument.

Taurine It is an amino acid suspected as being a neurotransmitter.

Tautophone. It is a projective device wherein the subject listens to a recording of unintelligible sounds and is asked to elaborate on what they seem to be saying.

Taylor-Russell Tables. A set of tables which enables on to assess the value of a particular test in selecting individuals.

Tay-Sach's Disease. An inherited disease which is characterized by severe neurological deterioration and accompanying mental and physical retardation.

T Data. Refers to any data based on the use of standardized testing procedures.

Telencephalon. It is a major subdivision of the forebrain. Its principal structures.

Teat. Refers to the nipple of a mammary gland.

Telencephalon. It is a major subdivision of the forebrain. Its principal structures contain the cerebral cortex, the basal ganglia and the limbic system. Also know as the *end brain.*

Telecopisa. A visual disorder wherein objects are perceived as being further away then they are and the sense of depth generally is exaggerated.

Teleotherapeutics. Refers to the use of hypnotic suggestion in therapy.

Telepathy. Refers to the hypothesized ability for direct mental contact between two or more persons.

Telesthesia. Refers to hyphothesized paranormal abilities to perceive events, objects thoughts, etc. without the use of normal sensory systems, *e.g., clairvayance, telepathy.*

Teletractor. It is a device which augments sound waves and converts them into vibration patterns which can be felt on the skin. It is used as an aid in teaching speech and language skills to the deaf.

Temporary Threshold Shift (TTS). Means the temporary (upward) shift in the threshold for a stimulus.

Tendon. Refers to fibrous connective tissue by which muscles are attached to bones.

Teratology. It is the study of birth defects, particularly the biochemical agents that cause them.

Territoriality. Refers to the tendency to defend or protect one's space ageinst invasion or incursion.

Test Battery. A collection of tests whose results can be combined to produce a single score.

Testee. Refers one who takes a test.

Testis. A male gonad or sex organ. One of two reproductive glands located in the scrotum that produce spermatozoa and the male hormone.

Test Scaling. It is the process of setting up a scale for a given test. The usual procedure is to administer the test to a sample group of persons and assign values to each item based on the scores obtained from the sample individuals.

Test Sophistication. Refers to the extent to which a person has had experience with (psychological) tests and hence is aware of the general nature and procedures in use.

Tetanizing Shock. Refers to electric shock strong enough to cause *tetanus*.

Tetanus. Sustained tonic muscular spasms or an acute infectious disease caused by the tetanus bacillus, the primary symptom of which is a state of painful, persistent, tonic spasms of serveral voluntary muscles.

Tetany. It is a condition marked by intermittent tonic muscular spasms, generally in the extermities.

Tetartanopia. An extremely rare from of *dichromatism* where in reds and greens are seen normally but blues and yellows are poorly distinguished, with yellow.

Tetrahydrocannabinol (THC). The paychoactive ingredient in marijuana and hashish, which are made from plants of the cannabis family.

Textual. Refers to which are a class of verbal operants controlled by visual verbal stimuli like words or symbols.

Thalamotomy. It is a form of psychosurgery wherein thalamic fibers are severed.

Thanatology. It is the study of the psychological and medical aspects surrounding death and dying.

Thanatomania. Refers to homicidal or suicidal maina or wasting away and ultimate death following awareness that one has transgressed seriously some societal taboo or believing that one has been bewitched.

Thanatophobia. Refers to morbid, pathological fear to death or an irrational fear of dead things, specially human corpses.

Thanatospy. Refers to examination following death to determine its cause, an autopsy.

Thelarche. Refers to the onset of breast development at puberty.

Thematic Apperception Test (TAT), A projective technique developed by Henry A. Murray and his co-workers. The person being tested is given a number of black-and-white pictures of various settings which are capable of being interpreted in any number of ways and is asked to tell a story about each. The stories are analyzed in terms of the *thema* which the person introduces into each narrative. The thema are, according to Murray's theory of personality. Considered to reflect deep needs, desires, fears, conflicts, etc.

Theomania. Delusionary condition wherein the individual considers that he or she is God or has, more modestly, direct, divine inspiration for thoughts and actions.

Theophobia. Refers to irrational fear of retribution from God for one's sins.

Therapeutics. Refers to any branch of science or medicine concerned with treatment and cure of disease or other abornal conditions.

Therapeutic Window. In psychopharma cology refers to the range of plasma concentration of a drug which has significant therapeutic value.

Therapy. Refers to all manners and formers of treatment of disease or disorder.

Theriomorphism. The attribution to humans of nonhuman traits which are characteristics and qualities.

Thermanalgesia. A pathological condition wherein the normal painful reaction to hot stimuli is not experienced.

Thermanesthesia. It is the insensitivity to temperature changes ; an inability to experience normal warmth and cold.

Thorndike Puzzle Box. One of the earliest (if not the earliest) pieces of laboratory apparatus specifically designed to study learning.

Thought Impulses. Refers to those aspects of dreams hypothesized to result from the ordinary stresses and experiences of everyday life.

Thought Withdrawal. It is experience which somehow one's thoughts have been taken away, from one's head.

Thurstone-type Scales. Refers to a number of scales, constructed to measure attitudes. The general procedure for constructing such scales is to take a number of statements reflecting particular attitudes with respect to some topic and have a large number of persons sort them in piles ranging from most strongly agreeing with the statement to most strongly disagreeing with it. The percentage of judges placing each statement in the various piles is calculated and forms the basis for determining the scale values assigned to each statement.

Tissue. Refers to any organic structure consisting of cells with similar structures and common functions which are organized or bound together in some manner.

Titillate. Means to excite or arouse one sexually or tickle.

T-maze. A maze shaped like a T, make up of an approach alley and two arms, either one of which the subject may choose.

Toilet training. Means, training an infant to urinate and defecate in the socially accepted place and manner.

Tolerance, drug. Refers to a condition of diminished responsiveness to a particular drug due to repeated exposure to it. Once tolerance has developed, increased, increased doses are needed to produce the effects achieved earlier with small doses.

Tomography. An X-ray technique that enables one to obtain a picture of the three dimensional structure of tissue.

Topectomy. A variation of the frontal lobotomy where in small cuts are made through the thalamofrontal tracts.

Topological psychology. A descriptive term often used of Kurt Lewin's *field theory.*

Tourette's syndrome. A neurological disorder which characterized, in mild from, by involuntary tics and movements and, in advanced cases, by large involuntary bodily movements, noises like barks and whistles, and in many instances an uncontrollable urge to utter obscenities.

Toxemla. Refers to an abnormal condition produced by toxic substances carried throughout the body by the blodstream.

Tranquilizers. Refers to any of several classes of drugs all of which have one or more of the following properties: antianxiety, sedative musclerelaxant, anticonvulsant, antiagitation. Tranquilizers generally grouped into the *minor, tranquilizers,* which are used primarily for the treatment of anxiety, and the *major tranquilizers,* which are used for the more serious psychiatric disorders like schizophrenia and bipolar disorder.

Transactional Analysis (TA). It is a form of psychotherapy developed by Eric Brene. It is practiced in a straightforward group setting wherein the primary goal is to have the client achieve an adaptive, meature and realistic attitude twoward life.

Transactonal Phychology. An extension of the basic ideas of transactionalism from the study of perception to other areas of human behavior, notably social interaction.

Transcendental Meditation (TM). It is a form of meditation and the techniques for practicing it developed and most effectively promulgated by the Maharishi Mahesh Yogi.

Transducer. Refers to any device which converts energy from one from to another.

Transvestims. It is a condition marked by a persistent desire to dress in the clothes generally considered by society as appropriate for the other sex.

Trend Test. Refers to any of several statistical tests which assess whether two or more trends seen in the data can be said to be reliable different from each other.

Triage. It is the process of screening the sick, wounded or injured in times of crisis and classifying them into three groups: those who will likely recover eventually without therapy, those who are expected to die no matter what is done to assist them and those whose recovery is deemed to depend on their receiving adequate care.

Tribadism. Means rubbing together of the genitals, particularly when both partners are female.

Trichesthesia. Refers to the tactile sensation experienced in the skin when a hair is touched or moved.

Trichomans vaginalis. A form of vaginitis charactrized by itching, redness and burning, especially around the vulva. It is caused by the Trichmonas protozoa and, although it is not linked directly with sexual intercourse, it is often classified as a venereal disease because it can be communicated through intercourse.

Trichopathophobia. A from of *trichophobia* seen in women and manifested by abnormal anxiety surrounding any growth of facial hair.

Tricyclic Compounds. A group of *antidepressant drugs* which function by preventing the re-uptake of amines in cholinergic synapses. A host of these compounds is in use although the "parent" drug *imiprmine* is the most commonly prescribed.

Tridimensional Theory of Feeling. Woundt's theory according to which all feelings could be represented as being composed of three dimensions, pleasure-displeasure, excitement-depression and tension-relaxation.

Triple-X Sydrome. A chromosomal anomaly wherein three X chromosomes are present. Such individuals are phenotypically female, sexually normal and usually fertile, although menstrual problems and early menopause are common.

Triskaidekaphobia. Refers to fear of the number that results from the operation of subtracting 1 from 14.

Troilism. Refers to deep desire to have sexual relations in the presence of others.

Tropin. Combining from used to indicate the stimulating effect of a substance on an organ or other site.

Tryptophan. An amino acid needed for normal growth and development. It functions as a precursor in the production of the inhibitory neurotransmitter *serotonin.*

T. Score. A tipe of score based on the transformation of normalized standard scores to a scale based on a mean of 50 and a standard deviation of 10.

T test. Refers to me of a number of statistical tests of significance based upon the *t* statistic.

Turing's test. It is a "test" of the adequacy of an artificial intelligence device on the question whether or not it can be said to think.

Turner's syndrome. A cromosomal anomaly in phenotypic females. The basic genetic defect is a missing sex chromosome, so that the total the count is 45, X. The syndrome is marked by short stature and absence of ovaries. With female sex hormones administered at the age of puberty, normal secondary sex characteristics appear, although the sterility cannot be corrected.

Twitch. It is a simple, spasmodic muscular contraction.

Type A Personality. A temperament characterized by excessive drive and competitiveness, an unrealistic sense of time urgency, inappropriate ambition, a reluctance to provide self-evaluation, a tendency to emphasize quantity of output over quality and a need for control.

Type B Personality. A temprament charcterized, by a relaxed easy-going approach to life, a focus on quailitv over quantity, low competitiveness and a tendency for self-reflection.

U

UCR. Abbreviation of unconditional response.

UCS. Commonly used by psychoanalysts as the shortened form of *unconscious* stimulus or mind.

U Curve. See U-*shaped curve.*

UG. Probably it has been the worst acronym ever introduced into science, it stands for *universal grammar* and would not be included here at all except that such prominent theorists as Chomsky insist upon using it.

Ulnar Muscle. Muscle on inner side of forearm, frequently used as an area for experiments in touch localization.

Ulnar Reflex. Response when tendon of bent forearm is struck ; hence not strictly a reflex.

Ulous. A suffix which means *tending toward.*

Ultra. Combining form which means *going beyond, extreme* or *excessive.*

Ultradiad Rhythms. Refers to any of the many biologic rhythms that are shorter than one day.

Ultrasonic. (Literally, *beyond sound)* Pertaining to sound waves of frequencies beyond the range of human hearing—that is, greater than 20,000 Hz.

Ultraviolet. The electromagnetic radiation the wavelength of which is shorter than that to which the normal human eye responds, *e.g.*, below roughly 400 nm.

Ululation. Animal-like groans and cries of some mental defectives, hysterical persons, and psychotics.

Umbilical Cord. The cord connecting the fetus with the p. enta.

Umweg. Round about or circuitous.

Umweg Behaviour. The detour behaviour or roundabout behaviours.

Unambivalent. (*Psychoan.*) Not opposite in kind or nature—commonly applied to two motives or affects existing in the same person, as love and respect. In contrast, love and hate for a single object, person, or group are considered *ambivalent*. See also ambivalence.

Unbiased. A term used to characterize operations or processes which display no bias, *e.g.*, decision-making that reveals no prejudices.

Unbiased Estimate. Any estimate which is made on the basis of adequate and representative sampling.

Unbiased Estimator. Any statistic which, in principle, gives a value for any sample which is an unbiased estimate of the true value in the full population. The *mean* has been an unbiased estimator.

Uncertainty. 1. Generally, refers to the state of belief when one does not fully believe, when one is unsure. 2. In information theory, refers to the degree to which there are no constraints upon the choices one has available or upon the possible outcomes of a situation.

Uncinate Hallucinations. Taste and smell hallucinations, usually unpleasant, caused by pathological condition in the uncinate gyrus of the hippocampal convolution of the temporal lobe.

Uncinate Seizures. Convulsions which are caused by organic disease in the uncinate gyrus.

Uncomplicated Bereavement. Normal reaction to the death of a loved one in the form of various expressions of sadness, guilt, depression and the like that are deemed appropriate to one's experiences and interactions with the deceased while alive.

Unconditioned Response or Reflex. A response evoked by a stimulus without the necessity of learning. Thus, salivation to food is a natural, unlearned response that occurs at the beginning of a conditioning series, before learning trials have been initiated. Salivation to the sound of the bell, by contrast, is a *conditioned response*, dependent upon learning.

Unconditioned Stimulus. A stimulus that evokes a response without the necessity of learning or conditioning. In the example provided by Pavlov's dog-food-bell experiment, the food is the unconditioned stimulus, whereas the bell is the conditioned stimulus.

Unconscious. A loose term connoting activities which proceed without concomitant awareness, such as digestion, pupilary reflexes, or heart beats. In the older discussions of habit, references were made to the automaticity of well-established habits, no conscious control being considered necessary to maintain them. The adjective has a mentalistic connotation ; hence it is not used by objectivists.

Unconscious Cerebration. Thinking that occurs without awareness.

Unconscious Cognitive Process. Generally, any process which involves thinking, reasoning, judging, problem-solving, etc. which takes place without consciousness, without awareness.

Unconscious Drive. An in drive or need.

Unconscious Inference. A judgment that is not verbalized but is acted upon withous awareness.

Unconscious Knowledge. Knowledge that a person is not aware of possessing, knowledge that is *tacit.*

Unconscious Memory. (*Psychoan.*) Repressions ; memories that have been forced out of the conscious level of mind into the unconscious.

Unconscious Mind. A troublesome and controversial term used, metaphorically, by psychoanalysts to subsume the basic drives, repressed ideas, and unwelcome impulses ; it is the part of the psyche in which the id reigns supreme and which is dominated by the pleasure principle Free associations and dream analyses are said, by psychoanalysts, to be the royal road into the unconscious mind.

Unconscious Motivation. Motivation of which the individual has been unaware. For example, the individual may forget an unpleasant appointment, convinced that it was a mere accident. The depth psychologist believes that it is revealing of a wish to forget.

Unconsciousness. Refers to the state of being ***unconscious.***

Uncontrolled. Referring to variables not regulated or held constant by the experimenter.

Underachievement. Performance that does not measure up to the individual's level of aptitude.

Underachiever. A person who does not perform at the level which is indicated by his aptitude.

Underdetermined. Of situations in which there has been insufficient evidence, data or information to determine a value or the correct alternative in a set of choices, etc.

Undergeneralization. The term used for the use of a word for a smaller and more specialized category of objects, events or circumstances than it is normally used for. Such ***underextensions***, as they are also called, have been common in young children, for example restricting the label "kitty" to but one cat.

Underproductive. (*Rorschach*) Refers to unusually poor responses to the inkblots.

Understand. To comprehend, to appreciate the deep meaning of a thing or a process.

Understanding. 1. Refers to the process of apprehending meaning. 2. In historical writings, refers to the faculty by means of which the individual apprehends meaning. 3. Sympathy ; feeling for another's poins of view.

Underweight. Refers to a condition in which body weight is 10% or more below the norms for a person's body type and age.

Undifferentiated. Refers to tissues that have not yet developed into characteristic forms and structures according to their hereditary potential.

Undistributed Middle, Fallacy of. An argument which leads to an invalid conclusion because of the use of a premise that is not distributed. For example, given that "All Communists are atheists" and "Max is an atheist" to conclude that "Max is a Communist", would be to fall prey to the fallacy. To rescue the syllogism one would need to have an additional premise such as, "All atheists are members of the Communist party." The obviously fallacious aspects are shown if the syllogism takes a more blatant form such as : "Max is a man," "Sam is a man," therefore, "Max is Sam."

Undoing The process whereby, according to psychoanalysts, the unconscious mind seeks to wipe out painful thoughts and memories.

Unfinished Business. Uncompleted tasks which do not get terminated with a desired degree of finality from the subject's point of view, and which become objects of continuing unpleasant concern or tension.

Unfolding. Refers to a type of ***multidimensional scaling*** developed by Clyde Coombs. The technique has been based on having a subject rank order a number of stimuli according to preference. The resulting preference ordering reflects an ideal point and the individual preferences are then "unfolded" mathematically to display the locations of the scaled objects in any number of dimensions relative to the ideal point.

Uni. Combining form which means *one, singular.*

Uniaural. Refers to a single ear, *monaural* (preferred).

Unicellular Organisms. Those which have but a single cell. *Protozoa.*

Unidextrous. Preferring one hand over the other for most actions. Also called *handedness.*

Uniformity. In social psychology, refers to a condition in which there occurs widespread ("uniform") agreement concerning some belief, practice or fact.

Unilateral. Affecting or pertaining to one side. Opposite of *bilateral.*

Unimodal. A frequency curve with a single mode or peak.

Unintentional Act. According to psychoanalysts, an act which, though consciously unintended, really expresses an unconscious wish.

Unintentional Humor. Psychoanalytic theory which holds that amusing slips of tongue are releases for unconscious, repressed tensions. The humor, usually having double meaning, resolves or reveals thwarted sex trends. Condensation and displacement occur in unintentional humor, just as they do in dreams.

Uniocular. Refers to a single eye ; *monocular* (preferred).

Unipolar Cell (or Neuron). A neuron having a single stalk leading from the soma. This neural process branches with the dendrites at one end and the axonal terminals at the other.

Unigue Factor. A factor found in only one test of correlation matrix. *Syn.* specific factor.

Unique Trait. 1. A personality trait which is found only in a single individual, 2. a trait that shows a zero correlation with all other traite being measured.

Unitary Trait A pattern of behaviour that functions as a whole.

Unisexual. Characteristic of a species in which each individual organism has been either male or female but not both.

Unit. 1. One of something which is taken as a whole, a datum. 2. A standard amount which is used as the basis of measurement.

Unitary Type. An individual whose afterimages, memory images, and eidetic images are similar in type.

Unit Character. In genetics, a biological characteristic that if transmitted to an offspring, appears as a whole, not partially.

Unity. 1. The state of consisting of one element, without parts or divisions, 2. harmony or concord in literary or artistic works, 3. a totality or whole.

Univariate. Having but one variable. An experiment using only one variable may be called a *univariate study*, although the term *single-factor study* (or *experiment*) is more common.

Universal. 1. adj. Refers to *universe* in any of that term's meanings. 2. adj. Refers to those underlying aspects or characteristics of human beings, their psychological make-up, their modes of thought, action and affect, that have been presumed to be common among all despite the vast observed array of manifestations of them. 3. n. Any one of those aspects which are assumed to be universal. 4. n. In logic, a proposition which is predicated of all members of a class.

Universal Complex. Any complex derived from any instinct.

Universalism. In sociology, refers to an approach to social theory in which standards of conduct are determined according to sets of principles assumed to reflect universal ethical standards. In this approach the tendency has been to disregard mitigating circumstances or individual contexts.

Universality. The property of being *universal*, in any of that term's meanings.

Universals. A term which is used collectively for any of those aspects of the human condition that the user is asserting are *universal*.

Universals, Linguistic. Refer to those linguistic aspects that are common to all *natural languages*. These hypothesized universals have been usually viewed as being of two types, *substantive universals*, which are common aspects of description of natural languages such as distinctive features, catalogs of word classes, sets of semantic features, etc., and *formal universals*, which represent the nature of generative rules found in natural languages, such as transformations.

Universe. 1. Most generally, refers to all things everywhere taken as a totality. 2. More specifically, also refers to a collection of things, taken together according to some defining features(s) or characteristic(s). This meaning is close to that of *set* (1).

Universe of Discourse. Refers to the full set of things under consideration in a given discussion, study or experiment.

Universe, Statistical. Refers to the full population from which samples are drawn and about which inferences from the samples are made.

Unlearned. Refers to behavior that does not depend upon practice or experience for its appearance. However, all behavior is modified by learning and is dependent upon environmental conditions ; hence, the term *unlearned* is somewhat misleading.

Unlearning. A deliberate attempt to overcome the effect of previous learning—usually attempted in the case of undesirable habits.

Unnatural. Contrary to nature. The term is popular rather than scientific.

Unobtrusive Procedure. A general term for any research technique for gathering data without the individuals (persons or animals) being observed becoming aware of the procedures.

Unpack. A term borrowed from the computer sciences where it refers to the recovery of original data that have been stored (or "packed") with other data. It is used as a metaphor for the process of retrieval of specific memories from a large store of other memories and knowledge.

Unpleasant. Characterizing experiences that are disagreeable and which the subject would like to avoid.

Unpleasantness. (*Titchener*) with pleasantness, one of two poles of feeling or affective tone. Unpleasantness is characterized by dislike and ambient behavior ; pleasantness by adient behavior.

Unpleasure. Refers to the emotional experience that results from the exposure to stimuli that are *unpleasant*. This experience has been usually treated as basic and primitive and resistant to conscious, introspective analysis.

Unproductive Mania. Excitement and hyperactivity without the flight of ideas which usually accompanies mania.

Unreality, Sense (or Feeling) of. A feeling that things experienced are somehow not "real" or not "right". When it occurs occasionally in normal living it is usually interpreted as a failure to be able to integrate an experience with one's previous knowledge of things—and, indeed, the feeling occurs most often when encountering strange or novel situations. When it takes place frequently or continuously it is regarded as pathological.

Unreflective. Impulsive. With respect to cognitive style.

Unreliability. Ant. of *reliability* in any of the meanings of that term.

Unresolved. Generally, of conflicts or problems not yet worked out or "resolved". This meaning occurs in cognitive psychology with respect to problems not solved or decisions not made and in psychotherapeutic discourse for psychological problems or conflicts with which the client has not yet come to grips.

Unselected. A term which is used occasionally to characterize a sample that was drawn from a population strictly at random.

Unsocial or Unsociable. 1. Characterizing one who avoids the company of others or does not seek others out. 2. Characterizing one who does not fit into the social system.

Unspaced Practice. Refers to learning situations in which no rest periods are given between trials.

Unstable. 1. Unpredictable in behavior, particularly in moods, attitudes, or emotional behavior. 2. Suffering from intermittent periods of mental disorder. 3. Unreliable.

Unstressed. In linguistics, a syllable which receives minimal accentuation in a word, *e.g.*, the *-er-* in *brotherhood.*

Unstriated Muscles. Smooth muscles ; often called the involuntary muscles.

Unstructed Interview. Refers to interview in which the topics to be covered have been left unspecified at the outset and things are left to the unfolding interaction between the persons involved in the interview.

Unweighted. Refers to scores that have not been multiplied by a constant before being combined with other scores.

Up-and-down Method. In psychophysics, refers to a variation on the *method of limits* in which the ascending stimulus sequence is shifted to descending as soon as the subject changes response category and vice versa. Also termed as the *staircase method.*

Upper Category. In the method of single stimuli in psychophysical experiments, a class of reports that will outnumber other reports as the stimulus magnitude is increased.

"Uppers" (or "Ups"). Street slang for any drug which is having stimulating, arousing effects. Most of these drugs have been *amphetamines* or amphetamine-derived.

Upper Threshold. Refers to the upper bound of sensitivity for a particular stimulus dimension.

Upset. Loss of complacency. The drive to action is an upset in the optimum balance ; the end or goal of behavior is the drive to maintain or regain balance.

UR. Abbreviation of *unconditioned response.*

Ur. A prefix from the German which means *original* or *primitive.* Used roughly synonymously with *proto.*

Uranism. Homosexuality, Karl Heinrichs coined the term in 1862, denoting the male homosexual *uraning* and the female *urinde.*

Uresis. Passing urine.

Urethra. The tube which runs from the bladder through which urine is passed.

Urethral Complex. H.A. Murray's hypothesized syndrome involving urinal soiling, enuresis and urethral eroticism. Murray regarded it as a minor complex but theorized that it might be related to the *Icarus complex.*

Urethral Eroticism. Sexual pleasure by the male in urination. According to psychoanalysts, the male can experience greater pleasure from the act because the urethra is about 8 to 9 inches long in the male ; in the female, it is only about 1½ inches long.

Urge. Non-technical term for any strong desire.

Urethral Eroticism. (*Psychoan*) The centering of sexual feeling in the urethra.

Urning. A male homosexual who takes the role of a woman toward other males.

Urolagnia. The association of sexual excitement with urination or urine.

Urophilia. A *paraphilia* characterized by the deriving of erotic stimulation from the smell or taste of urine or from the viewing of a person urinating, to the extent that such stimulation has been necessary for maintaining arousal and to achieve orgasm. Also called *urolagnia* and *undinism.*

US. Abbreviation of *unconditioned stimulus.*

Use, Law of. The generalization that, all other factors being equal, an association that is practiced will be strengthened.

User. Lit , one who uses a thing. The most common reference has been to one who takes a drug, with the connotation that it is taken excessively.

Uterine. Pertaining to the *uterus.*

Uterine Fantasy. In psychoanalysis, any fantasy which is associated with the uterus, the most common being a fantasy about returning to the womb with its warmth and protection.

Uterus. The womb. In mammals, the female organ in which the embryo is contained and nourished during gestation.

U Test. A nonparametric test for the significance of differences between means and unmatched groups.

Utility. 1. The fitness of an organ or of a genetic modification in terms of biological survival value. In general, the practical usefulness of a test or discovery.

Utilization. 1. Generally, the use to which something is put or its useful value. 2. In studies of *feeding behavior*, the variety of physiological processes involved in the consumption of food, including digestion, absorption, metabolism and excretion.

Utopia. The ideal society. Taken from Thomas More's 1516 work of the same name, the term refers to any visionary system of social, political and personal perfection. Various persons since More have had their hand in utopian prescriptions, the American behaviorist, B.F. Skinner being among them.

Utricle. The saclike structure of the inner ear containing the receptors that react to changes in head position.

Utterance. Very generally, a unit of speech or of talk. An utterance may be anything from a single simple vocal sound ("uh-huh") to an extended, multisentence discourse. Determining exactly where a particular utterance begins and ends is no easy matter.

Uvula. The term used for the soft structure that hangs from the back of the soft palate in the midline of the mouth.

V

V 1. Variable stimulus (also *v.*) **2.** ⇒*Variance.* 3. *Photopic luminosity coefficient* ; var. (3), $V\lambda$.

V 1. Variable stimulus (also *V*). **2.** Volume. 3. Volt.

Vaccinate. To produce immunity to a disease by inoculation.

Vacuum Activity. Refers to the occurrence of a *fixed action pattern* in the absence of its usual external stimulus (or *releaser*). The assumption has been that *action-specific energy* builds up, breaks through the inhibitory function of the *innate releasing mechanism* and causes the fixed action pattern to occur spontaneously. A classic example is the darting.

Vacuum Activity. Behavior which occurs in the absence of apropriate stimuli and believed by ethologists to be the result of a high drive state.

Vagina. The passage which is leading from the uterus to the exterior of the body.

Vaginismus or Vaginism. A painful and involuntary contraction of the muscles which is associated with the vagina. The disorder may prevent coitus and is believed to be the result of psychological factors.

Vagitus. The term used for the first crying of a newborn.

Vagotomy. A sectioning of the vagus nerve.

Vagotonia. Condition of vasomotor instability which is caused by overaction of the vagus nerve.

Vagus Nerve. The Xth *cranial nerve.* A mixed nerve with widely distributed afferent and efferent branches, it innervates the external ear, pharynx, larynx, lunds, heart kidneys, spleen, liver, stomach and intestines.

Valence. (*Lewin*) psychological attractiveness of objects. Positive valence signifies attractiveness ; negative valence. unattractiveness.

Valence Substitute. The valence which is associated with an object that has, for any number of possible reasons, come to serve as a substitute for an original but unreached object.

Valid. Denoting the circumstances in which, by the principles of logic, a statement has been unambiguously implied by the premises.

Validation 1. Refers to the process of determining whether a measuring instrument measures what it had been designed to measure. 2. More generally, refers to the process of establishing the objective proof of a proposition, process, measuring instrument, etc.

Validity. Refers to the characteristic of a proposition, logical argument, etc., that it is founded on truth or is consistent with law or fact. 2. Refers to the property of a measuring device that it measures in fact what it is intended to measure. Validity could be established by correlating the results of the test with an outside criterion or independent measure. If the test has been designed to measure aptitude for medical school, then it should correlate highly with grades earned in medical school.

Validity Coefficient. Refers to the correlation coefficient between a measuring instrument and an outside or independent measure of the function that the test was designed to measure. If those who stand high on the test stand high on the outside criterion, and those who stand low on the test are low on the outside criterion, the test is valid. Most investigators believe that a coefficient of .70 or higher is necessary for a single test to show validity. If a battery of tests is being used, a multiple correlation of .50 may be worthwhile as a predictor, particular if large numbers of cases are involved.

Validity Criterion. An outside or independent measure of what a test has been designed to measure. The correlation between the test and the criterion is taken as an index of the test's validity.

Valium. A trade name for diazepam, a tranquilizer.

Value. 1. Refers to a quantitative measure of score. 2. The worth or excellence of anything. 3. A social end or goal considered desirable of achievement. 4. In color descriptions, brilliance.

Value Analysis. Refers to a type of content analysis in which the proportion of expressions referring to a certain value get tabulated.

Value Judgment. A reaction to persons, objects, aesthetic products, etc., in terms of their value or worth, as opposed to their objective characteristics.

1. Property of being true, correct, in conformity with reality. This meaning, common in ordinary parlance, is typically *not* intended in the technical literature. 2. In logic the property of an argument or conclusion that it is deemed to be ⇒ *valid* because it conforms with proper, logical principles. The fundamental notion here is that the reasoning process itself must be correct; an argument may have validity in this sense and not correspond with reality but the fault will lie with assumptions and not the reasoning process. ⇔ *logic.* 3. In testing, the property of any measuring instrument, device or test that it measures what it purports to measure. Validity here is not a simple notion and it is not a simple "either-or"

property as in sense 2 and to some extent in sense 1. In the field to tests and measurements a large number of procedures has been developed to assess the validity of testing instruments, the most widely used to which are given below.

Validity, a Priori A kind of preliminary, intuitive estimate of the ⇒ *content *validity* of a test. The degree to which the items on the test seem to have an intuitive. a priori relationship to the behaviors that are assumed to be being tested. Also called *common-sense validity.*

Validity Coefficient Of. An index of test's ⇒ *validity* (3) ; the coefficient of correlation between the scores on the test and a set of ⇒ *criterion scores* which are taken as reflective of the variable(s) the test is purported to measure. For example, for a test designed to assess scholastic aptitude the correlation would be between the test scores and academic performance as assessed by grade-point average (the criterion scores) and it would provide a measure of the test's validity.

Validity, Common-sense. ⇒ *a priori *validity.*

Validity, Concurrent. A kind of ⇒ *criterion-related *validity* in which the relationship between the test scores and the criterion scores is established at the same time. Although similar in spirit to ⇒ *predictive validity,* the procedure really uses "post-diction" rather than "prediction." For example, one way of evaluating the validity of, say, a test for clerical skills would be to see how scores on the test correlate with the known "new math."

Validity, Convergent and Discriminant. The degree to which any particular testing instrument has validity will reflect the extent to which scores on the test (*a*) correlate highly with factors that they, in principle, should correlate highly with, and (*b*) correlate poorly with factors that they, in principle, should correlate poorly with. *Convergent validity* is manifested by the former ; *discriminant validity* by the latter.

Validity, Criterion. The independent measure that a given test is designed to assess. See the discussion under ⇒ *criterion-related *validity.*

Validity, Criterion-related. Validity of a testing instrument assessed by determining the relationships between scores on the test and some independent, nontest criterion ; ⇒ *concurrent *validity* and ⇒ *predictive *validity* are examples here. Also called *external *validity* ⇒ *empirical *validity.*

Validity, Definitional. In principle, validity of a test that is given by the fact that the items comprising it up are, by definition, items that reflect the aspects being measured. A glance at the entry for ⇒ *definition(s)* should alert one to the fact that, in practice, there is more to this notion than meets the eye. See and compare with ⇒ *construct *validity.*

Validity, Differential. The validity of a test battery as assessed by its ability to predict differences in performance on two (or more) criteria.

Validity, Discriminant. ⇒ *convergent and discriminant *validity.*

Validity, Ecological. ⇒ *ecological validity.*

Validity, Empirical. The validity of a test as determined by empirical means ; the degree to which the test actually works with real cases in a real sample of individual subjects. A common procedure here is to calculate a ⇒ *coefficient of *validity* based on a set of criterion scores ; see here ⇒ *criterion-related *validity.*

Validity, External. ⇒ *criterion-related *validity.*

Validity, Face. Validity assessed by having "experts" review the contents of a test to see if they seem appropriate "on their face." It really is a rather fuzzy procedure for validating a test, and, because of inherent subjectivity, is typically used only during the initial phases of test construction. Note that, while face validity seems superficially similar to ⇒ *content *validity,* the procedures are quite different, the latter being a systematic procedure, the former closer to ⇒ *a priori *validity.*

Validity, Factorial. A type of ⇒ *construct *validity* whereby several tests purported to measure the same underlying traits or constructs are factor-analyzed to determine whether they share common variance and thus can be said to be tapping the same underlying constructs.

Validity, Incremental. With respect to various tests of personality, the amount of additional, valid information provided by a test beyond that obtained by other procedures.

Validity, Internal. An informal procedure for determining the validity of a test by looking over each item and assessing the degree to which it is fulfilling its intended role in the test.

Validity, Intrinsic. Validity of a testing instrument based on the items of the test manifestly displaying the fact that they are

clerical skills of a group of clerks whose performance has been evaluated in actual working conditions. Also called ***status validity.***

Validity, Congruent. A method of establishing the validity of a new test by correlating scores from it with scores from another test of established validity. The most typical case here is in intelligence testing, where newly developed tests are compared with the well-known tests like the Stanford-Binet or the Wechsler.

Validity, Consensual. An informal procedure for assessing validity based upon the notion of consensus ; that is, it the more persons who concur in a proposition, the more likely is to be valid or the more persons who agree on a perception the more probable that it is real. The term is rarely used in tests and measurements research ; it is typically found in social psychology to characterize the principle that systamatic support of a particular position grants a greater acceptability to others. ⇒ ***consensual validation.***

Validity, Construct. A set of procedures for evaluating the validity of a testing instrument based on the determination of the degree to which the test items capture the hypothetical quality or trait (*i.e.*, *construct*) it was designed to measure. Thus, for example, if a test is supposed to provide a measure of intelligence one should ask : (*a*) What traits or qualities (constructs) actually characterize intelligence ? And (*b*) do the test items actually tap such constructs ? The initial stages of test construction are usually concerned with construct validity. Note that it provides neither a quantitative nor a static measure of validity unlike measures that depend on a ⇒ ***correlation of *validity,*** there are no mathematical bases for determining validity and unlike measures that depend on known patterns of behavior (*e.g.*, ⇒ ***criterion-related *validity***) the estimates of construct validity is always changing with the accumulation of further evidence about the traits and qualities that underlie the construct. ⇒ ***contant *validity,*** of which it is but one form.

Validity, Content. An estimate of the validity of a testing instrument based on a detailed examination of the contents of the test items. By contents here is meant the actual constituent materials of the test items ; the evaluation of them is carried out by reviewing each item to determine whether it is appropriate to the test and by assessing the overall cohesiveness of the several test items. For example, a test of mathematical abilities, in order to have a respectable level of content validity, should not phrase the items in such a way that verbal abilities are critical for the person taking the test to understand what is being asked. Further, the contents should be balanced so that all tested aspects are represented appropriately; the test should not be overloaded with, say, multiplication items to the neglect of addition items.

Establishing content validity is a largely subjective operation and relies on the judgments of "experts" concerning the relevance of the materials used. It is also situation-specific and estimates made in one circumstance may not carry over to others. For example, a test of arithmetic skills developed and content validated for a traditional school may have very low content validity if applied to a school using the so-called indeed evaluating the designated trait. For example, an item that asks the testee to spell a word is an intrinsically valid item on a test of spelling ability. ⇒ *a priori *validity* and *face *validity.*

Validity, Nomological. A variation of ⇒ *canstruct *validity* that derives from the argument that construct validity actually involves two separate endeavors : one that focuses on validating the constructs or traits (often called *trait validity*) and one that is concerned with validating the test within a larger theoretical framework—this latter is known as *nomological validity.*

Validity, Predictive. A type of ⇒ *empirical *validity* based on determining the extent to which the scores on a test are predictive of actual performance. A test designed to measure, say, clerical skills will have high predictive validity if it predicts who will and will not succeed in crerical jobs. Compare with ⇒ *concurrent *validity.*

Validity, Sampling. A variety of ⇒ *content *validity* based on an assessment of the extent to which the various traits assumed to underlie what is being measured are represented in the test. It is, in practice, more of a control procedure to guard against introducing a bias into a test than a real measure of the test's validity.

Validity, Status. ⇒ *concurrent *validity.*

Validity, Synthetic. Validity of a complex testing instrument or of a full test battery based on the relationship between a composite score that is taken to represent the various factors that are represented on the test and actual performance. The term derives from the notion that one has synthesized many elements or factors into a single value.

Validity, Trait. A component of the larger process of establishing *construct *validity*, the determination of the extent to which the underlying traits the test is presumably measuring are indeed being measured. Compare with ⇒ *nomological *validity.*

Valium. ⇒ *diazepam.*

Value. 1 n. The quality or property of a thing that makes it useful, desired or esteemed, Note the pragmatic aspect implied by this definition ; the value of a thing is given by its role in a (social) transaction, the thing itself does not posses value. 2 n. An abstract and general principle concerning the patterns of behavior within a particular culture or society which through the process of socialization, the members of that society hold in high regard. These *social values*, as they are often called, form central principles around which individual and societal goals can become integrated. Classic examples are freedom, justice, education, etc. 3 n. In economics, the net worth of a thing as determined by what it will bring in exchange, either in other goods or in some medium of exchange – usually money. This meaning. combined with 1 above, is very close to the meaning of the term ⇒ *utility*, especially 3. 4 n. In mathematics, a quantity or magnitude as represented by a number. 5 n. In the Munsell system for classifying colors, the position along the brightness dimension. 6 vb. To assess the worth of a thing. 7 vb. To hold something in esteem based upon one's evaluation of it.

Value, Absolute. A number or ⇒ *value* (4) expressed without regard to its sign. The absolute value of -3 is the same as $+3$ and is denoted as $|3|$.

Value Analysis. A type of *content analysis* which focuses on the tabulation of the frequency with which particular values are expressed in the message.

Value Judgement. A perspective toward a person, object, principle, etc. based on how one values the properties or characteristics thereof.

Values Clarification. A variation on moral education which emphasizes awareness and clarification of moral judgements and ethical considerations. Compare with *values education.*

Values Education. An aspect of education focusing on specific instruction in moral and ethical values in society. The term is usually associated with the work of L. Kohlberg on *moral development*, which is based on the assumption that some moral positions are inherently better than others. Hence, the educational curriculum here is oriented toward raising the child's level of morality. Compare with *values clarification.*

Value, Social. *Value* (2).

Value System. Loosely, any reasonably coherent set of values. They may be treated as individual, societal or absolute.

Value, True. *True score.*

Variability. The characteristic of being subject to change whether continuous or discontinuous. In descriptive statistics, the common measures of variability are the standard deviation, average deviation, and the range.

Variability Coefficient. See variation coefficient.

Variable. 1. A quantity that may increase or decrease. 2. A factor dependent upon other factors. See independent variable; dependent variable.

Variable Error. The deviation of a measure from the mean. Variable errors occur on either side of the mean. Their extent may be predicted by the measures of dispersion, but they cannot be corrected. *Syn.* chance error. *Contr.* constant error.

Variable Interval Reinforcement. Reinforcement delivered according to a random sequence of time intervals. Typically the intervals lie between prearranged arbitrary values with a fixed mean. *Contr.* fixed interval reinforcement.

Variable Ratio Reinforcement. A type of intermittent reinforcement in which the animal is given reinforcement, such as a pellet of food, after a certain number of responses, the number of responses varying from trial to trial but lying between arbitrary values with a fixed average.

Variable Stumulus. In psychological experiments, any one of the set of stimuli that are systematically compared with a constant stimulus.

Variance. The square of the standard deviation employed as a measure of the extent to which individual scores in a set of scores differ from each other. *Syns.* mean-square deviation: mean-square error.

Variate. The value of a variable.

Variation. 1. Change in condition. 2. A difference. 3. Biological differences between organisms. 4, Differences among statistical constants.

Variation Coefficient. A measure of relative variability given by the formula $V=\frac{100\sigma}{M}$

Variation Tone. The tone heard when the source of sound is interrupted rapidly.

Vas. A duct.

Vascular. 1. Pertaining to blood vessels. 2. Characterizing tissue richly endowed with blood vessels.

Vascular Theory or Thermal Sensitivity. (*Nafe*) The theory that thermal sensations are correlated with changes in the constriction and dilation of arterioles and veinules.

Vasoconstriction. The constriction or closing of the diameter of a blood vessel.

Vasodilation. The opening or enlargement of the diameter of a blood vessel.

Vasomotor. Pertaining to vasoconstriction and vasodilation.

Vasopressin. A hormone produced by the posterior pituitary gland that increases blood pressure and decreases the production of urine.

Vector. 1. A directed line or magnitude. 2. In field theory, a symbol of motivation or a representation of a force that causes locomotion toward or away from an incentive. 3. In statistics, the representation of a score by means of a line having direction and length.

Vector Field. (*Lewin*) A field in which there is direction and magnitude of all forces (vectors). Vectors, or directed lines, represent motivational forces in field theory.

Vector Psychology. (*Lewin*) an analysis of motivation or dynamic psychology with the use of vectors. Vector theory is a part of topology or field theory.

Veg. A psychophysical unit of measurement in a scale for perceived weight constructed by the method of equal-appearing intervals.

Vegetative 1. Pertaining to plants or the growth of plants. 2. pertaining to physiological activities such as respiration, digestion, growth, etc.

Vegetative Nervous System. The autonomic nervous system.

Vegetative Neurosis. (*Psychoan.*) A neurosis expressed as a disturbance of the vegetative functions.

Veith-Muller Circle. A circle centered at the visual origin for a set of points at a constant visual distance.

Velocity. The rate of motion in a given direction.

Ventral. Pertaining to the anterior or abdominal side of the body. *Contr*, dorsal.

Ventricle. 1. Any one of the cavities within the brain that form a continuous channel for the flow of the cerebrospinal fluids. 2. One of the chambers within the heart. 3. More generally, any cavity within an organ of the body.

Verbal. Pertaining to words in any form—oral, written, printed, etc.

Verbal Generalization. 1. A universal or widely held principle. 2. In verbal conditioning, stimulus generalization ; that is, responding in the same way to words with the same general meaning.

Verbal Image. A representation in verbal terms of a memory or remembered object.

Verbal Intelligence. The ability to deal effectively with words and symbols, the ability to solve problems utilizing verbal symbols. *Contr.* concrete intelligence.

Verbalism. 1. Undue reliance on words in thinking, without reference to what lies behind the words. 2. Uncritical acceptance of definitions in place of explanations.

Verbalization. 1. A statement or expression in the form of words. 2. Expressing oneself in words instead of action. 3. wordiness ; verbosity.

Verbal Learning. The learning of lists or words, nonsense syllables, etc. Verbal learning is often contrasted with conditioning, maze learning, and perceptual-motor learning.

Verbal Scale-test. A scale that utilizes words in the administration and taking of the test. *Contr.* performance test.

Verbal Summator. A projective technique in which an instrument produces low-intensity vowel sounds in response to which the subject is asked to tell what words he hears.

Verbigeration. A pathological condition characterized by meaningless and stereotyped repetition of words.

Verbomania. Pathological volubility that is typically incoherent. *Syn.* logorrhea.

Verbone. (*Murray*) a verbal action pattern.

Vergence. Any truning movement of the eyeballs.

Veridical. Corresponding to objective reality.

Verification. 1. The collecting of empirical data for the purpose of testing a hypothesis. 2. One of the states of creative or artistic thinking in which the thinker evaluates the results.

Vermis. The median connecting lobe of the cerebellum.

Vernacular. The everyday, colloquial speech of a group of persons or in a circumscribed area.

Vernier. A small, finely graduated scale used as an auxiliary scale to give a measuring device greater adjustment accuracy.

Vernier acuity. *Acuity, vernier.*

Vertebra. Any one of the 33 bony segments of the *spinal column*, pl., *vertebrae* ; adj., *vertebral.*

Vertex. 1. Generally, the top or summit of something. 2. In anatomy, the uppermost peak of the head. 3. In geometry, the point furthest from the base. adj., *vertical.*

Vertical. 1. Pertaining to the vertex, specifically the uppermost point of a thing. 2. By extension, pertaining to the line or plane perpendicular to the ground or to the base of an object. 3. Upright.

Vertical Decalage. *Decalage.*

Vertical Group. *Group, vertical.*

Vertical Growth. *Growth, vertical.*

Vertical Mobility. Mobility between social or occupational classes. The term covers movement up or down in the social system, but it is most commonly used with the connotation of upward movement. Also called *vertical social mobility.*

Vertical Sampling. *Sampling, vertical.*

Vertigo. 1. Loosely, dizziness. 2. Technically, an inappropriate sensation of bodily movement (*subjective vertigo*) or object movement (*objective vertigo*) caused by disturbances of the sensory mechanism for equilibrium. Mostly it is result of middle-ear disease but it also occurs in toxic conditions (*e.g.*, excessive alcohol intake).

Vesanic. Loosely, pertaining to insanity, particularly to clearly marked psychoses.

Vesicle. Generally, any small sac containing fluid.

Vesicle, Seminal. Either of the two sacs at the base of the bladder which store semen.

Vesicle, Synaptic. *Synaptic, vesicle.*

Vessel. Generally, any duct, tube or canal through which flows some bodily fluid.

Vestibular Apparatus. The bony cavity in the labyrinth of the inner ear, including the two vestibular sacs (the *utricle* and the *saccule*) and the three *semicircular canals*. See each for details on how the system functions as the sensory mechanism for the perception of head position, acceleration and deceleration. *vestibule* (2), which is occasionally used as a synonym.

Vestibular Canal. *Scala vestibuli.*

Vestibular Nerve. *Auditory nerve.*

Vestibule. 1. Generally, any small cavity at the front of a canal. 2. Specifically, the middle part of the inner ear in front of the semicircular canals containing the utricle and saccule. Occasionally the term is used to include the whole of the *vestibular apparatus*, which see for details.

Vestibulocochlear Nerve. *Auditory nerve.*

Vestige. 1. Generally, a thing that in its present form is a degenerate or imperfect representation of a fully developed form which existed in the past. 2. Specifically, in biology, an organ or organ part showing such characteristics.

Vexierversuch. The original German term for what is known as a *catch trial.*

VI. Abbrev. for *variable interval.* See the discussion under *schedules of reinforcement.*

Viable. 1. Of an organism, likely to live. 2. Of a seed or spore, likely to germinate. 3. Metaphorically, characterizing a theory or a hypothesis likely to stand up under stringent experimental test.

VIB. Abbrev. for *vocational interest blank,* most frequently the reference is to the *Strong Vocational Interest Blank.*

Vibration. Generally, periodic motion of matter. A full vibration cycle is from a given point through the full cycle and back to the original point, as in a sine wave, *vibration rate.*

Vibration, Forced (or Induced or Sympathetic). *Resonance* (1).

Vibration Frequency. *Vibration rate.*

Vibration Rate. The frequency of vibrations per unit of time (usually seconds). The years have witnessed several changes in the official notation used with respect to the rate of vibrating stimuli. Originally, a full vibration cycle was called a *double vibration* (or *d.v.*) and references to frequency of vibrations (as, for example, in the measurement of tones) were noted as *d.v.s.* (double vibrations per sound). Later this rather cumbersome system was simplified to *cycle* and frequency was abbreviated as *cps* (cycles per second). Today the term of choice for vibrations per second is *Hertz*, abbreviated *Hz* ; see that entry for details.

Vibratory Sense. A hypothesized sense that was assumed to have its own receptors and neural conduction system and which responded to a vibrating source. Most physiological psychologists now feel that it is not a separate sense but an aspect of other skin senses and is best thought of as rapidly moving *pressure* on the skin.

Vicarious. Pertaining to a substitute. May be used in the sense of a mother attempting to obtain substitutive satisfaction from her daughter's social activities, or in connection with brain mechanisms where one part of the brain may function in place of another that has been injured.

Vicarious Function. The substitution of one psychological process for another.

Vicarious Trial and Error. The substitution of mental performance for overt performance. The average chess player engages in a good deal of vicarious trial and error before making a move.

Viennese School. Freud's followers in the theory and practice of psychoanalysis.

Vierordt's Law. The principle that the more mobile the part of the body, the lower the two-point threshold.

Viewing Angle. The angle formed by the line of regard from the eye to an observed surface.

Viewing Conditions. Stimulus, retinal, and surrounding factors at the time of making a visual observation.

Vigilance Function. See arousal.

Vigotsky Test. A concept-formation test that requires the subject to sort out blocks of various shapes, colors, and sizes.

Vincent Curve. A group curve constructed by a technique for making comparable the learning curves of different subjects by dividing the individual curves into equal fractions (such as fifths or sixths) and averaging the results, on the assumption that an equal fraction of the total time or trials is equivalent from one individual to another.

Vineland Social Maturity Scale. A rating scale of maturity, based on samples of behavior characteristic of individuals at specified ages.

Violet. The visual sensation aroused by wavelengths of about 433 nm and shorter.

Viraginity. The characteristic in a woman of being like a man.

Virile. Having the qualities of the mature male ; manly.

Virile Reflex. The erection of the penis in the male.

Virilism. The development in a woman of the secondary sexual characteristics of the male.

Virtue. The habit of conforming to the moral code, particularly in regard to sexual matters.

Virulent. 1. Pertaining to the olfactory sensation represented by the odor of morphine, 2. Deadly or poisonous : destructive.

Viscera. The organs enclosed in the abdominal and thoracic cavities.

Visceral. 1. Pertaining to the viscera. 2. Pertaining to the functioning of the organs that make up the viscera.

Visceral Drive. A drive orginating in a physiological need.

Visceral Sense. The organic sense ; a sensation arising from the viscera.

Visceroreceptor. A receptor of the visceral organs.

Viscerogenic. Having its origin in the viscera.

Viscerotonia. See Sheldon's constitutional theory of personality.

Visibility. 1. In a short range of electromagnetic or radiant energy, the property of being capable of exciting the retinal receptors. 2. the property of being easily seen.

Visibility Coefficient. A numerical designation of the relative visibility of radiant energy, especially of a certain spectral-wavelength. The relative visibility coefficient has as its stnadard the maximum visibility of a wavelength of approximately 554 nm.

Visibility Curve. A graphic representation of the relative visibility of radiant energy plotted in relation to wavelength.

Visible Speech. The representation of units of spoken sound by means of patterns of black, white, and gray. Sound waves are transformed into visible light and then photographed for the purpose of making speech visible.

Visile. An individual or class of individuals whose imagery is primarily visual.

Vision. 1. The sense of sight whose receptor is the eye and whose stimulus is radiant energy ranging from approximately 400 to 760 nm. 2. That which is seen. 3. A visual hallucination.

Vision Theory. See color theories ; duplicity theory.

Visual, Pertaining to vision.

Visual Acuity. The ability of the retina to separate or discriminate stimuli. Acuity may be measured by acuity gratings or, more commonly, by means of the Snellen Chart, which employs letters of graded size. If the individual can discriminate letters that can just be discriminated by the normal eye at the standard distance of 20 feet, he is said to have 20/20, or normal, vision. A rating of 20/200 signifies that at 20 feet the individual is able to discriminate only what the normal person can discriminate at 00 feet. Correspondingly, 15/20 signifies that the individual can discriminate at 20 feet what the normal eye cannot discriminate at more than 15 feet.

Visual Adaptation. The tendency for the retina to adjust to conditions of continued stimulation or lack of stimulation. For specific types of adaptation, see dark adaptation ; brightness adaptation ; chromatic adaptation.

Visual Agnosia. Inability to interpret visual stimuli, resulting from injuries to the visual association areas (parastriate ; peristriate).

Visual Angle. The angle formed by lines from opposite extreme points of an object to the nodal point of the eye.

Visual Axis. A straight line passing through the external point of fixation and the nodal point of the eye to the fovea.

Visual Cliff. An instrument for testing whether depth perception is inherent by presenting the infant or baby animal with a situation in which he must crawl toward the experimenter over a heavy sheet of glass that bridges a sharp drop-off or cliff. If depth perception is inherent, the subject should refuse to cross the glass ; if not, he should unhesitatingly go over the "cliff".

Visual Displacement. The angles at which the eyes deviate either vertically or horizontally from the primary position when viewing objects.

Visual Field. 1. The totality of all objects available to the unmoving eye at any given time. 2. The subjective, three-dimensional space in which objects are perceived.

Visual Fixation. The turning of the eyes so that images fall on the foveas.

Visual Induction. The influence of stimulation of one part of the retina on another part. Thus, a small yellow square will make a surrounding gray field take on a bluish tinge.

Visualization. The ability to perceive things in terms of visual imagery.

Visual Motor Gestalt Test. See bender gestalt test.

Visual Organization. In Gestalt psychology, the fact that the perceived visual field appears organized and meaningful.

Visual Process. 1. The operation of seeing. 2. Any function—receptor, nervous, cortical—involved in the process of seeing.

Visual Projection. The process of attributing objective location to a visually perceived object.

Visual Purple. See rhodopsin.

Visual-righting Reflexes. Reflexes associated with the orientation of the head according to the fixation of objects in the visual field.

Visual Space. The visual field or the three-dimensional subjective space in which objects are perceived.

Visual Type. An individual whose imagery is primarily visual.

Visual Yellow. See retinene.

Vitalism. The theory that living substances contain a nonmaterial entity crucial to their existence.

Vitality. 1. The property of being alive or of being able to stay alive. 2. Vigor ; energy ; power of endurance.

Vital Statistics. Data about the rate of birth and death of human beings.

Vitreous Humor. The transparent, jellylike material that fills the eyeball between the retina and the lens. *Contr.* aqueous humor.

Vocabulary. 1. Any list of words. 2. The totality of words employed in a language. 3. The individual's stock of words as measured by a test.

Vocabulary Test. A test designed to assess the number of words that a person can use or understand. Vocabulary tests may be either part of an aptitude test or part of a language achievement test.

Vocal. 1. Pertaining to the voice. 2. A propensity for giving verbal expression to one's feelings or opinions.

Vocal Cords. The ligaments in the larynx concerned with the production of sounds.

Vocalization. The utterance of sounds, as in speaking, babbling, screaming, etc.

Vocal Organs. The totality of the organs involved in speech.

Vocal Register. The tonal range, or compass of pitch, of an individual's voice.

Vocation. 1. The manner in which one earns his living. 2. In religious writing, a call to the religious life.

Vocational Adjustment. The degree to which the individual is suited to his job or profession.

Vocational Aptitude. Potential or predicted achievement in a particular job or profession.

Vocational Aptitude Test. A test designed to evaluate, through measurement of ability, personality traits, interests, and potential achievement or success in a specific occupation or profession.

Vocational Counseling. Counseling as applied to the problems of vocational adjustment. Theoretically, vocational counseling involves only problems connected with employment, but vocational counselors find that personal problems and home conditions play an important role in job satisfaction.

Vocational Education. Training designed to fit a person for a particular job or profession.

Vocational Guidance. The process of assisting an individual to choose a vocation. Vocational guidance involves interviews, the use of aptitude and personality tests, and interest blanks.

Vocational Interest Blank. See strong-campbell interest inventory.

Vocational Maladjustment. A condition resulting from an individual's attempting to work in a job or profession for which he is unsuited.

Vocational Preference Inventory, An interest inventory for grades 12-16 and adults. The examines indicates like or dislike for 160 occupational titles. There are also built-in personality scales.

Vocational Selection. A choice made among applicants for a job or profession in terms of the individual most likely to succeed.

Voice Key. A switch, used in reaction time experiments, that automatically activates a clock when the subject speaks.

Voice Onset Time (VOT). The time between the beginning of the uttering of a sound and the vibration of the vocal cords. The easiest way to appreciate VOT is to say "ba" and "pa" with your fingers lightly touching your throat. The vocal cords vibrate at almost the same instant the lips are opened for "ba" but there is a short lag (about 50-100 msec) in voicing for "pa". This lag time is the VOT.

Voiceprint. *Spectrograph* and *spectrographic evidence.*

Voicing. In phonetics, a *distinctive feature* (2) marked by the presence or absence of vibration of the vocal cords. In English all vowels are voiced and several consonants can be distinguished from each other purely by this feature, *e.g.*, the voiceless *t* in "ta" compared with the voiced *d* in "da".

Vol. The unit of measurement of the psychological continuum of perceived volume of an auditory stimulus. A vol is defined as the apparent volume of a 1,000-Hz tone at 40 db. *Volume.*

Volar. *Palmar.*

Volition. 1. Generally and loosely, conscious, voluntary selection of particular action or choice from many potential actions or choices. 2. In the writings of the early introspectionists, a complex arrangement of kinesthetic sensations and images that occurred along with a conceptualized goal or end of one's actions or thoughts.

Volley. The (near) simultaneous or synchronized firing of a number of neural impulses.

Volley Theory of Hearing. *Theories of hearing*.

Volume. In psychophysics, the sense of how much space a stimulus appears to take up; the psychological equivalent of the physicist's definition. Volume is experienced most clearly with sounds, where high-pitched tones are perceived as "thin" and hence low in volume and low-pitched tones feel "larger" or "fuller" and hence as more voluminous. The unit for volume is the *vol.* The persistence of some radio and television manufacturers to mislabel the *loudness* control *volume* (a confusing practice arising from a mislabeling of the control for compensating for the human ear's deficiencies at low- and high-pitched tones as *loudness*) has produced more than its share of confusion. Many olfactory sensations will also have a voluminous quality.

Volume Color. *Color, volume.*

Volumetric Thirst. *Thirst, volumetric.*

Voluntarism. The metaphysical doctrine that volition or free will is the prime force in reality. See, for more on this issue, *free will* and *determinism*.

Voluntary. 1. Characterizing that which is internally motivated, freely chosen, volitianal. 2. Characterizing those psychological processes or behavior patterns that are under cortical control. Voluntary behaviors or processes are *emitted* by an organism and can be shaped using operant conditioning. Compare with *involuntary*.

Voluntary Admission. Admission into a psychiatric institute or hospital undertaken voluntarily by the individual. While there are cases such as this, the term is also used as a euphemism for many borderline instances in which the individual may be told by the appropriate authorities that either they request "voluntary" admission or a court order will be sought to impose admission. See here *commitment*.

Voluntary Muscle. Any muscle under voluntary control ; for the most part, *striate muscles*.

Voluntary Parenthood. *Planned parenthood.*

Volunteer Bias. A potential bias in any study where the subjects are volunteers rather than persans who have been selected from the population using sampling procedures that protect against non-representativeness. There is considerable evidence that volunteers are a typical ; they are generally more highly motivated and tend to perform at a higher level on most tasks than control subjects who are selected at random.

Von Restorff Effect. The generalization that if, given a series of stimuli to be learned (*e.g.*, a list of words), one of them is made physically distinctive in some way (*e,g.*, printed in large type or in a different color from the others) it will be easier to learn and recall, Also called the *isolation effect*.

Voodoo Death. *Thanatomania.*

VOT. *Voice onset time.*

Vowel. A speech sound produced by vibrating the vocal cords without obstructing the passage of air through the vocal tract. Contrast with *consonant*.

Voyeurism. A *paraphilia* characterized by a pattern of sexual behavior in which one's preferred means of sexual arousal is clandestine observing of others when they are disorbing, nude or actually engaged in sexual activity. Interestingly, a voyeur does not usually derive pleasure from strip-tease shows, public nudity or pornography ; arousal is dependent upon the observed person(s) not being aware of their being observed. *scopophilia*.

VR. Abbrev, for *variable ratio.* See the discussion under *schedules of reinforcement.*

VTE. *Vicarious trial and error.*

Vulnerable. Easily injured. Used with respect to physical, psychological or sociological circumstances.

Vulva. The external parts of the female genitals, consisting of the major and minor labia and the outer part of the vagina.

Vygetsky Blocks. A set of 32 wooden blocks differing in shape, height, horizontal width and color. On the underside of each a nonsense word is written. In the standard design there are four nonsense words, one for all tall wide blocks, one for all low wide blocks, one for the tall thin ones and one for the low thin ones. Color and shape are irrelevant. The blocks have been used in a variety of concept-formation studies and experiments on thinking, primarily with children as subjects. Interestingly, although they are called Vygotsky blocks after the Russian philologist, psychologist and philosopher, L.S. Vygotsky, who used them extensively in his work, Vygotsky himself credited a colleague L.S. Sakharov with developing them. The use of the full set of blocks is occasionally called a *Vogotsky test*, var., *Vigotsky.*

Vygotsky Test. *Vygotsky blocks.*

W

W. Weight or weighting factor.

Wakefulness of Choice. The wakefulness of a sleep cycle which gets resulted from learning : normally a single walking period each day.

Wakefulness of Necessity. Wakefulness from bodily need or discomfort.

Waking Center. A brain center in the posterior hypothalmus which is presumed to regulate sleeping and waking.

Wald-Wolfowitz Runs Test. It is a nonparametric statistical test that evaluates whether two samples of data can be considered to be drawn from the same population. The test analyzes the pattern of *runs* in the two samples and visualises differences between them.

Wallerian Degeneration. The degeneration of an axon when it gets separated from its cell body. The myelin sheath degenerates into a chain of small lipoid drops which can get stained, a procedure that allows the tracing of the course of the injured fibres. The neurilemma, if left intact, forms a hollow tube through which the axon could regenerate.

Walleye. 1. An eye having abnormally light-colored or white iris. 2. An eye having dense, opaque cornea.

Ward. A large room in a hospital for the use of many patients.

Warming-up Period. In learning and motor tasks it refers to an initial stage in which the individual starts out slowly and has been inexact in his responses even though familiar with the tasks but then rapidly regains his efficiency.

Warm Spot. A spot on the skin which has been particularly sensitive to warm stimuli.

Warmth. 1. Refers to one of the skin senses. 2. The sensory experience which is resulting from a stimulus above the normal temperature of the skin (roughly 89° F or 32° C).

Warm-up Period. In many complex learning situations refers to a period of time during which movements and responses have been tentative and inexact, var., *warming-up period*.

Wassermann Test. A test made of a blood sample or of a sample of cerebrospinal fluid for the presence of the sphilis spirochete.

Watch Test. A rough test of auditory activity which is carried out by moving a ticking watch toward and away from the subject until the threshold gets ascertained.

Waterfall Illusion. Refers to a motion after-effect which is most easily demonstrated by viewing a set of horizontal stripes moving downward (as in a waterfall) for a time.

Water-jar Problem(s). Refers to a set of problems involving three jars of varying capacity. The problems are usually presented as paper-and-pencil tests, although on occasion actual jars are used. They have been extensively used in the study of cognitive set in problem-solving.

Watson's Behaviorism. Watson defines psychology as the science of behavior. The aim of behaviorism has been able to predict responses from a knowledge of stimulus conditions and conversely, knowing responses, to be able to predict the antecedent stimulus conditions. Watson gave four characteristic methods to be utilized by behaviourists in their investigations ; (1) observation, with and without instrumental controls ; (2) method of conditioned reflexes developed by Palvov ; (3) verbal report method ; (4) testing methods. The verbal-report method is of special interest, since by introducing it. Watson hoped to be able to deal with such mentalistic phenomena, such as thinking, feeling, imagery, etc., which had been in the stronghold of the structuralistic psychologists.

Wave of Excitation. 1. Generally, refers to any neuronal impulse. 2. Also, refers to the propagation of an electrochemical charge along a neuron. 3. The excitatory impulses which travel through the conductile tissue of the ventricles of the heart, resulting in the contraction of the chambers.

WAY Technique. A projective technique in which the individual writes out shot answers to the questions, "*Who Are You* ?"

W Computation. Refers to the tendency to utilise all of the cards for a content description.

Weaning. Refers to the gradual process of acostoming a child to do without its mother's milk (or substitute thereof).

Weaning Psychological. 1. The term used for the process of gradually weakening and (one hopes) eventually breaking a child's psychological dependence upon the parents. 2. By extension, a client's gradual achievement of Psychological independence from his or her psychotherapist ; the process of dissolving *tranference*.

Weber-Fechner Law. An *Fachner's law* is derived from *Weber's law*, this combined term is occasionally used to encompass both generalizations. There occus also some confusion in the older literature over whose law has been called by which name, no little of it stemming from Fechner himself, in his generously referring to what we now call *Fechner's law* as *Weber's law* on the grounds that his general principle was a simple derivation from the law Weber had previously proposed.

Weber's Law. A psychophysical generalization which has been attributed due to the German physioligist Ernst Heinrich Weber (1795—1875). It states that the *just-noticeable differences* in stimuli are proportional to be magnitude of the original stimulus. Formally, $\triangle I/I=k$, where I denotes the intensity of the comparision stimulus, $\triangle I$ denotes the increment in intensity just detectable and k is a constant. The law holds true reasonably for the mid-range of most stimulus dimensions but tends to break down when very low- or very high-intensity stimuli have been used ; *e.g.*, for very low-intensity tones the Weber fraction is somewhat larger than it is for moderately loud tones. Note that the ratio has been often rendered as $\triangle R/R$, where R *stands for* Reiz (German for *stimulus*) and as $\triangle S/S$, where S stands for *stimulus*.

Wechsler Adult Intelligence Scale (WAIS). An individual general intelligence test which is similar to the stamord-Binet but which yields both verbal and performance IQ's as well as a total IQ. The test has been also believed to have diagnostic significance for certain psychiatric problem.

Wechsler Intelligence Scale for Children (WISC). An individual intelligence test for children 6-12 years of age similar in mature to the Wechsler Adult intelligence Scale. A preschool test is also available.

Wechler Preschool and Primary Scale of Intelligence (WPPSI). An intelligence which has been designed for use with children below the use of 6.

Wechsler Scales. A general label for the various Wechsler teste of intelligence, each of which has been given above. Note that all the Wechsler scales have been individually administered tests.

We Group. The group to which the individual who expresses similar ideas, goals, and feelings belongs. *Contr.* they group; out group.

Weight. 1. A multiplicative factor which has been designed to give more or less relative importance to a score. 2. The relative contribution of a factor toward the final result.

Weighting. The process of determinating the relative inflnence each item or score in a series should have in determining the total score.

Weight-lifting Experiment. A psychophysical experiment in which subjects judge the difference in magnitude between small weights.

Weigl-Goldstein-Scheerer Test. A concept-formation test that needs the subject to sort blocks according to color and shape. Goldstein has employed this and other similar tests in his studies of brain-studies people.

Well-Adjusted. A state of hormoneous relationship with one's social and physical environments.

Weltanschauung. (literally, *world view*). One's total outlook or philosophy of life. Freud's latter period is often termed as his *Weltanschauung* period.

Weltschmerz. (literally, *world sorrow*). A sentimental type of sorrow over the state of world.

Wernicke's Area. A cerebral area which is comprising parts of the first and second temporal gyri and the supramarginal angular gyrus: formerly regarded to be the area for understanding spoken language.

Wernicke's Syndrome. The term used for an acute brain disorder with eye movement dysfunctions, ataxia, orientation problems and general mental confusion being the primary symptoms.

It gets related to severe alcoholism and is, in the classic case, followed by *alcholic amnestic disorder*, although this sequela can occassionally be prevented large doses of thiamine. Also called *Wernicke's encephalopathy*.

Wet Dream. A dream which accompanied by seminal emission. A such dreams usually occur at night, they are also called *nocturnal emissions*.

Wetzel Grid. A device which is used for plotting height, weight and age with norms for development based on the interrelationships among these factors.

Wever-Bray Effect. Electrical activities which are generated in the cochlea in response to external stimulus. It is also known as aural micro-phonics.

Wherry-Doolittle Method. A shortcut for selecting a small number of tests that will give a correlation with a criterion only slightly smaller than the multiple correlation obtained with a large numbers of tests.

Whisper Test. A crude hearing test in which the subject, with one ear plugged, stands 20 feet away from the examiner who pronounces test words in a distinct whisper. The subject is not allowed to watch the examiner's lips during the test.

White. The visual sensations evoked by a mixture of radient wavelengths approximating those whose physiological action is equivalent to that stimulated by natural daylight, the extreme of the bright end of the series comprising the black-gray-white dimension of visius experience.

White Matter. A general term which is used for those parts of the spinal cord and the brain that have a predominance of myelinated fibers.

Whole-Learning Method. Simply, learning material (usually verbal) in its entirety as opposed to learning it one small piece at a time—the so-called *part-learning method*.

Whole Object. A person as an object of love.

Whole-word Method. A method of reading instruction in which the focus has been on the relationships between particular configurations of letters (the "whole word") and its pronounciation. Often termed as the *look-say method*.

Wholism. *Holism*.

Whorfian Hypothesis. As put forward by the American linguist Benjamin Lee Worf (1897—1941), the claim that different in linguistic habits make differences in non-linguistic behaviour.

Wh-question. In linguistics, any interrogative based on one of the "wh-" words, *what, which, where, when, why, who, whose* and *(w)how*. Wh-questions have been always "information-seeking" as compared with *yes-no questions*.

Wide-band Procedure. A term applied to the more subjective testing and evaluation procedures such as *projective techniques* and *interviews*. The term was borrowed from information theory.

Wilcoxon Test. The term is used for an extension the *sign test*, which evaluates the magnitude of differences as well as their direction in assessing the significance of differences between matched pairs of scores. Also termed as the *mached-pairs signed-ranks test*.

Wild Boy of Aveyron. One of the more famous case studies in psychology. Victor a wild *child*, was found near the town of Aveyron. Estimated to be about 7 years old at the time, he was extensively studied by the French physician/educator Jean-Marc-Gaspard Itard (1774—1838). The growth and development of Victor intellectually, socially and, to a modest extent, verbally, was discussed in loving detail by Itard over a period of many years and had a profound impact on educational theory and practice. The most likely explanation is that such children were subnormal to begin with and had been taken out and abandoned by the parents.

Will. 1. Generally, the internal, personal capacity for free determination of choice or action. 2. The totality of the person.

Willfulness. Refers to a negative reactivity, a tendency to resist the suggestions and/or attempts at manipulation of others.

Will Power. A non-technical term for self-control or the ability to resist temptation.

Will to Power. Adler's term for the desire to dominate others or the striving for superiority over them.

Windigo. A culture-specific syndrome observed in Algonquin Indians where a hunter thinks that he is in the power of a flesh-eating supernatural monster.

Win-stay Loso-shift Strategy. The term used for a commonly observed strategy in two-alternative choice experiments whereby the subject continues to make a response which receives reinforcement ("winstay") but abruptly switches to the other choice if reinforcement does not take place ("lose-shift").

Wisconsin General Test Apparatus (WGTA). A piece of laboratory apparatus which has been designed at the primate research lab at the University of Wisconsin. It houses a single monkey in a cage and is having a fairly flexible set of trays and platforms which hold various stimulus items for presetation to the subject.

Wish. 1. Generally, and longing or desire. 2. The object of the desire.

Wish Filfullment. 1. In psychoanalysis, a complex process whereby id impulses get satisfied and, because of psychic tension gets reduced. 2. More loosely and less technically refers to the satisfactory acceptance of any secondary goal following a thwarting of attempts to achieve the primary goal.

Wishful Thinking. Thinking which directed by, and along this lines of one's wishes and desires rather than upon the objective constraints of reality.

Witchcraft. Refers to the occult practice or sorcery. Beliefs concerning witchcraft and the role of its practioners which have found in many societies and with a with a wide range of variation ranging from evil or "black" to beneficent or "white" witches.

Witch's Milk. An archaic term for the milk-like secretion which is occassionally exuded from an infant's breast. It gets stimulated by locating hormone from the mother.

Withdrawal. 1. A pattern of behavior which is characterized by the person removing him or herself from normal day-to-day functioning—with all of its attendent frustrations, tensions, and disappointments. 2. A conscious removing of oneself from particular situations. 3. In ethology, a pattern of behavior which is exhibited by the loser of a battle, who gives a display of *submission* and is allowed to leave the scene unmolested. 4. In psychopharmacology, refers to the cessation of administration of a drug, especially one for which the individual has developed a dependence.

Withdrawal Delirium. Delirium which is caused by the withdrawal of a drug upon which one had built up a severe dependence.

Withdrawal Symptoms. Including any of the effects of the cessation of administration of a substance upon which one has built up a dependence.

Wolf Child. See *feral child.*

Wolffian Ducts. The structures in the embryo, that develop into the male internal sex organs.

Wolffian System. In the developing embryo, refers to the precusors of internal male sex organs.

Wolf-man. Refers to the sobriquet of one of Freud's more famous patients, a man whose dominant symptom was a recurrin dream involving a marked fear of wolves. He was a Russ nobleman whom Freud analyzed intensely and from whom he gathered much of his "evidence" for childhood sexuality and the Oedipus complex.

Woodworth-Matthews Personal Data Sheet. A neurotic inventory used largely for screening children or adolescents in educational institutions.

Word-building Test. A variation on an *anagram* task in which the subject has been asked to construct as many words as possible from a given letter set

Word Configuration. The term used for the overall shape of a word, its length, location of ascending and descending letters, placement of capital letters, etc.

Word Count. Any systematic assessment of the frequency of occurrence of words in written and/or spoken language. Often such counts have been restricted to specific linguistic domains, *e.g.*, first-year primers, parent-child interactions.

Word Salad. A meaningless jumble of words. Word salad has been a characteristic of certain schizophrenic disorder.

Work. 1. physically, the action of a force acting against a resistance. 2. physiologically, the expenditure of enery during activity. 3. psychologically, the completion of a task.

Work Decrement. A drop in output per unit of time.

Working Mean. The assumed mean.

Working Through. (*Psychoan*). The process of having the patient thoroughly explore and master the conflict that brought him to therapy.

Work-limit Test. A test in which each subject carries out the same task and the subjects are evaluated on the length of time required to complete the tasks.

Work Psychology. A term preferred by many European psychologists to *industrial/organizational psychology*.

Work Sample. A selected operation which is taken as representative of an individual's job. Work samples may be used to select new employees or as criteria for the purpose of validating other tests.

Worry. An emotional attitude which is characterized by anxiety about the outcome of future events.

Work Sample. Quite literally, a sample of work which is taken as representative of the work of an individual.

Work-up. Refers to the process of getting as much data as possible for diagnosing a disease or a psychological disorder.

Writer's Cramp. A spasm of the muscels used in writing, usually considered to be a functional disorder.

Wurzburg School. A group of researchers at Wurzburg University led by Oswald Kulpe, work around the turn of the century. Although they were *introspectionists* they extended their scope of research beyond that the Wundtian form of *structuralism* and focused on the so-called "higher mental processes" of thinking, problem-solving, cognitive set and the like.

X

X 1. Refers to any given raw score or, when the distinction has to be made, a raw score of the x-distribution. 2. Also, refers given value of the independent variable.

X. Refers to the arithmetic mean of a set of scores.

Xanthrocyanopsia. Insensitivity to light-waves for red (by some writers, for green as well).

Xanthropsia. The condition in which objects are sensed as having a yellowish hue, as in jundice.

Xenoglossia. (1) Speaking in unknown tongues (2) Unintelligible talk by persons who are in a condition of religious ecstasy or excitement ; (3) According to occultists, the power of a person to speak or to understand languages while in a trance which would be incomprehensible while the person is in a normal state.

Xanthopsin. Visual yellow, a visual pigment which is produced when *rhodopsin* is bleached by light.

X Chromosome. See under *chromosome.*

Xeno. Combining form from the Greek for *strange* or *foreign*, var., *zeno*.

Xenogenous. Refers to that which gets caused by a foreign body.

Xenoglossophilia. The use of strange, foreign, or pretentious words.

Xenoglossophobia. A pathological fear of foreign languages.

Xenomania. Morbid preference for foreign words, customs, or dress. It is said to indicate a wish to attract attention or to maintain prestige-status by an inidividual who has an inferiority feeling.

Xenophobia. Great fear of foreigners or of foreign practices. It is said to indicate an over-identification with the in group on the part of an insecure personality.

Xenorexia. The term used for a pathological condition which is characterized by the persistent swallowing of non-food objects.

Xenophebia. The term used for a pathological fear of strangers.

X-O Test. (*Pressey*). A test of attitudes and interests in which the individual either crosses out or circles certain preferences.

XX. In genetics refers to the shorthand notation for the normal genotypic pattern for a human female in which two sex chromosome have been present.

XXX Syndrome. See *triple-X syndrome*.

XXXY Syndrome. A variant of *Klinefelter's syndrome*.

XXY Syndrome. See *Klinefelter's syndrome*.

X^{V} In genetion refers to the shorthand notation for the normal genotypic pattern for a human male in which two sex chromosome have been present ; *chromosome*.

XYY Syndrome. The term used for a *chromosomal anomaly* in which three sex chromosomes have been present. Persons with the anomaly have been phenotypically male, of above average height and with normal genital development, but their fertility may be low because of reduced sperm production.

XYZ Pattern. A gentic abnormality which is believed to be related to criminal or aggressive behavior.

XYZ System. The term used for a system of standard primaries taken as mathematical abstractions for a formal specification of color. Unlike the *RGB system* wherein the *color equation* has based on "real colors, the *XYZ* primaries are not real colors but exist only as mathematical expressions.

Y

Y 1. Any given raw score of the *y* distribution. 2. Any given value of the dependent variable.

Y. Refers to a deviation from the mean of the *y* variable.

Yantra. A visual pattern used in meditation.

YAVIS Syndrome. The term used for an acronym for young, attractive. verbal, intelligent, successful. A half-joking term used to describe the type of client that psychotherapists, in painfully simple terms, prefer to have in therapy. Persons displaying this syndrome make wonderful clients for a variety of reasons, not the least of which has been that successful therapy is highly likely.

Y Chromosome. See chromosome.

Yellow. Response to wave-lengths of about 585 nm and one of the "primaries."

Yellow-blindness. The most uncommon form of color-blindness.

Yellow-sighted. Pertaining to a pathological condition in which there is a heightened sensitivity to yellow.

Yellow Spot. A small area (also known as *macula flava* or *macula lutea*) which lies in the central posterior section of the retina. The small depression in the "yellow spot" is known as the *fovea centralis*.

Yerkish. The artificial language which was developed by D. Rambaugh and co-workers for communication with chimpanzees. It consists of a set of arbitrary symbols that denote words or concepts and some simple grammatical rules for ordering symbols to express meaning. The name derived from the Yerkes laboratory in Georgia, USA, where the has been work was done.

Yes-no Question. The term used for any interrogative that takes either "yes" or "no" as the prescribed answer. There have been three basic forms for such interrogatives : *auxiliary inversion* ("Did you do that ? "), *tag questions* ("You did that, didn't you ? ") and a *rising-intonation contour* ("You did *that* ? ").

Y Maze. A *maze* shaped like a Y having a single approach alley and two arms one of which the subject must choose.

Yoga. (1) Formalized techniques of abstract contemplation by Indian philosophers ; (2) System of practices including formalized postures of body, breathing exercises, and diets, which are said to facilitate self-hypnosis and trances.

Yerkes Bridges Point Scale. Refers to an early adaptation of the Binet Scale utilizing points instead of months of mental age.

Yerkes-Dodson Law. The generalization that moderate levels of arousal or motivation yield optimal performance.

Yoked Control. Refers to any experimental control technique in which two subjects, an experimental and a control, get linked or yoked so that whenever the experimental subject receives some reinforcement or punishment it is also administered to the control subject. The timing and total number of reinforcement and/or punishments has been thus the same for both but their delivery has been contingent only on the behavior of the experimental subjects.

Young-Helmholtz Theory of Colour Vision. A theory which postulates the existence of three types of receptors (or nerve fibers) responding, respectively, so wave-length for red, green, and violte. All other color sensations are analyzable into combinations of these fundamentals. This theory has gained wide acceptance among physicists. It was first proposed by Thomas Young (1807), an English physiologist, and developed by Herman von Helmholtz (1860), German physicists and physiologist.

Youth. Usually defined as the period between childhood and maturity.

Z

Z. See *z-scode.*

Zeigarnik Effect. The relatively greater retention of interrupted tasks than of completed tasks. B. Zeigarnik, German psychologist, reported the experiments in 1927.

Zeitgeber. German for *time giver.* In the study of *circadian rhythms* it has been used for whatever particular stimulus configuration offers the neural mechanisms of a particular species with information about temporal cycles. For most mammals, *light* has been the *Zeitgeber.*

Zeitgeist. Germam for *spirit of the timee.* The term has been used in a rather loose metaphysical manner to characterize the rich and varied matrix of ideas, trends, philosophies, economics, social structures,-political climate, etc., that make up the tone of a culture during a given era. In historiographical work, the so-called *naturalistic approach* emphasizes the role of the *Zeitgeist* in directing and controlling events and usually gets balanced against the so-called *personalistis approach* which emphasizes the role of particular individuals.

Zen Buddism. The term used for a meditative school of Buddhism which focuses upou the "stilling of the mind" with the aim of reaching the enlightened state (satori) in which one appreciates the true, mystical, unanalyzed nature of things beyond the normal, rational conscious manner of "ordinary" knowing.

Zoophilia. Abnormal degree of affection for animals or a particular animal.

Zoophobia. Intense fear of animals or a particular species of animal.

Z-score. Type of standard score in which deviations of raw scores from the mean are expressed in terms of the standard deviation of the distribution.

Zurich School Psychiatrists of Zurich, Switzerland, who, under the leadership of C.G. Jung and E. Bleuler, were among the first to recognize the worth of Freud's contributions.

Zener Cards. A deck of 25 cards which find use in research on extrasensory perception. Each card in the deck is having one of five symbols (star, plus sign, wavy lines, circle, square) on it with each symbol appearing on five cards. Also known as *ESP deck* (or *cards*) and *Rhine deck* (or *cards*) after J.B. Rhine who used them extensively in his work in *parapsychology*.

Zero, Absolute. Refers to the true zero point on any dimension; the point at which nothing of the variable under examination exist.

Zero-Order. Referring to ordinary correlation coefficients, *i.e.*, coefficients calculated from the original data where none of the variables have been held constant as is the case with *partial correlations*.

Zero, Psychological (1) The point at which, theoretically, psychological behavior just barely commences to function; (2) the theoretical point at which mental age is o; (3) the temperature of the surface of the skin (normally about 85-90 degrees Fahrenheit), which is the point of references in judgments of coldness or warmth of objects (though the temperature shift from time to time).

Zero Population Growth (ZPG). The term used for the demographic condition in which the number of deaths in a population approximates the number of viable births, so that the total population does not change over a period of time.

Zeta (ξ). Refers to the difference between the squares of the correlation ratio and the correlation coefficient. In terms of a formula :